Praise for
Someday My Prince Will Come

"Fine's writing is pithy and funny . . . a fresh twist on the tired tales of offbeat girls in search of their dream." —*USA Today*

"A charming and humorous story . . . showing that the strength of one's conviction can be the strongest predictor of one's fate."
—*Publishers Weekly*

"It's impossible not to root for the unlikely heroine in this rip-roaring adventure." — *Daily News* (New York)

"It inspires readers to believe and go after the impossible, while still trusting in happily ever after . . ."
—*Social Life Magazine* (The Hamptons)

"Any woman who has spent any time searching for a good man will enjoy this real life adventure, warts and all." —*New York Post*

"Jerramy Fine is almost too good to be true: a beautiful, intelligent American girl who thinks there's something attractive and romantic about upper-class Englishmen. It's heartwarming to know that there are still people out there who think of England as a fairy tale kingdom."

—Toby Young, author of
How to Lose Friends and Alienate People

"Jerramy Fine doesn't need a prince to corner the market on 'charming.' *Someday My Prince Will Come* is a real-life fairy tale with twists and delights on every page. Tuck it in your beach bag . . . right next to your tiara." —Jen Lancaster, author of *Bitter Is the New Black*

Born in 1977, Jerramy Fine grew up in western Colorado. (Yet she still maintains there was a dreadful hospital mix-up and she was switched at birth with the baby daughter of English aristocrats.) She attended the University of Rochester, where she spent her semester abroad working in the House of Commons, and later completed her master's at the London School of Economics. She now lives in London with her English boyfriend. He's not royal, but she forgives him.

www.jerramyfine.com

Someday My Prince Will Come

True Adventures of a Wannabe Princess

JERRAMY FINE

To Our Princess —
(not a wannabe —)

GOTHAM BOOKS

Love Mommy
and Daddy ☺

GOTHAM BOOKS
Published by Penguin Group (USA) Inc.
375 Hudson Street, New York, New York 10014, U.S.A.
Penguin Group (Canada), 90 Eglinton Avenue East, Suite 700, Toronto, Ontario M4P
2Y3, Canada (a division of Pearson Penguin Canada Inc.) • Penguin Books Ltd, 80
Strand, London WC2R 0RL, England. Penguin Ireland, 25 St Stephen's Green, Dublin 2,
Ireland (a division of Penguin Books Ltd) • Penguin Group (Australia), 250 Camberwell
Road, Camberwell, Victoria 3124, Australia (a division of Pearson Australia Group Pty
Ltd) • Penguin Books India Pvt Ltd, 11 Community Centre, Panchsheel Park, New Delhi
– 110 017, India • Penguin Group (NZ), 67 Apollo Drive, Rosedale, North Shore 0632,
New Zealand (a division of Pearson New Zealand Ltd) • Penguin Books (South Africa)
(Pty) Ltd, 24 Sturdee Avenue, Rosebank, Johannesburg 2196, South Africa

Penguin Books Ltd, Registered Offices: 80 Strand, London WC2R 0RL, England

Published by Gotham Books, a member of Penguin Group (USA) Inc.

Previously published as a Gotham Books hardcover edition

First trade paperback printing, January 2009
10   9   8   7   6   5   4

Gotham Books and the skyscraper logo are trademarks of Penguin Group (USA) Inc.

Permissions appear on page 308 and constitute an extension of the copyright page.

The Library of Congress has cataloged the hardcover edition of this book as follows:

Fine, Jerramy, 1977–
    Someday my prince will come: true adventures of a wannabe princess / by Jerramy Fine.
        p.   cm.
    ISBN 978-1-592-40352-3 (hardcover)   978-1-592-40433-9 (paperback)
    1. Fine, Jerramy, 1977–   2. Fine, Jerramy, 1977– Childhood and youth. 3. Young
women—Colorado—Denver—Biography.   4. Young women—England—London—
Biography.   5. Fantasy—Case studies.   6. Phillips, Peter Mark Andrew, 1977–
7. Anne, Princess Royal, daughter of Elizabeth II, Queen of Great Britain, 1950– Family.
8. Windsor, House of—Miscellanea.   9. London (England)—Social life and customs.
10. London (England)—Biography.   I. Title.
    CT275.F5542A3   2008
    978.8'83—dc22   2007033967

Printed in the United States of America
Set in Granjon   •   Designed by Elke Sigal

To my Knights in Shining Armor:
Michael Seymour, Jason Reeves, Iain Quirk,
Julian Connerty, and Richard Elsen

Without the limitless kindness, generosity, and dedication of these amazing men, this book literally could not have been written. Not only did they lead me through the darkness, but they renewed my faith in the power of good—and for both I will always be grateful.

Note from the Author

This is a true story. You have my word on that. But it is also a memoir—meaning I've described events how I remember them and how I perceived them. I'm not a fan of legal battles, so I've changed some names and identifying details, created composites when necessary, and occasionally modified the timeline to suit the narrative flow. This book is meant to do nothing but entertain readers and inspire them—and I hope it is always viewed in the harmless way in which it was written.

Someday My Prince Will Come

"There is no use trying," said Alice. "One can't believe impossible things." "I daresay you haven't had much practice," said the Queen. "Why when I was your age, I always did it for half an hour a day. Why, sometimes I've believed as many as six impossible things before breakfast."

—LEWIS CARROLL

Prologue

*"When someone makes a decision, he is diving into a strong cur-
rent that will carry him to places he never dreamed of when
first making that decision."*

—PAULO COELHO

I was very young, but I was drawn to my destiny as if by a
magnet.

Lying on my bedroom floor and propped up on my elbows, I
studied every word in that precious library book. The font was
tiny and the pages themselves were almost half the size of my six-
year-old self, but my future depended on this so I had to stay
focused.

I carefully followed the intricate lines of the Windsor family
tree and individually assessed each male name to see if it was
suitable. So far, I had found an earl who was almost nine. An earl
was okay, but nine was kind of old. Then there was the lord. The
lord might have worked, but he was only four, probably still in
preschool.

My finger slowly traced over each name and birth date, searching for the perfect combination. Then, as if it was being magically guided, my hand suddenly stopped.

Peter Mark Andrew Phillips. Born 1977.

He was my age! The only eligible English royal in the world that was my age.

I circled his name over and over with my little fingertip. And in that moment, for better or worse, I felt the direction of my life changing irrevocably.

One

*"There are some people who live in a dream world, and there
are some who face reality. Then there are those who turn one
into the other."*

—Douglas Everett

"Jerramy, as a friend, I'm telling you that you're absolutely
delusional."

Max's voice boomed in the quiet Indian restaurant. No matter
where we went in London, his loud New York accent never failed
to make a scene, but I'd given up pleading with him to tone it
down.

"No, I'm not," I said defiantly. "Think about it. How many
girls actually say they want to become a princess and how many
actually *go out there and try to do it?*"

Max looked me straight in the eye. "And how many of those
girls are under the age of seven?"

Well, I guess he had a point. I was not under the age of seven.
In fact, I was sixteen years older than seven. I'd had sixteen years
to come to my senses. But the simple fact remained: I was twenty-
three years old and still believed that one day I would become a
princess.

To be honest with you, I have no idea how it started. I cannot
remember a time in my life when becoming a princess was not
my main ambition. There was a time, I believe it was preschool,
when all of my friends dreamed of becoming princesses too. But

later, when my friends moved on and dreamed of becoming ac-
tresses, astronauts, and flight attendants, I *still* wanted to be a
princess. Those same girls actually grew up and became lawyers,
fashion buyers, and management consultants. I was still trying
to become a princess.

I wasn't stupid. I knew this wasn't a career that my high
school guidance counselor could help me with. I knew perfectly
well that I couldn't just go out and get a Ph.D. in princess studies
or buy a royal title off eBay and crown myself at my own coronation. If only! No, I was painfully aware that breaking into my
chosen vocation was going to be far trickier than that.

But the thing was, unless I could biologically prove that I
had real royal blood in my veins (which, for the record, I was
working on), becoming a princess was sadly something I couldn't
achieve through my own independent efforts. To legitimize my
particular professional dream, I had to marry a prince. Simple
as that.

Now many would point out that I live in the twenty-first
century and that princes aren't exactly a dime a dozen anymore.
In fact, for the most part, they are pretty much obsolete. So?
Eighteenth-century Chippendale dressing tables aren't exactly
a dime a dozen either, but that doesn't mean I couldn't go out
and find one if I tried hard enough. Granted, limited-edition,
antique English furniture is slightly easier to track down than a
twentysomething, eligible male royal, but the point is, it's not impossible, and I explained this to Max.

"Do you know how stupid you sound when you say that?" Max
taunted. "Saying your ideal career is to be a princess is just as
ridiculous as saying your ideal career is to be First Lady."

I laughed. "First Lady is a good plan B!"

Sometimes I had no idea why I was friends with Max. But I
appreciated his bluntness, no matter how brazen or obnoxious.

"Okay," Max continued, "let's say that *hypothetically* you really do meet one of these royal assholes. How are you going to get his attention? You're hot, but you're not the hottest girl I've ever met. You might be able to pull off a one-night stand with a prince, but for more than that, you'd have to be super, super hot. I'm talking uberhot."

I rolled my eyes. I knew better than to be insulted. "Thanks, Max."

The waiter came and placed half a dozen steaming dishes onto our little table. I piled some rice onto my plate while Max helped himself to chicken jalfrezi.

"Jerramy," Max sighed, "for a girl as intelligent as I know you are, you really worry me. One of these days, you're gonna have to start living in the real world."

I took a large gulp of white wine.

Honestly, if I had an ounce of royal blood for every time someone mentioned the "real world" to me, I'd *be* a princess by now.

Most of my family and some of my very closest friends had at least learned to humor me; they saw my princess complex as a quirky and rather amusing endearment. But pretty much everyone else just laughed, shook their heads, and looked at me with pity—exactly what Max was doing at that very moment.

I knew what everyone was thinking: How could such a bright girl have such a ridiculously frivolous and downright impossible goal? And (here it comes) when was she going to grow up and start living in the real world?

My question was this: What's so wrong with living in a fantasy world? Seriously. What's so wrong about ignoring the conventions and practicalities of the so-called real world, and actually pursuing your childhood dream? Sometimes I think the "real world" is just a phrase invented by adults to give credibility to the miserable lives they've created for themselves. Feel free to call me delusional, but I was someone on this planet who, no matter how silly it seemed, was actually listening to my heart—I trusted it, believed it, and followed it. And in my opinion, there was nothing more "real" in this world than that.

So no matter how much I was teased, or how many obstacles I faced, or how many birthdays I celebrated past the age of seven, my singular desire to become a princess remained firmly in my heart. And I often thought it would take nothing short of an exorcism to remove it.

⤜⤏

I had an odd fixation with Snow White when I was a child. In fact, I had accumulated such a huge collection of Snow White memorabilia that the Denver Children's Museum put it on display. I insisted on dressing up as Snow White for Halloween five years in a row, and *every day* after preschool I'd rush home to listen to my Snow White record on my Fisher Price record player. (I wasn't allowed TV, so it was the next best thing to the video.)

Don't forget that back in the seventies, there was no such thing as a Disney Store; there were no Princess Collection aisles filled with everything a little girl like me could only dream of playing with. For my second birthday party, my mom had to scour the party shops to find anything vaguely Snow White themed, and when she finally found plastic Snow White cake-toppers, she thought she had hit the jackpot. I was so happy, I didn't even notice that my health-nut parents were serving me a sugarless carrot cake with sugarless icing.

I guess you could say that Snow White was my best (albeit imaginary) friend, and whenever I was upset about my nonroyal life I would confide in her. My mom said she overheard me all the time: "Snow White," I would sob, "you are *the only one who understands*!"

Looking back on it, it makes perfect sense. Snow White was an orphaned princess. And so was I.

⟶

I was born in Denver, Colorado, a city filled with a rather bland collection of modern architecture. The one exception was the state capitol building, which, compared to the dull structures surrounding it, seemed positively majestic with its marble steps, huge Roman columns, and golden dome. The first time I saw it in all its stately splendor, I was a toddler strapped into the backseat of the family station wagon. As we drove closer to it and eventually past it, my mother said I had burst into tears. When she asked me what was the matter, I had whimpered simply, "I . . . I . . . didn't see the Queen."

Evidently, I was so upset that she didn't have the heart to tell me that the building wasn't a palace and that the "Queen" didn't live there, or more importantly, that Colorado had no reigning monarchy. I was left to discover these devastating facts on my own and for the next few months, every time we drove past the capitol, I would continue to scan the windows anxiously looking for royal family members I might recognize. And not just any royal family members. My *own* royal family members.

In the beginning, my parents thought I was just unusually precocious or perhaps blessed with an overactive imagination. I wasn't getting my royal ideas from TV—I wasn't allowed television. I wasn't getting my ideas from books—I couldn't read yet. But as my toddler behavior became ever more bizarre, they began to worry.

One day, when my mom dug out her old photo albums and showed me pages from her early years in Europe, I wouldn't rest until she let me put the tattered postcards from her visit to the Crown Jewels on my bedroom wall.

My mom tells stories of how she would wake me up in the

morning for nursery school, how I'd eerily gaze up at her without a hint of recognition, and say, "You're not the woman who dresses me."

Or another time when, I toddled up to her with my tiny hands placed haughtily on my tiny hips and asked, "Where is my armoire?"

"What's an armoire?" my dad had to ask me.

My poor parents. Apparently, I constantly addressed them with an arrogance and superiority unheard of in a two-year-old—as if I were doing them a favor living amongst them in their humble home. And to be honest, that's exactly how I felt. My whole world always seemed like an altogether foreign environment to me. And as a little girl, I felt increasingly frustrated that no one seemed to understand *who I was*, even if I wasn't entirely sure myself.

It wasn't long before my parents saw a pattern. Not only was I obsessed with royalty, I *behaved* like royalty. It couldn't have been easy for them—but very much to their credit, my mom and dad were never insulted that their little girl frequently treated them like lowly commoners. And in retrospect, I actually have to concede that my parents were extremely open-minded in their assessment of me. After much reading on the subject and discussion with their friends, they decided that the explanation was relatively simple. I had been a princess, or some type of high-ranking royalty, in a past life. Because I was so young, past-life memories were surfacing regularly and I was having difficulty adjusting to the new nonroyal life that I was currently living. This explained why I was confused about the lack of palace furniture (armoires, for example); this explained why first thing in the morning, I often confused my mother with my chambermaid; this explained my intense relationships with Disney princesses; and most of all, this explained my incessant desire to escape or "go home."

Never underestimating my toddler intelligence, my parents sat me down and carefully explained their past-life theory to me. Afterward, they looked at me expectantly, perhaps hoping to see an instant transformation now that I understood what I'd been going through. I looked right back at them. I had to admit, their theory had its merits. But it didn't change anything, did it? Whether I'd been a princess in a past life or not, I still wanted to be a princess in *this life*.

As I grew a bit older, it wasn't long before I developed my *own* theory—and in my opinion the evidence for this theory was equally overwhelming. I was obsessed with royalty and aristocracy from such a frighteningly young age that my parents often joked that I couldn't possibly have been spawned by flower-power, equality-loving children of the sixties like themselves. And ironically, I couldn't have agreed with them more.

If truth be told, as a child, as a teenager, and even into my twenties, I was never *one hundred percent convinced* that the people I called Mom and Dad were actually my real, biological parents. I know it sounds like a clichéd movie plot, but I'm being totally serious. You want proof? All you had to do was look at them.

Both of my parents had hair way past their elbows. That's right. *Both of them*. My dad, with his long ponytail and thick dark beard, always looked like a cross between some kind of Indian guru and ZZ Top. And as for my mom, well, she was pretty, but the way she pranced around in her long ethnic skirts and embroidered peasant blouses, she looked like she'd been raised in some kind of psychedelic pixie forest. Then there was me: an innocent child, a helpless victim of their hippie lifestyle. They dressed me in tie-dye and hemp fiber, fed me tofu and quinoa, and soothed me to sleep with the dulcet tones of Janis Joplin and Jimi Hendrix.

And as if living with the hippies wasn't enough, they had to go and give me a hippie name. Not only that, they had to give me a *boy's* name. There is no logical explanation for it. I was named Jerramy for no other reason than "it sounded pretty." I'm sure that after years of listening to nonstop Janis Joplin and Jimi Hendrix anything sounds pretty, but that's hardly an excuse.

And don't even get me started on my middle name. It's Sage. As in the grayish green cooking spice. My parents claim it represents wisdom, but as far as I'm concerned, they might as well have named me Jerramy Oregano. Or Jerramy Garlic.

Deep down, I bet my parents questioned the biological facts of the situation too. I mean, surely if I were their *real* daughter, I would not be actively plotting an escape to a life of royal elitism, but instead would be fantasizing about a selfless existence in the Peace Corps. At the very least, my parents hoped that one day I'd tear myself away from my books on royal protocol and get as excited as they did about grinding their own flour every night. But despite all evidence to the contrary, they continued to claim that I was conceived one starry night in a rundown miners' cabin deep in the Breckenridge Mountains—by them.

So my girlhood theory was this: The day I was born, a dreadful hospital mix-up occurred. The mix-up involved two young aristocrats from England, two ultraliberal hippies from America and two beautiful baby girls. Somehow, on this historic day, my infant self ended up in the hippie Colorado home rather than the glorious stately home in the English countryside.

More than twenty years later, both my parents still have hair longer than I do. And let's just say that if tomorrow I were to be approached in the street by an elegant British couple who insist that in 1977 a certain Denver hospital made a terrible mistake, and that, how shall they break it to me, I am their real daughter— I won't be the least bit surprised.

⟶

Of course I loved them dearly, but from day one I knew that my parents were hardly a pair that would seamlessly fit into the daily life of a royal palace to which I knew I was going to become accustomed. I actually had recurring nightmares about how they might behave at my future royal wedding. Can you imagine my bearded ZZ Top father escorting me down the aisle of St. Paul's Cathedral in front of all of Europe's reigning royal families? The thought was too painful to bear.

I survived my nonroyal childhood by focusing on my escape— which included planning my royal betrothal and studying the culture of the future kingdom I would help to reign.

I subscribed to *Royalty* magazine—it was six dollars per issue because it was printed in the U.K., but to me, it was worth every penny of my monthly allowance and I studied it voraciously.

It helped that I already knew exactly which royal I was going to marry. And I have to say, as royal boys my age went, he was pretty close to perfect. His name was Peter Mark Andrew Phillips. (How romantically regal is that?) Son of the Princess Royal, Peter was Queen Elizabeth II's oldest grandchild, and at the time, he was seventh in line to the throne.[1]

You may think that six is quite young to make such a huge decision about one's future husband, but the minute I saw his name in that royal family tree . . . well, I can't explain it. I just *knew*. I knew, without a shadow of a doubt, that I would marry that boy. I just had to find him.

---

1 With the subsequent births of HRH Princess Beatrice (1988), HRH Princess Eugenie (1990), Lady Louise (2003), and Viscount Severn (2007), Peter eventually moved to tenth place in the line of succession.

But finding Peter was going to take time and I quickly realized that it was going to take even more time if I allowed there to be an ocean between us. Studying magazines was not going to cut it. I knew that if I were serious about fulfilling my destiny, I had better get myself out of that hippie house and over to England ASAP.

But considering I was only six years old, this was easier said than done. Luckily, I had a plan. So far, I wasn't impressed with my Denver kindergarten, and in fact, I found it so unchallenging that my teacher wanted me to skip it and go straight to first grade. Whereas I wanted to skip the American school system entirely and go straight to British boarding school.

Again, not quite sure how I knew British boarding school existed, but my parents were horrified when I suggested it. What child begs to be shipped off to boarding school thousands of miles away from home? But as I repeatedly tried to explain to them, I didn't think going to England would be *leaving* home, I thought of it as *going* home.

But it was like arguing with a brick wall. The hippie parents would have been far happier sending me off to live in a nude commune than a snooty, class-ridden girls' boarding school that would no doubt fill my head with all sorts of ancient, antifeminist, right-wing ideas. And despite my constant persuasive efforts on the subject, getting the hippies to agree with my plan was absolutely futile.

"You'd be miserable," they insisted. "For starters, they'd make you wear a uniform."

"But I love pleated skirts!" I wailed.

"You'd have to eat things like cold, burnt porridge."

"Doesn't matter."

"You'd be bored out of your mind, Jerramy!" my mom tried in vain to tell me. "These hoity-toity English schools you think you want to go to aren't known for academics. You'll learn nothing but how to curtsy and plan a dinner party. They're designed purely to help girls marry the correct husband." She said this last bit with visible disgust. Women's lib was still very close to her heart. (To this day she still refuses to wear a bra.)

But to her dismay, I nodded excitedly. "Exactly! That's why I want to go!"

She looked at me sternly. "Jerramy, you're simply too intelligent for your dad and me to justify sending you off to a place that would do nothing but melt your brain cells. End of discussion."

See? It's no wonder Snow White and I got along so well. If that no-English-boarding-school mandate wasn't classic evil stepmother behavior, I didn't know what was. Just like my beloved Disney princess, I was a prisoner in my own home.

Two

"Everyone, when they are young, knows what their destiny is. Back then, everything is clear and everything seems possible."

—Paulo Coelho

I remember the first time I found a proper photo of Peter.

Sure, I managed to spot him in the official photos of Fergie and Andrew's wedding,[2] but you can't really judge a future husband if he is wearing a ruffly, navy blue page boy outfit with little gold buttons and sitting cross-legged on the floor in the corner of a magazine picture. Basically, all I knew about my prince for the first few years was that he had a cute boyish face and shiny golden hair. And I knew between my hair and his, we would have beautiful blond children together.

Peter wasn't old enough (or well-known enough) to attract any significant attention from the press—especially in America. But if I scoured the English magazines hard enough, every now and then his face would pop up in the background.

Then, one day, I saw him in his full glory. This time it wasn't just his tiny blond head in the corner of the page that some photo editor had neglected to crop. No, this time the photo cropper hadn't even touched him! And suddenly I found myself looking

---

2 Peter was one of four pages at the wedding of the Duke and Duchess of York on July 23, 1986. Press reports described him as "a pageboy in midshipman blue."

at a photograph of the most handsome ten-year-old boy I had ever seen. In fact, considering the male morons I was in school with at the time, he was the only handsome ten-year-old boy I had ever seen.

He was walking with his family to church. His posture was casually dauntless, his gray suit was immaculate, his Windsor knot was perfect, his profile was striking, and his complexion was positively glowing beneath those English rosy cheeks. I fell deeper in love than ever that day. And as I carefully cut out his regal image and taped it to my bulletin board, I knew that my six-year-old decision was the right one.

Meanwhile, life with the hippies was not improving. If truth be told, once my parents decided to move us out of Denver to a Colorado mountain town in the middle of nowhere, it seemed to be getting progressively worse. They told me they wanted to raise me and Ezra (my new baby brother) in a "safe, country environment" away from the pollution and crime of the city; they told me they wanted to "get back in touch with the land."

What they didn't tell me was they were going to assemble a full-size Native American tipi[3] in our backyard, buy goats and chickens so we could "play farm," and send me to school with a bunch of junior rodeo champions who drove to school with hunting rifles displayed in the back of their pickup trucks. Our new house was charmingly set near a small hill called the Hog Back and my new town's biggest attraction was a two-headed stuffed lamb, which was on display at the local farming equipment store—just in case you wanted to gawk at some freak taxidermy while shopping for your pitchforks.

Years later at a London engagement party, I mentioned the

---

3 My godparents owned one of the largest tipi factories in North America.

name of this cowpoke town to an American I'd just been introduced to and I was amazed when he said he'd heard of it.

"You're from *there?*" he asked incredulously. "Wow. That
place has like *zero* outside influence."

Tell me about it.

When I was finally old enough to buy alcohol at the town
liquor store, I produced my passport as ID, and the clerk was
mystified. He'd never seen one before.

"Ma'am," he said with suspicion, "I'm gonna need to see some
state ID."

"But this is *international* ID," I tried to explain.

"Sorry, ma'am," he said. And I left empty-handed.

As a child, I was miserable. One freezing winter morning in
first grade, I was waiting for the school bus with a bunch of other
kids, when the farmer who lived across the street came out of his
house holding a large rifle. We watched silently as he walked into
the adjacent pasture and proceeded to shoot his herd of cows, one
by one, right in front of us. It must have been butchering season or
something, but he was such a hard-core farmer it didn't even occur to him to wait until his young audience had gone to school.

A year or so later, I went over to a friend's house so we could
try out our new roller skates and was horrified to see the dead
body of an elk (we're talking antlers, hooves, and all) lying across
her kitchen counter.

"My dad shot it this morning," my little friend said breezily
as we walked by.

I'll never forget those glassy elk eyes staring at me as my friend's
mom happily removed its bloody guts with a knife as naturally as
if she were baking cookies.

In school, I was ostracized quite early on by the majority of
kids because I had no intention of joining the Future Farmers of
America or training to become a rodeo princess. (That was *not*

the kind of royalty I had in mind!) Sure I could wander through the cornfields by myself at night without fear of being murdered, but so what? If the Red Barn and Big Barn were the only restaurants in town (and if deep fried bulls' testicles[4] were the regional specialty), I wasn't convinced the low murder rate mattered so much.

Yet my parents seemed to love their new home and their new earthy lifestyle. They loved being away from the Denver smog, raising their own animals, and growing their own food. Still, I don't think they realized how much work a hippie farm was going to be, because as part of this unwavering quest for utopia, suddenly my list of chores expanded exponentially.

My new responsibilities included clearing out the rabbit hutch and the chicken coop; collecting the chicken eggs; cleaning up the goat's pen; and feeding the rabbits, the ducks, the cats, the dog, the fish, the gerbils, and the garter snake. And that's just what I had to do after school. On the weekends I had to wash and put away the (mismatched) dishes, pick tomatoes from the organic garden, pick apricots from the trees (and pick up the gross gooey ones that fell on the ground), water my mother's billions of flower gardens (that were lined with Tibetan prayer flags), and help make whole-wheat pastry for the never-ending vegetarian quiches. Did I mention that in addition to Snow White I also identified with Cinderella?

Both of my parents grew up in major cities so I kind of understood their desire to play farm when they finally moved to the middle of nowhere. But at least when Marie Antoinette played farm at her Petite hameau in Versailles, her staff made sure that all her livestock had been sprayed with eau de toilette and that

---

4 Also known as "Rocky Mountain Oysters."

the chicken eggs had been carefully washed before she went to collect them!

One Saturday morning, I was busy watering the vegetable garden, when our mother duck and her new team of fluffy ducklings waddled past me, quacking their heads off.

I turned to see what the newest duck-related commotion could possibly be about and noticed the strangest thing: A baby gosling had joined their group. Tottering on his new webbed feet, he was trying his best to march in line with the rest of them. His gray goose down stood out among the bright yellow fluff of the baby ducks, and even though he was probably their same age, his gosling body towered above them, standing almost as tall as the mother. Poor guy. He'd obviously been separated from his real goose parents, wandered onto our property, and suddenly found himself part of a very strange and very different feathered family from the one he was used to. My heart ached for him—I knew exactly how he felt.

⁓

My little brother didn't mind life on the farm half as much as I did. He played baseball with the rotten duck eggs, played frisbee with the cow pies, and often got in trouble for throwing the chickens out of the tree house to see if they could fly. For a five-year-old boy, all that dirt and mud was fun! But not for me. I dreamed of the sophisticated outdoor pleasures you might find on a royal estate: a backyard filled with splashing fountains, elegant topiaries, and manicured lawns where I could play croquet.

I dreamed about trips to museums and nights out at the theater, of box seats at the ballet or the opera—but my only options were nights out at the Big Barn or bleacher seats at the monster truck show. Yet my constant requests to move out of hickville to at least a vaguely cosmopolitan environment went virtually unnoticed.

I just didn't get it. I mean, didn't my parents *care* that the local farmers made fun of their hippie clothes and the fact that they rode their bikes to work? Didn't they find it *strange* that the town had more churches than restaurants? Didn't it *bother* my dad that he was asked to leave a certain eating establishment because of his long hair? Apparently not.

"Just look at *the mountains*," my parents would say to me with sweeping gestures and a scary, almost evangelical passion. "It's just *so beautiful* here!"

So they were raising me in a provincial vacuum for the sake of beauty?

My fantasies about being shipped off to English boarding school or discovered by my real English parents increased. But even if my real English parents were actively looking for me, my town was so far away from any civilization (the nearest city was a six-hour drive in any direction), there was no way they'd be able to find me. To cope, I stayed away from the cornfields and the rodeos and threw myself into English society novels, books on the rules of hereditary titles, and any information I could find on the lives of all reigning royals throughout the world.

"Jerramy, stop reading and go outside and play!" my parents would plead.

But to no avail. There was no way I was ever going to play in that tipi. There was no way I was ever going to think scattering chicken feed was fun.

⌐

I have to say that my many years of cornfield avoidance and self-imposed royal research eventually paid off, because one of the most important things I learned along the way was this: Contrary to popular belief, you don't have to come from aristocratic stock to marry a prince. And considering the "stock" I had been allotted, thank God for that!

As I grew older, I continued to scan the media and religiously study the trends of contemporary royal marriages as well as the credentials of the few remaining modern-day princesses. And I had to admit, things were looking up. It was almost like some kind of progressive princess movement was taking hold.

No disrespect to the late Princess Diana (as I positively adored her), but modern princes were no longer after wide-eyed nineteen-year-olds straight out of Swiss finishing school. Blue blood didn't seem to matter like it used to. And crown princes didn't just want beauty in a royal bride; they now wanted brains as well. Thousands of years of royal tradition had suddenly gone topsy-turvy—and all in my favor. We were entering a new royal era. And the more modern princesses I read about, the more I was sure that my theory was correct.

Take Princess Masako of Japan, one of the very first royal rule-breakers to enter the scene. Another ditzy aristocrat? Hardly. This girl went to Harvard *and* Oxford. She spoke four languages. She used to negotiate international trade accords. And, just like me, at her American high school she had a 4.0 GPA and was in the National Honor Society. She was only the second commoner ever to enter the Japanese imperial household, but despite this lack of noble breeding, Princess Masako is next in line to become Empress of Japan! Not too shabby for a high school bookworm.

Then there was the fabulously chic Princess Mette-Marit of Norway. This girl inspired me to no end. Think you have to be a virgin to spawn a future king? Think you have to have a flawless, angelic past? Not anymore. This stylish princess used to date a *drug dealer*! And if being associated with such a shady character isn't bad enough, she (gasp!) had a kid with him (gasp!) out of wedlock! A single-mother princess with a child fathered by a convicted felon? How could it possibly be? Well, when the handsome, free-thinking Crown Prince Haakon set eyes on this elegant Hitchcock blonde at a rock concert, he didn't think twice about her less-than-perfect past. Totally smitten, the prince welcomed Mette-Marit and her young son into his home, and within months he proposed to her. Isn't that one of the most romantic royal love stories you've ever heard?

And Norway was not the only Scandinavian country to shun royal convention, because next came Princess Mary of Denmark, who looks just like Charlotte from *Sex and the City*. But despite her classic understated glamour, Mary is hardly a European noblewoman. Nope, she hails from Australia—a country founded by convicts, for godsake! And her résumé boasts more than the usual string of curtsys and dinner parties—after graduating from college, Mary moved swiftly into a dazzling advertising career. Prior to marrying Crown Prince Frederik of Denmark (whom she met in an Australian *pub*!), Mary worked for high-flying companies like Young & Rubicam and Microsoft. Like I said, teenage princesses right out of finishing school with no worldly experience were rapidly becoming a thing of the past.

It wasn't long before it became almost *trendy* for European royals to marry beautiful commoners. And Spanish Princess Letizia of Asturias, the most recent addition to my collection of modern-day princesses, illustrated my theory yet again. Once more, this princess was not just a pretty Audrey Hepburn face— she was one smart cookie. Letizia was an award-winning television reporter, who had worked on the front lines of Iraq and Ground Zero. She met the tall, dark, and handsome Crown Prince Felipe when she was sent to northern Spain to cover the sinking of an oil tanker. Not only did His Royal Highness fall head over heels for her, but the Catholic Church forgave her for being a divorcée! That wouldn't have happened a few centuries ago, let me tell you!

So there you have it. Bookworms, single mothers, divorcées, even Australians! Traditionalists were probably outraged, but from the looks of it, at some point princesshood had become an equal opportunity industry.

As I continued to pore over my royal magazines, I'd gaze longingly at the sumptuous gowns, elegant day dresses, and tailored Chanel suits that filled page after glorious page. Then I'd compare them to the macramé peace-march outfits worn by my parents, and to the ten-gallon hats, bib-fronted shirts, and Wrangler jeans worn by my peers. Let's just say that when it came to pursuing my royal dream, it became more and more obvious that I had better take matters into my own hands.

With the help of my royal research, I decided to put together a small list of the new essential qualities required to be a successful modern-day princess. For those that missed it the first time, let me repeat that you don't have to come from an aristocratic background. (As you can tell, I was extremely happy about this discovery!) Rather, from what I could see, there were only three prerequisites for successful prince-snagging in the new millennium:

1. Immaculate grooming
2. Impeccable style
3. A brilliant career

Simple as that. In fact, the more I read over the tiny list of princess criteria, the more it seemed to be almost ridiculously easy. I mean, it wasn't like I had to run marathons or master quantum equations or learn to read hieroglyphics or anything grueling like that. With a bit of work, the princess criteria were actually very attainable!

I figured if Masako, Mette-Marit, Mary, and Letizia could do it, by God, so could a girl raised by hippies in the middle of nowhere. (I just probably wouldn't be mentioning the tipi, the chickens, or the rodeo to my future royal in-laws if I could help it.)

⌒

Like I said, pretty much everyone laughed at my desire to marry a prince. One day, my best friend Chloe and I were playing with our Barbies after school. I loved Barbies (talk about immaculate grooming, impeccable style, and a brilliant career—Barbie had it all!), and amazingly, my feminist mother allowed me to play with them. Granted, I had to sneak over to Chloe's house if I wanted to watch Miss America or Miss Universe, but at least I was allowed Barbies.

Anyway, Chloe and I were sitting in the sea of miniature dresses and flesh-colored plastic that covered my bedroom floor when she asked me, "Jerramy, who is that boy?"

I tugged at Astronaut Barbie's perfect, creamy blond hair with the flimsy pink brush and looked up.

"What boy?" I asked absently.

"That one," said Chloe, pointing to my bulletin board.

There among the Disney birthday cards and old royal postcards, and next to my favorite Chinese fortunes that read *You'll be invited to a royal dancing party and meet your first lover* and *You'll be chosen to be heir of a kingdom in Europe* was the small picture of a young boy wearing a suit—my miracle find. My only real photo of Peter.

"Oh, him? That's Prince Peter. That's who I'm going to marry. He's my age so it's perfect." I put Astronaut Barbie down and began choosing an outfit for Malibu Barbie.

Chloe rolled her blue eyes. "Jerramy, you're not really going to marry a prince."

"Of course I am," I said calmly. "I'm going to marry *that*

prince. I was so excited to finally find a picture of him. There's never any pictures of him in any of my royal magazines."

Chloe laughed out loud and looked at me with baffled skepticism.

"Jerramy," she said, "do you mean to tell me that this cutout prince with this piece of Scotch tape on his head is going to be your husband?"

I shrugged. "Yes. Why couldn't he be?"

Chloe shook her head in amusement and returned to assembling the Barbie cosmetic counter.

"Jerramy, one day when you really do get married, I am going to give you that cutout, Scotch-taped prince as a wedding present—to remind you of how crazy you are!"

Right then and there, I made a promise to myself: I would prove Chloe wrong. When she came to my royal wedding at St. Paul's Cathedral she would be amazed not only at my beautiful designer wedding dress and the elaborate flower arrangements and the poignant organ music, but at how wrong she was to think, even for a moment, that dreams don't come true.

⟶

There was only one time of year that was more exciting than rodeo season or the Sweet Corn Festival—and that was the County Fair.

To the town locals, the County Fair seemed to bring all the social thrills of an NRA meeting, a quilting bee, and the ever-popular "black-tie bingo" all rolled into one. Not to mention the added bonus of hotly contested competitions on almost every element of livestock and agriculture you can imagine. Where else could you find hay-baling contests alongside prize-winning broccoli? Or pistol matches sponsored by the local beef-jerky company?

My family went every year. And I went with them because I was too young to stay home by myself.

As we wandered through the endless stalls, I tried to avoid stepping in manure as I stared in bewilderment at all the cowboys and cowgirls doing what their families had done for generations. I watched boys from my third grade class expertly leading their pet pigs around the show ring, happily sending them to their death for the highest bidder. I watched girls my age or younger carefully washing and grooming their cows, filing their hooves, and teasing the ends of their tails into perfect bovine puffballs—all to ensure that the beef would sell for a handsome price.

I could never do what they did. I may have hated the manual labor that came with my own farm animals, but I'd become so attached to them and their little barnyard personalities, there was *no way* I could calmly prepare for their slaughter!

Still, these ranching children seemed *so happy* doing these things, so happy following in their parents' footsteps. They even dressed exactly like their parents with their tight jeans and miniature cowboy boots. The County Fair was their world and they loved it. They fit right into it, never questioned it, and I could tell that they couldn't imagine ever doing anything else.

"It must be nice," I thought to myself.

I looked at my dad with his shocking waist-length beard and his long dark hair that stuck out in every direction, tumbling down his back like a lion's mane. I looked at my brother, Ezra, who was just starting kindergarten. He was wearing tie-dyed shorts and sporting a wacky Mohawk hairdo. I looked at my mom, whose hair was so long she could sit on it, and who had purposely decided to wear her *Love Animals, Don't Eat Them* T-shirt because she loved causing controversy.

I tried to dress differently from them, tried to look normal: I curled my bangs like the other girls, rolled up the cuffs of my jeans, and wore bright white Keds.

My mom always offered to sew any item of clothing for me that I wanted (no point in supporting the establishment and buying anything new, she'd tell me), but I stubbornly insisted that everything in my preteen wardrobe was store-bought and factory-made. (I *lived* for that annual trip to the Denver mall where my grandmother would let me buy new, nonhippie clothes with my birthday money.)

But it was no use. No matter how I dressed, people knew that this long-haired, motley crew was my family and I was constantly reminded of it.

As we toured the County Fair's sheep-shearing exhibit, kids from my elementary school (as well as their parents) would stare at us and whisper and giggle behind their hands. Why did my family have to be so embarrassing? How was I supposed to fit into this town when they made it so difficult for me?

One year, it was even worse. My mom obtained permission to set up a giant tipi on the fairgrounds. Inside this tipi, she offered face painting and simple art projects for any of the children that had grown bored of wandering through the rabbit displays or the corn bread contests. With my mom's help, children had the option of making their own magic wand or creating an origami butterfly (which came complete with a mini lesson on metamorphosis). But the tipi was up for less than a day, before the town's people started to complain: How dare this woman preach evolution to our children? How dare she encourage them to practice black magic?

The whole county fair was buzzing with gossip about "the witch in the tipi," and as news reached kids from my fifth grade class, I wanted the straw-covered fairground to swallow me up. And my parents thought living with a daughter like *me* was difficult? Did they have any idea what it was like living with *them*?

(In retrospect, this uproar shouldn't have come as a surprise. Plans to build a new library had been halted for years because the gothic gargoyles in the architect's design were thought to be satanic. Never mind that most gargoyles are found on ancient churches!)

At dinner that night, I picked at my salad and fried tempeh and announced to my parents that I was cutting my long blond hair and getting a classic shoulder-length hairstyle.

"But why?" my mom asked. "Your hair is beautiful! It's just like Lady Godiva's!"[5]

"I don't want to be part of the 'crazy long-haired family,'" I whimpered. "Everyone makes fun of us."

"It doesn't matter what other people think," my mom said. "Sounds like they're the ones with the problem—not you."

"Our hair makes people stop and think," my Dad added. "It forces them to realize that there is more to life than appearances."

To my near-teenage self, this statement made absolutely no sense. In middle school, appearances were *everything*! Didn't they understand that?

"Can I least have some pink Keds like Chloe has?" I asked, practically in tears.

"You already have white Keds," my mom answered, "and you're already extremely lucky to have those. Do you know how little those factory workers got paid to make those shoes?"

"But they're going out of style!" I wailed. "I need pink ones."

"You're lucky you have feet," said my dad.

And with that, yet another boring, sugar-free dessert of freshly picked apricots was served. I shook my head in hungry despair.

---

5 According to legend, Lady Godiva was an eleventh-century noblewoman who rode naked through the streets of England with nothing but her long hair to cover her.

For a family that claimed to like Lady Godiva so much, they could at least let me have one of her chocolates once in a while.

Going grocery shopping with my mom was yet another example of pure hippie-related agony. I would gaze wistfully at the dazzling sugar cereals—the ones with exotic, mystical names like Cookie Crisp and Cinnamon Toast Crunch—knowing that I would never, ever be allowed to consume anything more exciting than homemade granola. I would stare longingly down the snack aisle (as we never even entered it), dreaming of Chips Ahoy and Soft Batch, of Cheetos, Doritos, and Ruffles—knowing full well that my school lunch box would never hold anything to munch on but raisins and celery sticks. I fantasized about gourmet chocolate, caviar, and foie gras, knowing I would have to sustain myself for years to come on nothing but soybeans, bulgur wheat, and dandelion leaves.

And if the constant food torture wasn't enough, it seemed like my mom actually made a point to embarrass me on these outings. She would pick up a sports drink bottle and proclaim at the top of her lungs, "Look, Jerramy—it says right here that this contains an ingredient known to cause cancer in rats!"

Everyone in the entire aisle would turn to stare at her, so she'd simply repeat herself even louder. A few minutes later she'd pick up a packet of hot dogs and stridently exclaim, "Did you know that these are made out of pigs' ears, lips, and eyelids?" (She never seemed to notice that her constant effort to educate the shoppers never stopped any of them from tossing the offending items into their carts.)

But whenever I told her that she was embarrassing me, her reply was always the same: "If I made even one person stop and think today, then embarrassing you was worth it."

And people wondered why I begged to be sent to English boarding school.

Three

"*Getting ahead in a difficult profession requires avid faith in yourself. You must be able to sustain yourself against staggering blows.*"

—SOPHIA LOREN

I have to admit that I used to write long doting letters to my future royal husband. I didn't tell many people about these letters at the time because, let's face it, they already thought I was crazy. But what did I have to lose? Nothing. If anything, I had the whole world to gain.

I was about fourteen when I sent my first letter to Buckingham Palace—when all the other girls my age were writing fan mail to teenybopper stars like Kirk Cameron and Rob Lowe. But aside from a crush I would later develop on Hugh Grant, I had zero interest in Hollywood heartthrobs. And zero interest in the pathetic high school dating scene. Why would I want to go to a Future Farmers of America dance or on a romantic date to the truck stop? Why would I want to pile into some guy's pickup, drink cheap beer, and make out in the woods? The local drive-in was fun—but unlike Chloe, I usually went for the movie, not for the boys. Eight years, ten years, even fifteen years after I'd found his name in that library book, Peter Phillips continued to be the only guy for me.

But unfortunately, Peter's address was not in the Yellow Pages. And Google hadn't even been invented yet, not that it would have been there either. So, despite my bookshelf full of royal resources, I was kind of at a loss—until the summer of eighth grade, when I was chosen to attend a youth leadership conference in Washington, D.C.

Government and political history had always been my best subjects (it's a huge aspect of royalty if you think about it) and I was ecstatic. That trip to Washington was life-changing for me. For the first time in my life I was surrounded by hundreds of honor students just like me and Princess Masako. For the first time in my life I wasn't shunned by my peers for not being a cowgirl. And for the first time in my life, no one knew about my hippie upbringing. Strutting through the halls of Congress in my first ever suit was pure bliss. And that's when I decided that until I made it to England, I would study political science. Worst-case scenario, I'd marry a senator.

One afternoon during the conference, our group of students was scheduled to visit the Bolivian Embassy and meet the ambassador. After politely listening to the ambassador's welcome speech, I made a bold move. I decided to skip the cake and punch reception, and breaking the conference rules, I ducked out early and scurried across the road to the British Consulate. Miraculously, it wasn't crowded inside and I was able to speak to someone right away.

Through the glass partition, I tried to explain my unusual request. I told the woman I was there with the leadership conference—that way I seemed nice and harmless. I told her that back at school I was working on an important honors project about the role of young royals in modern society and Peter's address would be very useful in my qualitative research. And to my surprise, she didn't tell me to leave immediately.

To be honest, I think it helped that I didn't mention Prince William. Most young girls were fanatically in love with Prince

William because he was cute and blond and got so much glamorous press coverage. And I'm sure British embassies around the world were barraged with soppy love letters for their country's future king. Part of me wonders if I had been closer to William's age (he was nearly five years younger than me), whether I might have been in love with him too, and part of me is very thankful that I am not. I mean, can you *imagine* the competition for William? Can you imagine all those social-climbing American mothers, hastily putting together their daughter's applications to St. Andrews University once William announced he was going there? If I were after William, I'd spend most of my time fighting off other girls! Admittedly, William was heir to throne—very much a bonus point for girls determined to be Queen—but, come on, I had to be realistic. Pursuing William was guaranteed to end in heartbreak. I was much happier with my subtler, lesser-known royal ambition. Not to mention that I didn't feel cosmically drawn to William in the way that I was to Peter.

Anyway, when I mentioned Peter Phillips, the Foreign Office woman seemed almost pleased that I even knew he existed. Still, she remained stern and professional and wasn't about to give away any information that she shouldn't. She suggested that I write to any member of the Royal family courtesy of Buckingham Palace and assured me that it would be delivered. She gave me the address and postcode; I happily thanked her and managed to find my seat on the conference bus moments before roll call was taken and we headed toward our next stop at the Supreme Court. I breathed a sigh of relief. Royal address attained. Mission accomplished.

〜

Back home in Colorado, I spent my summer days working at the local bookstore. Yes, believe it or not, my country bumpkin town actually had a bookstore—and as I slowly outgrew the minuscule local library, it became a place of refuge for me. With its soft normal carpeting, soft normal music, free coffee, and free cookies, that bookstore was the polar opposite of my family's crazy farmhouse (where cookies were never allowed unless they contained both wheat germ and carob).

Between the ages of nine and fourteen, I was reading up to three or four books per week. This was mainly because my parents finally broke down and bought a television, and the rule was that I had to read a full book for every half hour that I watched it. The second rule was that I had to mute all the commercials so I wouldn't be brainwashed into wanting products that I didn't need.

When I started reading nothing but Sweet Valley High and The Baby-sitters Club, my parents decided that sugary teenage books didn't count and that I had to read a literary "classic" for every half hour of television. My mom created elaborate (and oddly draconian) charts for my brother and me to keep track of all this. All I know is that suddenly I was plowing through Jane Austen and Charlotte Brontë as fast as I could—just so I could watch a measly hour of Saturday morning cartoons.

Anyway, I was in the local bookstore so often as a child, that the owner offered to hire me—and pay me in books. And when I was old enough to work for actual money, I realized I had landed the best summer job in town. While my peers worked in McDonald's or Wal-Mart (or roped cattle on someone's ranch), I was able to help the area elite with their literary purchases and I relished every second of it.

I remember pleading desperately with my parents that same summer to let me legally change my name to something girly and English—like Gwendolen or Cecily. (I clearly had just finished reading *The Importance of Being Earnest*). But more than anything, I remember sitting in my backyard and drafting the perfect letter to Peter.

It was quite tricky, actually. I didn't want it to sound like a love letter—that would come later. Rather, my plan was for us to be friends first. A few months as harmless pen pals perhaps— *then* the glorious romance could begin. So I had to sound fascinating enough for him to want to write me back—but on the other hand, I had to be careful not to sound so eager and interested in his life that I came across as some kind of crazy royal fanatic. Like I said, it was tricky.

I agonized over whether the letter should be typed or written in cursive, done in blue or black ink, with a fountain pen or a ballpoint. I experimented with all kinds of stationery, pondered the pros and cons of scenting it with perfume, and sifted through hundreds of photographs until I found one to send him that made me look sweet, pretty, and ever so slightly regal. I spent weeks and weeks working on it, crumpling up one draft after another. I *so* wish I had a copy of the letter that I finally mailed so I could tell you exactly what I wrote in the end, but alas, it was written by hand and I never thought of Xeroxing it for posterity.

I do remember wondering how to skirt the family issue. I wasn't about to tell my future husband that my parents still thought life was one giant Woodstock concert. Instead I wrote something about how my mother was Canadian and my father was from New York City—that way they sounded almost cosmopolitan and I was able to slip a Commonwealth reference in at the same time. Like me, the royals loved all things canine, so I made sure to mention my beloved dog, Jasper, as much as possible. I discussed Colorado in terms of world-class ski resorts and sprawling scenic ranches—as if the state was one giant alternative Switzerland instead of a place bursting with gun shows and goatropings. I remember focusing on how Peter and I were the same age and how fascinated I was with England and how wouldn't it be lovely if we could be transatlantic pen pals?

Once it was mailed, I felt confident that I was in command of my own destiny and that my life would finally start moving in the right direction. Soon, my prince and I would be happily corresponding. Soon after that we would inevitably meet up in a very romantic location, which would be followed by a starry-eyed courtship, a lengthy engagement and at last, a magnificent royal wedding, quite possibly without the hippies in attendance. As ever, I knew it was only a matter of time.

My parents, on the other hand, weren't so sure. They were increasingly worried about my incessant interest in royalty with its inherent class system and trappings of material wealth.

"The best thing that could happen to you, Jerramy," my mother would repeatedly tell me, "would be for you to fall in love with a homeless man. That's what you need to bring you back down to earth."

And I became increasingly worried that if I actually brought home a homeless man and announced that he was my new boyfriend, they would be overjoyed.

⟶

Every day, I walked the long length of the driveway from our farmhouse to our mailbox to see if Peter had replied. Jasper, my darling and devoted golden retriever (and quite frankly the only family member I could ever actually relate to) always came with me on those walks.

Like it was yesterday, I remember opening the little silver door of the mailbox one Saturday afternoon and pulling out the pile of mail—bills, *Mother Jones* magazine, the local newspaper with story after story about livestock, and, oh my God—there it was. It had hardly been two weeks! How could he have replied so quickly?

My address was neatly typed on the featherweight envelope. It had a blue airmail sticker in one corner and the postmark was from Buckingham Palace. *From Buckingham Palace!* For a long time, I just stood there. Holding the envelope and staring at the postmark. My heart thudded in my chest and the rural landscape swam around me as my mind spun with an overwhelming sense of destiny.

I almost wasn't brave enough to open it. It was much, much worse than when I had to open letters from Cornell or Georgetown a few years later to see if I'd been accepted. Because it mattered so much more.

Like the wonderful companion that he was, Jasper sat at my heels, patiently waiting to see what I would do next.

"Jasper," I whispered, "my prince has finally written to me."

His big brown eyes widened and he panted a wide smile back at me, full of moral support. At least Jasper didn't want me to marry a homeless man. If only my family understood me half as much as he did.

I walked slowly back to the house, mustering the courage to face whatever I might find inside that royal envelope. Jasper grabbed a stick with his mouth and ran the length of the driveway and back again before he realized a game was hopeless. Lost in my own world, I sat down in a wicker rocking chair in the front lawn and Jasper sprawled euphorically on the grass beside me. I carefully opened the envelope, took a deep breath, and pulled out a beautiful sheet of watermarked stationery.

Buckingham Palace

27 September 1993

Dear Jerramy,

The Princess Royal has asked me to write to thank you for your letter to Peter. I have been asked to send Her Royal

Highness's best wishes.

Yours Sincerely,

The Hon. xxx xxxxx
Assistant Private Secretary to HRH The Princess Royal

I must have read that letter a hundred times, refusing to believe it. There had to be more than a response from his mother's assistant secretary! There had to be! From the looks of it, Peter hadn't even been given the chance to read my letter! The perfect letter that I worked so hard on! How could this have happened? How could I not have foreseen this happening? The reality of my own naiveté hit me like a blow to the stomach and I trembled in an attempt to stop the tears.

It was going to be more challenging than I ever, ever realized.

I don't know how long I sat there, staring up into the blue sky, looking for answers. But after many deep breaths, I dried my eyes and regained my composure. I wasn't about to let this *minor* obstacle stop me. The only reason Peter didn't write back was because he didn't even *know* I had written to him! So I couldn't judge myself, or him, too harshly. I would just find some other way of making contact.

⤚

Once school started up again, I tried to take my mind off the whole princess thing. I took the dreaded ACT and SAT, joined the tennis team and the debate team, marched in the homecoming parade, and went to prom. (Chloe set me up with a very cute guy that could talk about nothing but Jesus and the military.)

Like a robot, I went through all the motions of any well-rounded American girl preparing for college. All these activities served as a welcome distraction, but my need to be in England never left me. Despite my attempts to ignore it or pretend I couldn't hear what the little voice inside me was saying, I knew I would never be able to keep it quiet. It was always there, forever repeating to me that England was where I must go.

Then one day, I saw the poster: 6TH–12TH-GRADE STUDENTS INTERESTED IN WEEKLONG EDUCATIONAL TRIP TO ENGLAND, PLEASE MEET ON TUESDAY AT 7 P.M. INFORMATION PACKS AVAILABLE IN THE MAIN OFFICE. Considering most of the kids I went to school with could benefit from a weeklong educational trip *anywhere* outside of our tiny town, I was in shock. I could not believe my cowboy school was even thinking of offering something so worldly and wonderful!

I ran to the office, got myself an information pack, and read every word. From Shakespeare plays at Stratford-Upon-Avon to the Changing of the Guard at Buckingham Palace, the trip covered everything I'd been dying to see. But not surprisingly, it was expensive. It would require begging my parents and grandparents for a loan. Still, I wasn't daunted. I would find the money somehow even if it meant babysitting every night of the week.

My parents came with me to that Tuesday night interest meeting to gather more details on who exactly would be accompanying me across the Atlantic. But when we arrived at the classroom it was practically empty. Out of the entire county school district, only one other person (a boy) was interested in this amazing once-in-a-lifetime trip to England. The two sponsoring teachers and four parents waited in silence another thirty minutes while the boy and I eyed each other with embarrassment. Finally, it was decided that only two students would not be worth the effort and the trip was declared canceled.

Perfect. Another door to my destiny slammed in my face. Was I ever going to make it to England?

At least Mike (the aforementioned boy) and I became friends. Mike was a year younger than me and even though I *never* say this about boys, he was a good ten times smarter than me. And to my utter astonishment, he thought my insane parents were amusing rather than terrifying.

Once Mike came over and ended up discussing Pink Floyd with my dad for hours. All the while I was worried to death of what he would think of me when he saw my house filled with all kinds of weird antiques, Guatemalan cushions, bizarre modern art sculptures, my dad's enormous paintings of indigenous people, the wall-to-wall hysterically patterned carpet that used to be in a 1930s movie theater that my parents found abandoned in a Denver alleyway, and the room that my mom decided to paint bright purple so it would look like a "Santa Fe sunset."

But shockingly, Mike loved it.

"Jerramy, your house is great!" he told me. "No stairs—it's perfect for parties!"

Those last years of high school weren't so bad once I learned that my peers would still speak to me after stepping inside what was essentially a hippie-fied carnival funhouse. And I guess there was one good thing about having hippie parents: As a teenager, I found that it was downright impossible to horrify them. And with this realization I started doing things that no one else my age would be allowed to do in a million years.

I was the only one in town allowed to throw "coed slumber parties" and my parents insisted if my friends were too drunk to drive home, or too afraid to face their parents after missing a curfew, they could always stay the night at our house (or in the tipi or the treehouse or the root cellar).

Personally, I possessed a very puritan view toward drugs and alcohol—probably because my parents didn't hesitate to share their past experiences, in detail, with me on everything from LSD to opium. So although I adored playing the perfect social hostess, I never smoked or drank a thing. And I guess that's one thing that horrified the parents, or at least puzzled them. That and the time I entered the Miss Teen Colorado pageant[6] without telling them. I have to admit that didn't go down particularly well either. Especially with the bra-burning feminist mother.

⟶

When I was in junior high, my mother made us have a family fire drill to practice escaping the farmhouse in case it ever went up in flames. But when the alarm sounded, instead of running straight to the front door as I'd been told, I threw open my closet, grabbed armfuls of my beloved clothes, and tossed them out my bedroom window—hangers and all.

"How could you put the safety of your clothes before the safety of your own life?" my mom demanded angrily. But to me, one didn't exist without the other.

Until Wal-Mart took over, for years the only places to buy clothes in our Podunk town were a small ranchwear boutique that catered to wealthy tourists and a store that offered about a billion styles of cowboy boots. Other than that, you were free to place orders from the Sears catalog just like you could if you were a rural farmer back in 1886.

But clearly none of this mattered one bit to my parents because their idea of shopping was rummaging through boxes at The Salvation Army and their idea of fashion was still stuck somewhere between Haight-Ashbury and the Summer of Love.

"Jerramy, what do you think I should wear to my job interview?" my mom would ask me.

"Um, how about *not* the batik skirt covered with feathers," I'd tell her.

My dad was even worse. I once bought him a brand-new

---

6 I didn't win the state title, but I won "Best Speech" and still got to wear a ball gown and tiara.

button-down shirt for Father's Day. He took one look at it, sneered at the pristine packaging, and returned it the very next day. Still, I was desperate to inject at least one item of clothing into his wardrobe that I approved of, so I waited a few weeks, went back to the store, and bought the same shirt again. Except this time I took off the tags, crumpled it into ball, put it in an old plastic bag, and told him I'd found it at The Salvation Army. Now he wears it all the time.

Clearly, when it came to fashion, I had no living role models—only my precious books and magazines—and so, like everything in my life, I set about teaching myself. I was about fifteen years old when I abandoned contemporary eighties trends and decided to pattern my wardrobe after Grace Kelly and Jacqueline Kennedy. True, they were somewhat before my time—but wasn't everything? Feeling I was born into the wrong era was hardly a new sensation! To me, these two magnificent women represented the absolute pinnacle of ladylike sophistication. And as a young girl stranded in the style abyss of the Rocky Mountains, I quickly took them on as my personal fashion mentors.

Admittedly, attaining their timeless style and impeccable grooming was rather difficult when I lived in the middle of nowhere and six hours away from something as basic as a Gap. But over time, my wardrobe began filling up with as many Grace and Jackie essentials as I could afford: sleeveless A-lines, three-quarter-length sleeves, pleated skirts, cashmere twin sets, bejeweled cardigans, coats with oversize buttons, and more cocktail dresses than I knew what to do with. Jewelry? Only pearls. Heels? Always. And if it were still acceptable to wear white gloves every day, believe me, I would.

What I loved so much about Grace and Jackie was the regal quality that permeated their personal style and the regal demeanor that allowed them to carry it off. The fact that one became a princess in real life, and the other became the Queen of

Camelot is no coincidence. They had dressed for their destinies and their destinies had been fulfilled.

I had every intention of doing the same.

⁓

High school seemed to move in geological time, but luckily the promise of college loomed before me. Accustomed to helping kids join the military or apply to local vocational and agricultural schools, my guidance counselor didn't have the faintest idea what to do with me when I told her I wanted to go to school out of state. So essentially, I was left alone with my college applications.

I had the required GPA, high test scores, and a résumé filled with the requisite clubs, teams, and token charity work. That stuff was easy. The hard part was the essay. It had to be eloquent, poignant, and most of all, brilliantly unique. Finally, I decided to write about my letter to Peter. I knew it was risky (other students were writing about lessons learned through raising prize-winning hogs), but I hoped that such an unconventional topic would get the attention of admission boards—and that the story of seeking out but failing to contact my prince would show my resourcefulness, my resilience, and my unshakable dedication.

It worked. I'd applied to several prestigious colleges across the east coast and received partial scholarships to them all. But when it came time to choose between them, it boiled down to one factor and one factor only: their study-abroad programs in England.

In the end, I chose the University of Rochester in upstate New York—not only did it have a very English name, but it ranked highly in political science, had fantastic study-abroad options, and best of all, you couldn't get much farther from Colorado without crossing the ocean. I was so close to escaping that blasted cow town I could hardly contain myself. All that was left between me and deliverance was the six-hour car ride to the Denver airport. And I only barely survived *that* with my sanity intact.

As we drove peacefully through the steep switchbacks of the Rocky Mountains, something came over my mother. She suddenly felt that it was her maternal duty to confess everything that she'd been holding back from me before I went away to college. Believe me, I didn't want to know. And believe me, I did my best not to listen. I really did try to spare myself. But stuck in the back of that station wagon, there was nowhere to run.

All my friends' parents had nicely framed wedding photos on display somewhere in their houses. These photos inevitably contained a bride in a white dress and a groom wearing a pale blue tuxedo with ruffles. Nice, normal 1970s photos. Then, in utter bewilderment, I would look at my parents' wedding album. These photos consisted of a picture of someone's bloodshot eye, a close-up of my parents' first dog, a close-up of what looked like the blue corner of a tablecloth, and another one showing nothing but a giant yin-yang of white flower petals. Based on this ridiculous group of snapshots, I couldn't even figure out what my mother had worn (not that I would have approved).

"Our wedding ceremony was beautiful" or "Our wedding reception was very cool" is all my parents would ever say about their mysterious San Francisco nuptials, and it drove me bonkers. I used to ask them over and over where on earth the normal pictures were so I could see this very cool ceremony for myself—but they simply refused to tell me.

Until that excruciating car ride.

"You know, Jerramy," said my mom as she looked at the expanse of mountain highway before her. "At our wedding, there was a dropper full of acid in the Japanese wine. Everyone was drinking it. So everyone was tripping. Even the photographer."

Ah.

I acted like I wasn't fazed by the news; like I wasn't screaming at her inside my head.

"Can you tell me what you and Dad *wore* to your wedding?" I asked, ignoring the acid comment altogether.

"Well," she answered dreamily, "I wore a hand-embroidered orange skirt and your dad wore pants that I sewed for him out of a tablecloth that we bought for fifteen cents at The Salvation Army."

I stared straight ahead of me, trying to stay calm. I'd had a countdown on my calendar for the last three years, religiously crossing off the 1,095 days until I left for college and could escape the insanity once and for all. It was the 1,094th day. Only one more to go.

"Now, Jerramy," my mom continued, "when you get to college, go ahead and experiment with drugs if you feel you need to. But please—please don't start drinking."

It wasn't long before my dorm room cocktail parties were legendary.

A girl's got to rebel somehow.

Four

*"The accent of our native country dwells in the heart and mind
as well as on the tongue."*

—FRANÇOIS DE LA ROCHEFOUCAULD

Lots of kids get homesick when they go away to college.
Not me.

In the sophisticated, east-coast atmosphere of Rochester academia, everything was as it should be; and everything was exactly what my past was not. It was like this magical, alternative universe that I'd always known existed but had finally been able to enter. College was one big blur of learning and laughter and until that point, I don't remember ever being happier. After eighteen painful years of enduring the hippies and hickville, I was finally able to breathe freely, finally able to be myself.

Every night, as I climbed into the loft bed above my desk, exhausted from another late night of studying or partying, I said a silent prayer—thanking some greater power for taking me away from Colorado and granting me this new life. I'd never really believed in God, but I always felt it was important to speak to whatever force out there might be listening. I firmly believed that if I continued to define the life that I wanted, continued to focus on it with all of my intention, and was ready to claim it with all of my heart, eventually the universe would provide it for me.

~

I also firmly believed you had to constantly visualize your inten-
tions if you truly wanted them to materialize. So I plastered
my side of the dorm room with dozens of glossy posters: beautiful prints of the State Dining Room and the Grand Staircase
at Buckingham Palace, turn-of-the-century black-and-white
photographs of the bronze lions in Trafalgar Square, sparkling
night skylines of the Houses of Parliament and Big Ben.

Late at night, when I became bored or delirious after reading
too much of my comparative politics textbook or something really horrible like my neuroscience notes, my tired eyes would always wander away from my desk and settle on my wonderful
English posters. In my sleep-deprived state, it sometimes seemed
that if I stared at those posters hard enough, I could somehow
transport myself into them. I could actually picture myself in that
royal dining room; I could hear the buzz of the society chitchat,
feel the heat of the golden candelabras, see the texture of my
nineteenth-century ball gown and the brocade on the footman's
arm as he served me from a giant silver platter. When I wanted to
procrastinate, my mind could wander for ages, swerving in and
out of my imaginary English life, moving from scene to scene,
epoch to epoch, and poster to poster.

Meanwhile, my Los Angeles roommate thought I was nuts;
her side of the room was covered with black-light Led Zeppelin
posters.

~

The first day Lindsay and I met, I was sitting on the floor of our
room trying to set up the voice mail on our shared phone.

"The six-digit password is 774623—or PRINCE," I told her
cheerily.

"Prince as in *Purple Rain*?" she asked.

"No, Prince as in Prince Charming," I answered.

At first glance, anyone would have guessed that as freshman roommates we must have despised each other. And I suppose this was an easy mistake to make because outwardly, we couldn't be more different. Lindsay wore jeans and big baggy T-shirts every day; I hated jeans and only wore big, baggy T-shirts to bed when I couldn't find my silk pajamas. Lindsay tried to teach me about heavy metal music while I tried to show her the joys of Broadway musicals and Disney soundtracks. For the campus-wide Halloween party, I dressed up as (big surprise) a princess, and she dressed up as the scary girl from *The Addams Family*.

Lindsay felt that college had ripped her away from her closest friends; I felt that college might be my first opportunity to make them. She missed home desperately; I dreaded the thought of ever returning. But after getting over each other's questionable tastes in music, fashion, and decor, Lindsay and I realized we had more in common than not. We were both extremely picky about boys, extremely serious about academics, and most importantly, extremely determined to attend college parties at least five nights a week. And believe me, it wasn't long before we were as thick as thieves.

Probably out of curiosity, boys and girls were drawn to our unlikely friendship and within days, our schizophrenically decorated room was the social epicenter of our coed hallway. Lindsay tried to get me to stop drinking beer with a straw and I tried to show her the classic glamour of perfectly mixed martinis. Night after night, we'd drink ourselves silly till 3 A.M. and then roll into class the next morning with astonishingly clear minds. We were too young to experience debilitating hangovers (I actually used to *enjoy* getting the bed spins!), but it's truly a wonder our brains didn't dissolve away completely with the amount of units we regularly consumed on an almost nightly basis. Our *pre-party* cocktail parties alone should have killed us. (Not to mention I have no idea how over fifty people squeezed into our tiny dorm room every night.)

But college wasn't all fun and games. Thanks to my parents' brilliance, I also spent a great deal of my time trying to explain to various university administrators that despite my misleading first name, I wasn't a boy—that I was actually a girl and extremely girly at that—and to please make sure that I was removed from the fraternity mailing list and to also make sure that no official records had my gender listed as male or my title as Mister. Lots of people tell me that I got off lucky. That I could've been named Rainbow or Peaches or Moonbeam. But at least those names are somewhat girly! At least with a name like Peaches, I wouldn't have been constantly invited to join a fraternity.

Like most moms, my mom sent me a college care package that first year. Along with giant bottles of vitamin C and echinacea, it contained a small, handmade wooden tray engraved with my initials. I had absolutely no idea what I was meant to do with it. Serve myself breakfast in bed? Lindsay took one look at it and burst out laughing.

"I can't believe your mom sent you a rolling tray!" she cackled. "A *personalized* rolling tray!"

"What do you mean 'rolling tray'?" I asked her. "What am I supposed to roll? Sushi or something?"

She was still laughing. "Joints, you silly blonde! It's for rolling joints!"

For the love of God. Why couldn't she send me cookies or muffins or something like everyone else's mothers? After all these years, did she *still* not realize I was never, ever going to embrace her beloved sixties counterculture? When she called me later that week I decided to confront her about it.

"Mom," I said carefully, "I appreciate the thought, but you know perfectly well that I don't smoke pot and never will."

"I know, honey," she said warmly. "I figured maybe you could use it as a cheese tray if you wanted to. In any case, it's good to support the hemp industry. Hemp crops are the solution to global warming, you know."

I'm telling you, my switched-at-birth theory did not come out of nowhere. The evidence came rolling in every day.

No pun intended.

⟶

Now please keep in mind that past lives aside, at this point in time, I had never met a real-live English person. I had never heard a real-live English accent that wasn't in a Hugh Grant movie, BBC costume drama, or an old rerun of *Fawlty Towers*. So when I overheard one in the beer-stained basement of a noisy fraternity house one night, I froze. The effect was positively hypnotic.

"I left my *mo-bile* at the bar . . ." the mystery voice was saying.

I felt like someone raised by wolves who had suddenly recognized the sound of my mother tongue even if I couldn't speak it myself. In a flash of delight, I was overwhelmed by a flood of bizarre sensations. I felt like the kid in *The Jungle Book* when he first saw another human. The sound evoked my deepest memories and innermost desires, and in that beautiful, emotionally charged moment, I became some kind of accent-addicted madwoman.

Whatever vibration occurred in the upper-crust English accent became the single largest aphrodisiac I was ever to experience. And for the rest of my life, I was irrationally overcome with the desperate need to hear it again and again.

Lindsay could have her carefree California boys. I had no interest in them, nor the hundreds of preppy guys from New England boarding schools that filled every frat party. I had a new plan as far as boys were concerned. From that day forward, I was going to seek out and seduce the few Englishmen roaming the campus. So help me God.

Unfortunately, soon after making this drunken announcement to my friends, I pored though the university student directory and based on the home addresses listed, discovered that the campus contained only two Englishmen for me to seek out. But I wasn't daunted. Quite intentionally, I went out and developed a crush on a chunky Englishman with a mole on his face, and another on a guy with dark beady eyes and a face like an eagle. It didn't matter what the boys looked like; it didn't matter what they talked to me about—all that mattered to me was the spellbinding sound of their beautiful English accents.

My obsession eventually seeped into my coursework. I convinced the registrar to let me take the History of Victorian England as an English credit (after all, I would be writing lots of papers *in English*) and always sat in the front row staring starry-eyed at the handsome, middle-aged professor. He was technically American but he'd lived and studied in England for so long that his accent had changed and when he said things like "Do you have any queries?" instead of "Do you have any questions?"—my heart would flutter.

When my friend Natalie told me her physics professor was English, I signed up for the class right away, knowing full well that I'd probably fail it. I didn't understand those scorpionlike equations for the life of me, and as expected, by the end of the semester most of the students had As and I had a D. But at least I got another dreaded science credit out the way, and my God, that English professor's accent made it all worth it.

Meanwhile, back in the world of student frat parties, I would strategically place myself near my two not-so-handsome English targets and hang on their every English-accented word. The fat one with the mole quickly dismissed me as yet another crazy

American (honestly, how could he?), but the Eagle and I got on rather well when we were drunk. And one night during my sophomore year I found myself sitting on his lap in a crowded car on the way to someone's house party. One thing led to another and somehow he ended up in my dorm room and I ended up letting him kiss me.

Mind you, because of the rather impossible criteria I insisted upon before letting a guy kiss me (i.e., kisser must be English or speak with an English accent), letting a guy kiss me didn't happen often. So, needless to say, I was quite excited that such a rare occasion had presented itself.

After a while, the Eagle came up for air and began to look around. It was the first time I had brought a boy back to my room, so until that moment, it hadn't really occurred to me how boys might react to my England-inspired decorating scheme. I mean, I have to admit, if Anglophilia were a crime, that dorm room contained more than enough evidence to arrest me and imprison me for life.

In my silly, cocktail-induced condition, I watched the Eagle's beady eyes move from my Union Jack flag to Tony Blair's smiling face (seriously, can you name a sexier world leader?) to my posters of London's dazzling skyline. My shelves full of vintage royal memorabilia, including an elaborate shrine to Diana, were behind him, which, in retrospect, was probably for the best.

"Fucking hell. You're *obsessed*," said the Eagle with a tone not as kind as it should have been.

"I like England." I shrugged with a giggle. I tried to pull his lips back to mine, but he pulled away, still looking at my posters.

"Jerramy," he said slowly, "you do realize it's *just a country*."

You see, that's where he was wrong.

"It's so much more than that!" I laughed when I said it. But I was serious.

The Eagle looked at me with visible fear, like he had just found out I was some kind of dangerous mental patient or something. Granted my lipstick was probably smudged like in *Whatever Happened to Baby Jane?*, but that was hardly a reason for him to look as frightened as he did.

As the door closed quickly behind him, I was left standing fully clothed with a bottle of beer still clenched in my hand, and staring bewilderedly at the *Life* magazine picture of Charles and Diana's famous wedding kiss that I had taped to the back of my door.

Never mind. It's not like the Eagle and I had a future together. He wasn't even royal.

⌒

During the first semester of my junior year, I was sitting in the campus coffeehouse when my radar ears picked something up from a nearby table.

"You think the exam was easy?" the mystery voice was asking his coffee companions. "Bollocks! It was a disast-a!"

Wait a minute. I'd already been through all the English guys on campus. Who was *this*?

I sneaked a glance. Our school was small and everyone lived on campus, so I definitely recognized him. In fact, I'd probably seen him hundreds of times in the last two years. But our social circles didn't cross very often and I'd never taken much notice to be honest.

But after hearing his very English accent, everything changed. Suddenly this stranger, whom I hadn't given a second glance to in the past, was extremely good-looking. (And to be fair, compared to Mr. Mole and the Eagle, he was practically a supermodel.) And just like that, my new English love interest was born.

Because of his trendy red sneakers, my nickname-loving friends quickly took to calling my newfound crush "Red Shoes."

And if any of them spotted Red Shoes in the library, they would call me right away so I could study in his section. This semistalking behavior went on for weeks. I even invited him anonymously to my sorority crush party—but he didn't show up.

Then came the traditional day[7] when the entire university gets up at dawn and drinks all day in the autumn sunshine. I'd swallowed two full thermoses of white wine by the time I got up the courage to walk across the Frat Quad and tell Red Shoes it was I who'd invited him to the crush party.

He looked at me through his trendy sunglasses and in his beautiful, glorious, sexy English accent, he said, "If I had known it was you, I would have come."

God, I love English guys. They can take the simplest sentences and make them sound like the most sophisticated, eloquent, and heartfelt combination of words you've ever heard in your entire life. Too bad the white wine erased all memory of everything we said to each other after that.

⟿

I suppose it's just as well our paths never crossed again after that short but ever so sweet drunken rendezvous—because my semester abroad had finally arrived and soon I'd be departing for the motherland! Gone were the days of chasing any hint of an English accent, because soon I'd be *drowning* in English accents!

But before I caught that first precious flight to London, before I was able to begin the rest of my life once and for all, I had to go back to Colorado for Christmas break.

---

7 Known as Dandelion Day or "D-Day." In the 1980s, *Newsweek* ranked it as one of the nation's top fifteen college parties.

Five

"Home is not where you live, but where they understand you."

—Christian Morgenstern

As usual, the blissful normality of college life slipped away as soon as I arrived in the Rocky Mountains. And, as usual, I was forced to endure the traditional Christmas Day family outing to the nearby clothing-optional hot springs. My parents loved that place. They walked around naked all the time at home, and I seriously think if they had their way, the whole world would be one giant nude commune.

Ezra, my little skater-punk brother, didn't seem to mind holidays at the hot springs. Quite annoyingly, he never minded half the zany stuff my parents did. (He didn't even mind his weird name, but then again at least his name was the correct gender.) But for me, the entire ordeal was absolutely mortifying.

While my family basked naked under the stars in the giant steaming pool with all their other naked friends, I would head indoors and sit by myself in the only pool on the premises where swimsuits were required—all the while knowing I would later be shunned for refusing to join in the family spirit of Christmas. Well, I'm sorry, but my Christmas spirit had its limits.

For as many Christmases as I can remember, I would float on my back all by myself in that tiny clothing-required pool, staring at the ceiling and dreaming about what life would've been like if I hadn't been switched at birth. I'd dream about the classic English Christmas my real parents were having somewhere in the English countryside and how they were probably all wearing clothes. I dreamed about being somewhere I *belonged*, somewhere that actually felt *like home*.

And the instant my flight touched down at Heathrow, I knew that I was.

⟿

I dropped my suitcases at the Earl's Court hotel, ignored my jet lag, and began making up for twenty years of lost time. I will never forget when I climbed the steps out of Westminster tube station and had my first good look at London. Big Ben towered above me, golden and gleaming, and for a few seconds I couldn't breathe. It was, without a doubt, the most beautiful thing I had ever seen. I just stood there. Dazed. Wondering why a giant *clock* had nearly knocked the wind out of me. Despite all my years of trying to escape everything around me, I suddenly felt something I'd never felt before: the desire to stay in one place forever. I suddenly felt certain that whatever I had been longing for my whole life was actually within my reach.

⟿

After being housed in a giant flat with nine other American girls, I was desperate to make it through the mandatory "cultural assimilation" week that my university had organized. I couldn't wait to escape the lectures on "How to Tell If You're Not Coping with the Stress of a Foreign Country,"[8] the dangerous differences between the U.K. and U.S. meanings of the word "pants,"[9] and

---

8 Apparently one of the indicative warning signs that you're not coping was "drinking too often."

9 "Pants" (plural noun) refers to underwear in the U.K. and what the English would call "trousers" in the U.S.

which way to look when crossing the street, and start my full-time internship at the House of Commons.

Quite romantically, the U.K. Parliament has evolved from the ancient medieval council that once advised the King. Just like America has representatives and senators, the U.K. has Members of Parliament (MPs) and lords. MPs are elected by the British public into the *House of Commons*—meaning this is where the "commoners" or nonaristocrats are represented.

The *House of Lords,* on the other hand, are not elected by the public—they merely *inherit* their political position from their aristocratic parents. There are over seven hundred aristocratic titles in the U.K. that can be inherited and most of these hereditary noblemen are entitled to a seat in the House of Lords—purely because of their birthright.[10]

Believe me, I tried to get an internship at the House of Lords so I could meet some nobility and eventually meet their sons, but unlike the U.S. Senate, the English upper house hadn't learned how to exploit free American labor quite yet and therefore had no internships available.

But I wasn't too disappointed. The dreamy Tony Blair had just come into power and I was going to be working for one of the newly elected "Blair Babes."[11] It was going to be great. Besides, I'd interned for a U.S. congresswoman when I was a sophomore so I figured at the very least, from an academic point of view, it would be a fascinating parallel experience.

As suspected, just like in Congress, my days were filled with replying to endless letters from fretful constituents. For example, "Dear Mr. English, Thank you so much for writing to Mrs. XXX

---

10 Since the nineteenth century, however, the powers of the House of Lords have been steadily declining, and in 1999, the automatic hereditary right to sit in the House of Lords was removed completely.

11 "Blair's Babes" refers to the dozens of female Labour MPs newly elected into the Commons in 1997.

MP to share your concerns regarding the bearskin hats used by the Queen's Guards. She has asked me to write and tell you how much she appreciates hearing your views. . . ."

But then there were the times when I was moved to tears knowing my footsteps were echoing along the very same government corridors as Churchill's—and those kinds of moments were worth every bit of my mundane office work. (Not to mention I got to see the dreamy Tony Blair in the flesh on more than one occasion.)

Still, compared to the decadence of the U.S. Congress, there were some major differences I hadn't bargained for in the British Parliament. Like how hard it would be to find a pencil. Or a Xerox machine that actually worked. The most basic modern technology (like e-mail) was only just beginning to seep into English governmental offices and most of my traditional English colleagues were highly skeptical of it.

One day, one of the English office assistants pulled me aside and whispered, "Jerramy, I hate to say it, but I do believe our good friend Bradley is somehow involved in the porn industry."

Bradley, one of the three American interns including me working in Parliament that year, was the most clean-cut, politically determined kid I'd ever met. I doubt he'd ever picked up a *Playboy* in his life. He was far too worried it might ruin his senatorial campaign twenty years down the road.

"Why?" I laughed. "What on earth makes you think that?"

"Well," the flustered Englishman continued, "I received something from Bradley this morning called *hot mail. HOT* mail! Can you believe he'd send something like that to me at work? I daren't open it. Very dodgy. Very dodgy indeed."

It took me a while to explain to him that most young Americans had Hotmail accounts and that most of them (back then anyway) had nothing to do with the porn industry, but he wasn't at all convinced. It didn't help that the Monica Lewinsky scandal had hit the British press that same week. Understandably, all American interns, however eager, were suddenly deemed a bit suspicious.

Yet while office supplies and twenty-first-century computer knowledge were severely lacking in the House of Commons, other things weren't. Bars, for instance. The Houses of Parliament are located within the Palace of Westminster, a historic royal palace and former residence of kings. The layout of the palace is intricate, with its existing buildings containing well over two miles of passages. And within this beautiful, ancient maze of a building, you will find twenty-three official bars.

I wasn't even old enough to legally drink back in America, and all of sudden I was spending night after night downing government subsidized gin-and-tonics with the U.K.'s most senior politicians.

By law, the bars had to stay open as long as the House was in session. So while the MPs and their staff sat around waiting for the voting bells to ring, they drank. Vote. Drink. Vote. Drink. Vote. Drink. It's no wonder their government ran like such a finely oiled machine.

No one was violently protesting about unborn children. No one was demanding the right to own semiautomatic weapons. No one was complaining about the topless women that appeared every day as a matter of course in several of the national newspapers. From what I could tell, England appeared to be an oasis of sheer calm and civilization under the watchful eye of Her Majesty the Queen. Only in the U.S. could you still have decidedly genuine and objective arguments about whether the death penalty was a moral obligation, whether stem cell research was sacrilegious, or whether gay humans were substandard to straight ones. I'm telling you, whatever connected contemporary British society to the ancient institution of royalty seemed to be working.

Much to my surprise (and everyone else's), chasing English boys wasn't a huge priority during my semester abroad. But to be honest, I wasn't surrounded by loads of temptation. Whereas all the young men working in U.S. Congress were tan, square-jawed, and positively Kennedy-esque, the English government didn't seem to be churning out quite so many youthfully handsome political lackeys. Besides, the very idea of chasing after random English boys seemed silly when I knew my physical proximity to Peter Phillips was closer than it had ever been before.

At any rate, I was already head over heels in love with London. I loved *everything* about it: the air, the accent, the people, the palaces, even the milky tea and the rainy weather. Determined to explore every single inch of that breathtaking city, I crammed every spare hour I had with sightseeing. Sadly, most of my American classmates were primarily interested in the novelty of the U.K.'s lower drinking age,[12] so getting people to tour the Royal Mews or Hampton Court Palace or Windsor Castle or the Crown Jewels or Diana's Dress Collection with me early on a Saturday morning wasn't always easy.

However, I did meet one nice English guy during that semester. Now don't get excited—he wasn't a love interest. Rupert was working for an MP during his gap year[13] and sat at the desk across from me in our little government office building next to Westminster Abbey. Although he insisted on calling me Jezza[14] and teased me endlessly about my royal obsession, Rupert was one of those guys who instantly became a surrogate brother to me. We might have had a momentary spark of attraction for each other in the early days, but our friendship became so close so quickly; it soon seemed utterly ridiculous to even consider anything else.

---

12 You can legally drink alcohol at the age of eighteen in the U.K..

13 A year off taken by British students after high school before matriculating into full-time university. Most gap-year students go backpacking around the world or gain work experience.

14 A weird British diminutive used for first names where the first of multiple syllables ends in an *r*. Hence, Karen becomes *Kazza* and Jerramy becomes *Jezza*.

Rupert and I would read the morning papers together, make countless cups of afternoon tea, complain about the eternally broken "photocopier," gossip about what had gone on in all the government bars the night before, and try to predict what year Bradley would be elected to the U.S. Senate. Knowing all the other students in my program were hanging out purely with other Americans in all-American sports bars, I felt genuinely lucky to have made a real English friend.

I was also lucky to have landed such an amazing internship— not only was it extremely social, but it granted me elite glimpses into British life. The MP I was working for always offered me her discarded invitations, giving me the option of attending in her place. And as a result, I went to all sorts of crazy things: receptions in support of cable television, receptions campaigning against circus animals, committee meetings on everything from fireworks safety to poverty in Africa. One morning my MP handed me an invitation to a housing awards ceremony taking place that afternoon and of course I agreed to go.

After lunch, when I looked at the invitation more carefully to see where I needed to be, I nearly fell out of my chair. Princess Anne, HRH The Princess Royal, *was going to be presenting one of the awards*! Princess Anne was the Queen's only daughter, Prince Charles's younger sister, and the mother of my beloved Peter!

Full-scale panic set in. I was going to come face to face with my *future mother-in-law*!

The awards were taking place in ten minutes. I had no time to prepare. Zero time to compose myself or create any kind of strategy. How on earth was I going to handle it? My palms were sweaty and my heart was pounding, but I had no choice but to stay calm as I entered the smart Westminster conference room, put on my nametag, and took my seat.

All through the awards, I felt like I was trapped in some kind of space-time continuum. I watched the presentation on all the good deeds the housing charities were doing across the country: the homeless teenagers they were sheltering, the life skills they were teaching to make sure the same kids never wandered back onto the streets again. It was all very moving. I watched it as if everything were perfectly normal. As if some critical juncture in my destiny wasn't unfolding before my very eyes.

More down-to-earth than the other royals, Princess Anne didn't necessarily have a reputation for elegance, but overall she was the type of woman that the British public considered to be a "good egg." I watched her intently as she stood patiently to the side before presenting the awards, wearing a navy wool suit and her signature white gloves. Now in her late forties, she had long, sturdy legs and her upswept bouffant hairstyle hadn't changed a bit since the 1970s. You had to admire her for refusing to give into fashion trends and focusing solely on her charity work. I read somewhere that she was associated with over two hundred charities and organizations in an official capacity. How could anyone be against the monarchy when faced with a statistic like that?

As I sat there, all my years of royal research became a dizzying blur. Let's say I was lucky enough to be presented to her. How was I supposed to address her? Your Highness? Your Royal Highness? Ma'am? Or was that only for Princess Margaret? Should I dip my head into a slight bow or was that only for men? Did I curtsy with my weight on my left foot or my right? I couldn't remember a thing. And if she did talk to me, what in the name of God was I going to say? Dare I mention I planned on marrying her son?

The awards ended, and tea and biscuits[15] were served. Every-

---

15 In the U.K., *biscuit* means "cookie"—it *does not* refer to the buttermilk biscuits you'd find at KFC.

one mingled about trying to get near the Princess Royal without looking like that's what they were trying to do and I was no exception. Aside from the few formerly homeless teenagers who had been invited to the event, I was by far the youngest person present—and I suppose that's what drew her to me.

I was introduced to her by one of the charity executives. "May I present Miss Fine, an intern in the House of Commons," she said, reading directly from my nametag.[16]

Everything became somewhat hazy after that. I was overcome with the significance those next few moments would hold for my future.

"Your Highness." I smiled, bobbing into a subtle curtsy and lightly touching the gloved fingertips of her outstretched hand. "How do you do."

(If they offer their hand, you shake their hand—at least I was focused enough to remember that bit of royal protocol!)

And before we could exchange any more pleasantries, before I could slip her my e-mail address to pass on to Peter, before she could see what a fantastic daughter-in-law I was going to make, she was swiftly introduced to the next person. And I was left alone with my teacup. Giddy beyond words.

〜

As I happily walked back to Parliament in a daze, I hummed the lines from my favorite *Little Mermaid* song. Back in Colorado, I used to listen to *The Little Mermaid* sound track on my Walkman at top volume whenever my parents assigned me the disgusting task of cleaning out the chicken coop. Those beautiful Disney songs were all I had to help me block out the fact that I (someone quite possibly of noble birth) was being forced to shovel hay and excrement.

---

16 One never introduces herself or himself to a royal; one must always wait to be formally presented.

But now, after meeting Princess Anne, the mother of my future husband, so soon after arriving in England, my beloved lyrics took on a whole new meaning and suddenly seemed as if they'd been written just for me.

> *"I don't know when, I don't know how,*
> *But I know something's starting right now!*
> *Watch and you'll see, someday I'll be, part of your world!"*

Just like Ariel after she had seen the shipwrecked Prince Eric, I could feel the weight of my destiny on my shoulders. And by the time I reached the office, I was quite worked up about it. Luckily most people had gone home for the day so only Rupert was there to witness my minor bout of hysteria.

"It's a small country," I muttered, frantically pacing back and forth across the room. "Therefore, statistically, it's only a matter of time. I mean, if I can meet Peter's mother in *less than one month* after arriving on English shores, surely, *surely* it's only a matter of time before I meet Peter."

I looked pointedly at Rupert. He was leaning back lazily in his desk chair, fingers interlaced behind his head, and watching me—utterly amused.

"Why don't you just climb into his bedroom window?" he teased. "Then you can meet Peter tonight."

I stamped my foot in protest. "Rupert! I'm serious about this!" (And besides, I wasn't yet entirely sure where Peter lived.)

"Ah, Jezza," Rupert sighed. "You're sweet. But you're barking.[17] Properly barking."

---

17 *Barking*: as in "barking mad." British slang used when the person referred to is so completely insane that he or she resembles a mad dog. Although I think rather unfairly used in this context.

Six

*"I hold my breath and cast my fate in the direction of my heart.
I will put on hold my lesser dreams and reach for what is truly
mine."*

—Marianne Williamson

My junior year was ending and as much as I tried to deny
it, that meant my semester abroad was ending too. Not only did it
mean leaving my beloved English homeland and returning to
monarchy-free America, it meant spending the rest of the summer in the cowboy-crammed mountains of Colorado. And let me
tell you, after six glittering months in London, neither location
seemed at all enticing.

I briefly and quite seriously considered throwing my passport
into the sea and staying in the U.K. forever as a citizen of the
world. But something told me I would be back. And much sooner
than anyone realized.

Look at it this way: I had always dreamed of visiting
England—and through nothing but sheer passion and tenacity I
had made it happen. If the simple power of intention was all that
was required, then surely I was capable of making *anything* happen. And I suppose it was this revelation that prompted me to try
my luck and write to Peter one more time.

I know what you're thinking. She's twenty-one years old for

godsake! She's about to be a senior in college! She should have known better! Besides, didn't she learn her lesson the first time?

This is true. When it came to previous royal correspondence, I'd been pretty badly burned. And I agree that by this point I really should have realized that acting like a wistful teenager and sending out yet another lovesick piece of fan mail to Buckingham Palace was not going to further my cause. I mean, what was I hoping to achieve? Another nonresponse from another assistant secretary?

Of course not. You see, this is where my maturity would be an asset. This is where my twenty-one years of experience would come into play to make sure that nothing as devastating as that would happen again.

I knew that meeting Peter's mother was no coincidence. And I simply wasn't willing to let a slice of serendipity as strong as that pass me by. Perhaps my letter was not meant to reach Peter all those years ago, but maybe now the moment was right.

When my semester in London was over, I backpacked[18] around Europe for a few weeks, and spent the rest of the summer waitressing and working on political campaigns in Denver. And, you guessed it, I also spent several days trying to draft the perfect letter to Peter. Talk about weird déjà vu! The only difference was this time I was writing on a laptop instead of on scented lavender stationery. And this time I didn't pause once to decide if dotting my *i*'s with little hearts was or wasn't a good idea.

But let's face it, modern twenty-one-year-old boys had no desire to become pen pals with strange girls, however alluring they may be, unless they were in jail or at war. So this time around, I decided to take a slightly different approach with my letter. I be-

---

18 Not that I would be caught dead with an actual backpack. My friends had them, but I insisted on a small piece of luggage with wheels. (I also insisted on packing a travel wardrobe that allowed me to blend in with native Europeans—nothing screams American more than sneakers, tracksuits, and baseball caps.)

gan by addressing it directly to "The Princess Royal's Assistant Private Secretary." I figured he'd be the one reading it anyway—so why pretend otherwise?

Attempting to use the same kind of cleverly persuasive language I'd learned about in my political speech writing class, I went about telling the assistant private secretary my story: I described my silly girlhood crush on Peter, the romantic letter I had painstakingly written, and the startling bureaucratic response I'd received from the Palace. I told the assistant private secretary how this peculiar chain of events had served as the subject matter for my college entrance essay and how wasn't it extraordinary that I met The Princess Royal as a direct result of my college acceptance?

I told him that although I understood letters of this nature were not traditionally passed on to children of Her Royal Highness, that perhaps, just this once, he would make an exception. I kindly asked him to please pass *this* letter on to Peter—to grant the childhood wish of a little girl and in doing so, to allow events to come full circle.

Like clockwork, a featherweight envelope arrived at my Denver doorstep exactly three weeks later. Recognizing the familiar watermark of the Royal Crest, I opened it with a heavy heart. It had arrived far too soon. I knew it wouldn't be from him.

Bracing myself for two lines of formal text, I was surprised to see nearly two full paragraphs:

Buckingham Palace

7 July 1998

Dear Miss Fine,

I regret that your fears, as you articulated in your letter of June 11 to Peter Phillips, are being realised, and, instead of hearing

*from him, you are getting an official response from me! I am
sorry about this but it is The Princess Royal's official policy.*

*I rather enjoyed reading your letter. It was well written, seri-
ous, and, I believe it to be very sincere, but I hope that you will
understand the principle behind Her Royal Highness wishing
to protect her family from the public gaze when they are still
studying.*

I wish you well in your government studies.

Yours sincerely,

XXXXX XXXXXXX, Esq.
Private Secretary to
HRH The Princess Royal

I carefully folded the letter and gently placed it back inside
the royal envelope—calm as calm can be. And why shouldn't I
have been? Not only had I received two well-thought-out paragraphs instead of two formulaic lines, but they had been personally composed by my future mother-in-law's *private* secretary—not
by some lowly assistant. Not only that, but it was clear that my
future mother-in-law's private secretary *liked me*. And I knew it
wouldn't be long before I had the entire royal household on my
side.

⌒

A month or so later, I happily returned to Rochester for my senior year of college. Painfully conscious that my blissful university
bubble would be popping soon, I studied hard and partied harder.
Acquaintances disappeared and my true friendships strength-
ened. I even allowed myself to kiss a few boys that didn't have
English accents!

I knew I was going to miss college terribly, but there wasn't a
second of my senior year when I wasn't carefully devising a way

to get myself back to England. I hadn't realized the true depth of my longing for that country, the true capacity of my heart to love—until England and I were forced to separate at the end of that precious London semester. I was certain that if I returned to the U.K. for a longer period of time, something extraordinary would happen. And I would finally understand why my heart kept pushing me there with such ferocity.

⌒

For quite some time, I pondered the idea of going to Swiss finishing school[19] after graduation. I'd always wanted to go to one—almost as much as I wanted to go to a British boarding school. The way I saw it, finishing school was a great excuse to return to Europe (and eventually to England) and an ideal venue for mixing with well-connected people. And from a cost perspective, it wasn't any more ridiculously expensive than the high-ranking law schools and grad schools that my friends were applying to.

But then I began to wonder what would happen if, for some reason, finishing school didn't catapult me into royal circles as planned? What then? What skills would I be left with? Menu writing? Seating charts? How to gracefully exit a sports car? Don't get me wrong—I truly believe these kinds of skills are tragically underrated in today's society, but I wasn't so sure they'd be taken seriously on my résumé if worst came to worst and I ended up back in America.

So, perfectly aware that I'd have to double the size of my student loan if I got in, I applied to a master's program at The London School of Economics. Ultimately I knew that going to such a

---

19 Finishing school is a private all-girls institution that prepares girls for life among the social elite and is intended to "complete" one's educational experience. The most famous finishing schools are in Switzerland and lessons include things like skiing, cooking, and French. While girls as young as sixteen can attend the average age for entrants is twenty. Princess Diana attended Swiss finishing school at the Institut Alpin Videmanette in 1977.

prestigious institution was my only hope of getting to England under a legitimate-sounding guise—one that wouldn't cause all the cynical people around me to raise their eyebrows at my motives. (I mean, it wasn't *my* fault the best school in the world for my subject matter *just happened* to be in London.) At LSE, I'd be able to escape all the accusations that I was being irresponsible and neglecting my career—and instead would be free to chase my dream.

I nearly fainted when I received my acceptance letter. Just like my momentary encounter with Princess Anne, it was a sign—an omen! With all these signs, it was clear that my heart was leading me down the right path after all. And it was also clear that the universe was conspiring to help me along every step of the way.

It shouldn't have surprised me, but explaining this to others was easier said than done. When I ran into various people in my hometown, usually the ones that worked at Wal-Mart, and they asked me what I was up to these days, they had absolutely no idea what I was talking about when I told them I would be attending LSE in the fall.

"You're goin' da London? Wow. That's in France, right?" Then the guy would spit a wad of chewing tobacco into the used Dr Pepper can he kept hidden under the cash register.

While my city-dwelling relatives could find both London and France on the globe, they still had their doubts about me going to LSE. And because they worried about my hippie parents' rather laissez-faire approach to parenting, my stricter and more traditional family members were more than happy to share their reservations with me at every opportunity.

"Aren't you sick of England already?" my uncle would ask. "You've already lived there for six whole months. We thought for sure you'd have it out of your system by now."

"What do you want to leave your own country for?" asked another. "You're an *American*. You belong in America!"

Mercifully, if my dad happened to overhear these tirades against me, he'd always come to my defense. "Jerramy drives on the wrong side of the road anyway," he'd say. "She always has. It's safer for everyone if she goes back to London."

Indeed, driving has never been my strong point. But personally, I think my dad was overjoyed that I'd be attending the same school as Mick Jagger.[20] Although I'd mentioned several times that LSE was also the alma mater of John F. Kennedy, Her Majesty Queen Margrethe of Denmark, Crown Prince Haakon of Norway,[21] and the uberintelligent Mrs. Tony Blair—for some reason it was only the celebrated Rolling Stones connection that seemed to stick in his mind.

"But what are you going to eat when you go over there?" asked my very worried aunt. "Do you need me to send you any tampons? I'm not sure you'll be able to buy them."

But more than anything, what I heard from everyone was this: "Are you sure getting into so much more debt is a good idea? Shouldn't you be getting a real job to pay off your first student loan before you take out another one? Isn't it about time you stopped floating around your crazy English dreamland and started living in the real world?"

The real world. You know my feelings on *that* place. And I had absolutely no intention of going there. Not when my heart constantly told me to go someplace entirely different.

---

20 Sir Mick Jagger was registered at the LSE between 1961 and 1963. But he ultimately opted for rock stardom over finishing his economics degree.

21 Husband of the aforementioned Crown Princess Mette-Marit

Seven

Fine, I'll admit it.

Maybe I'd been a tiny bit naïve. Maybe I'd been a tad unrealistic. Maybe, if I'm being entirely honest, I'll admit that I wasn't fully prepared to accept the fact that my life wouldn't magically become one giant, romantic Hugh Grant movie the minute I landed at Heathrow for the second time.

Still. That doesn't explain how my perfect plan had gone so dramatically off the rails.

Don't get me wrong; London was just as heartbreakingly beautiful as I remembered. And it was still brimming with all the splendor and sparkle that I knew my life was going to have once I figured out how to grab onto it. It's just, well, how should I put this? It's just that there didn't seem to be many Hugh Grants wandering around. In fact, there didn't seem to be *any* Hugh Grants wandering around.

I'm not joking.

I (a fairly presentable girl) had been in London nearly a month, and I'd yet to meet a single English person. Not one. Neither male nor female. And considering my plan, and subsequently my entire future, explicitly depended on meeting

English people, I found this state of affairs to be more than slightly alarming.

⌒

It all started when I hopped into a black cab at Heathrow and it pulled up in front of what looked like a menacing six-story bomb shelter instead of a smart and leafy West London address. Could this ugly stack of gray concrete blocks really be my LSE residence hall?

Still, I tried to stay positive. So what if I had to endure less than ideal housing conditions for a while? No big deal. Everyone has to struggle a bit before living happily ever after and if that meant I had to live in a bomb shelter for a while, so be it.

I paid the ridiculously high taxi fare[22] and lugged my three bulging suitcases to the entrance. Once through the doors, I felt better. The lobby was bright and cheery, almost modern—making me think that calling it a bomb shelter might have been a slight overreaction on my part. I signed in with the grumpy man at the front desk and picked up my welcome packet. "Lydia Parson Hall," read the cover of the tenant handbook, "A University Residence for Postgraduates Only."

Instantly, my mind swam with visions of the postgraduate Englishmen I would meet: devastatingly handsome ones in tailored suits from Savile Row[23] who would invite me to polo matches; devastatingly clever ones in smart tweed jackets who would read to me in Latin. I would sit in old libraries and chic coffeehouses with all of them, poring over our political studies together, pausing only to gaze into each other's eyes or engage in deep, academic conversations about how we were going to single-handedly solve

---

22 £45 = approximately $88. Converting pounds to dollars is never a good idea if one wants to enjoy the U.K.

23 Savile Row is a famous London street known for its many shops offering traditional bespoke tailoring.

world poverty and social exclusion. Before I knew it I was going to be whisked away into a whirlwind of glittering English society and leave Colorado firmly in the dust.

I squeezed myself into the tiny elevator (or *lift* as the Brits would say), noting with amusement how I could barely fit inside, much less with my luggage. Granted each of my bags was as big as I was, but I knew an elevator incapable of holding more than one small person and a single suitcase would probably cause any other American to throw a temper tantrum and launch into the usual stream of complaints: "The sheer inconvenience and inefficiency of it all! Think of the fire hazards! The potential lawsuits! It's no wonder this country lost the revolutionary war! It's no wonder they lost the empire!"

It's not that I was unaware of the stark contrast between convenience and efficiency in the U.S. and the lack of convenience and efficiency in the U.K.; it's just that, well, I'd always found Old World–style incompetence to be vaguely entertaining (charming even)—so much so that it never seemed to annoy me.

Squeezed into the corner under the weight of my giant duffel bag (I'd have to go back for the others) and thanking God I wasn't claustrophobic, I eventually managed to press floor number five.[24] The lift jolted and buzzed and moved awkwardly upward, and when the doors finally opened, I wanted more than anything for them to close again.

Let's just say that calling this place a bomb shelter was putting it nicely. Unbelievably nicely. Because what I saw through those rickety elevator doors was so scary it literally made me gasp out loud. This was no bomb shelter. This was a mental institution from a 1950s horror movie.

---

24 Which was really floor number six since the Brits strangely insist on calling the first floor the ground floor, and the second floor the first floor

I know you think I'm exaggerating. My parents certainly did. But really I'm not. The narrow corridor in front of me was so long it bordered on infinite and I half expected a matronly nurse to rush through any second with some moaning lunatic buckled to a stretcher. Beneath the eerie green glow of the fluorescent lights, what I could only hope was Indian food dripped from a section of the wafer-board ceiling, and the walls, covered in layer upon layer of dirt, peeling paint, and quite possibly urine, looked like something you'd find in an abandoned crack house. The thought of staying in that place overnight made me physically sick.

I nearly gave in. I nearly turned around and marched back into that microscopic elevator. I nearly picked up the phone in that deceptively modern lobby and bought a plane ticket back to America using my last bit of credit on my only unmaxed credit card. I was this close to giving up and giving in. This close to admitting to everyone that they were right and that coming back to London had been nothing but a terrible mistake. This. Close.

But something stopped me. Something made me stand still. Something made me take a long deep breath and exhale extra slowly like I used to do in my yoga class. Okay, I told myself. Try to stay calm. Try not to be frightened. Try not throw up. And try to think clearly.

So I wouldn't be living in London's plushest residence. I could handle it. My freshman dorm in Rochester wasn't exactly in the best condition either and yet it had become central to one of the best years of my life. It's the people you live with that matter, not the quality of your living conditions. (Right?)

I thought back to all those times in my isolated farm town when I'd insisted that living off your vision was more powerful than living off your circumstances. That just because you come from a place full of Sweet Corn Festivals and NRA meetings doesn't mean you have to stay there forever. Or just because you come from a family that made you carry tofu salad to school in a homemade cardboard lunch box and drink a disgusting "living brew" of fermented Kombucha iced tea,[25] doesn't mean that one day you can't have your lunch at the best restaurants in the world or someday drink your tea with the Queen. Everyone, despite their circumstances, has the power to become the person they were meant to be, and the power to follow the dreams that dwell inside their heart. You just have to be brave and stay focused.

That's what I used to tell my friends in high school, anyway—when they'd tell me they couldn't imagine going to college out of state. And that's what I used to tell my more cynical relatives. And as I stood there in that disgusting bomb shelter on the verge of hysterical tears, I knew I had better start following my own crazy advice.

I mean, really, how hard could it be? I'd already conquered the loony circumstances of my childhood enough to propel myself to London. *Twice!* And all based on the strength of my vision. Surely I could conquer a stint in this bomb shelter long enough to propel myself into the English life I had dreamed of.

I leaned against the filthy wall of the empty corridor, stared into the fluorescent glare of the dusty ceiling lights, and interrogated myself quite sternly—begging myself to let me in on what I was truly up to. Eventually, I could hear something—it was barely audible, but it was there.

"You're home," my heart whispered softly. "You've come home."

---

25 Kombucha is derived from a strange mushroomlike fungus (a symbiotic culture of yeast and other microorganisms), which, when nourished with the right amount of black tea and sugar, reproduces a "baby" fungus in a rather disturbing fashion. Ancient Chinese and Russian medicine claims that drinking the liquid by-product has unparalleled health benefits. Personally, I'm not convinced. And actually rather traumatized.

And you know what? It was right.

I couldn't flee from my destiny. Not now. Not so soon. My *circumstances* might have resembled a terrifying Orwellian mental institution-cum-crack den, but my *vision* of English happiness and royal romance was still very much intact. And, just as it always had, I knew that it would see me through.

So as I dragged my massive luggage down the scary hallway, I told myself that once I met all my fellow postgraduates and we all became close bomb-shelter-dwelling buddies, I wouldn't even notice the huge tangle of exposed electrical wires strung across the entire length of the wall. And as I unlocked the heavy wooden door to my room, I told myself that soon we'd be helping each other out with our course work, watching silly movies and playing drinking games together. We'd borrow each other's clothes, counsel each other, comfort each other, and love each other until this mental institution of a dorm was a virtual haven of postgraduate friendship and learning.

So determined not to indulge any more negative thoughts, and remembering that "mustn't grumble" was one of the golden rules of Englishness, I set about unpacking my things and arranging them in my dusty, cavelike room.

~

It wasn't long before I realized that something very important was missing from my cave-room. Although I had been provided with an electric teakettle and a heated towel rack (both of which I had lived twenty-two years so far without ever needing or missing), I had not been provided with a study desk of any kind. I was, after all, a student living in a student residence hall. Was I being a spoiled American to presume I would need such a luxury?

I sighed. Maybe a bit of music would help. (I had to do *something* to stop my mind from making constant sarcastic comments to itself.) I'd left my stereo in Colorado, but luckily I had my trusty clock radio. For some reason English electricity is like a million times stronger than U.S. electricity, so if you don't want big electrical explosions, you have to have special adapters and special transformers if you're planning on connecting anything American to a U.K. outlet. It took me a while to figure out how everything worked, but finally my struggles paid off and I was rewarded with a loud burst of the Spice Girls.

This was quickly followed by a large puff of black smoke, then silence. Fine. So music wasn't an option.

As I attempted to scrub the brownish gray smudges off my bedroom walls, I tried to concentrate on the bright side of things. Like the almost certain fact that a handsome blond aristocrat was living in a room on that very same scary hallway. And how almost certainly he would be studying something sexy like corporate responsibility—meaning that despite his massive personal wealth, he still cared deeply for the welfare of others. As I scoured decades of mold out of my shower, I concentrated hard on how we would get along beautifully, and how our lovely, boarding school–educated children would frolic in the manicured grounds of our estate in the English countryside.

And even as smoke continued to stream from my clock radio and it slowly short-circuited before my very eyes, I told myself that everything was going according to plan. And that I would never look back.

⟶

You probably didn't think it was possible (I certainly didn't think it was possible), but things got worse. For one, I discovered that 75 percent of the residence hall was designated specifically for married student housing—meaning I was surrounded by armies of mute, gloomy couples who would glare at me if I dared to glance at their spouse in a friendly way.

For two, from what I could tell, the remaining 25 percent of the students, regardless of their unmarried status, refused to socialize on any level whatsoever. Seriously. No eye contact. No smiles. Not one stab at pleasant conversation. They just wandered around silently, squinting and looking haggard, like they'd all just stumbled out of the same dark hole.

Finally, and to me this was the most distressing of all, is that I had lived in that godforsaken dorm for over two weeks and had yet to catch sight of a single English resident. Much less talk to one. Much less be invited to a polo match.

I wasn't asking for Animal House. But between the distinct lack of tailored suits from Savile Row and all the dreary husbands and wives lurking in the shadows, I was miserable. I have to say that it was becoming increasingly difficult to stay optimistic about meeting my future royal husband in such a depressing atmosphere.

Still, I gave it my best shot. Classes hadn't started yet, so I tried my best to be as social and as approachable as possible until they did. Every morning I'd read *The Times* and *The Guardian* in the dingy reading room; and every night I'd sit by myself on the filthy, battered furniture in the dingy student bar hoping to strike up a friendly conversation. But the only social interaction I ever received on these evenings always came from the same hairy Eastern European guy who would leer at me lecherously, paw at my blond hair, and then ask me over and over, "Vut do you staadee?"—never understanding a word I said to him in return.

I even went so far as to eat all of my dinners in the cheaply priced student cafeteria even though the badly translated menu was full of entrees like Lamb Fingers with Raisin Sauce or Apricots dressed with Cracked Eggs. You'd think the cafeteria would be a great place to meet people but it was more like participating in a scene from the movie *Awakenings*. Everyone sat at tables by themselves, slowly moving their plastic forks to their mouths and staring silently into the space in front of them. It was as if the mental-institution surroundings were rubbing off on people by osmosis and I seriously began to wonder if this creepy comatose state was in store for me if I stayed there long enough.

⁓

It was around week three when I met Max. An English aristo-crat? If only! More like a loud-mouthed, half-Jewish New Yorker suffering from severe privilege and severe only-child syndrome. But he could talk! And that's a hell of a lot more than anyone else in the building seemed capable of doing.

I first saw Max in the cafeteria. He was staring at the food op-tions with a mixture of confusion and disgust, wearing baggy khakis and a crooked baseball cap. Obviously American.

I was filling my plastic cup with tepid drinking water when he came up to me and said, "You're like the third best-looking girl in this building. Wanna borrow my IKEA catalog? It will help this place not seem so much like the fucking prison that it is."

They were the first sentences spoken to me in unbroken En-glish since I'd arrived in the bomb shelter and I nearly cried with happiness. It was like Max was some sort of bizarre angel sent down by the gods to snap me out of my solitude. And although he was just as obnoxious as he was hilarious, I'd be lying if I said I wasn't grateful when he decided to befriend me.

I kept telling myself that things would improve once classes started up at LSE. But they didn't. There were a few African stu-dents in my lectures and a handful from Scandinavia and Eastern Europe. But the rest of my classmates were one hundred percent American. Instead of the gorgeous, polo-playing, English aristo-crats that I had anticipated, every master's program was full of American kids that had Kraft macaroni and cheese and Miracle

Whip mayonnaise shipped over from the U.S. because the U.K. versions weren't good enough. And rather than seek out native Londoners, my fellow countrymen spent every night drinking American beer with other Americans in Leicester Square's American-themed bars.

I didn't know which was worse: discussing London's tragic lack of authentic bagels with my compatriots at LSE, or talking to my bedroom wall back at the bomb shelter.

Every now and then, I'd buy an international phone card, venture into one of the red *Doctor Who*–style phone booths plastered with pictures of fat prostitutes, and call my parents. I'd sob to them about my wretched living conditions, my terrible social life, and general unhappiness—but extracting sympathy from them was useless.

"You'll be fine!" my mom said breezily. "Besides, isn't living in London what you've always wanted? Isn't it what you've always dreamed of?"

And that was the hardest part of all.

This was no one's fault but my own. Against all advice, I had followed my heart instead of my head—and now I was paying the price.

I had such wonderful friends at Rochester, girls and guys that understood me, loved me, and wholeheartedly encouraged me to follow my dreams, however crazy they seemed. But after graduation, we were scattered across the globe: L.A., Chicago, D.C., New York, London—the list of cities made it sound as if we were opening a chain of fashion boutiques. After being inseparable for so long, parting virtually overnight was a huge shock to the system and I missed them desperately.

My only solace took place in the dilapidated LSE computer lab, where I would send regular e-mail updates with tales of my

London woes. The girls replied to me with e-mails full of loyal sympathy (certainly more than my parents were offering) but Justin, a good friend from my writing class at Rochester, could take it no longer.

"Jerramy," he e-mailed, "what did you *expect* to happen on your return to London? Did you expect the ghost of Princess Diana to emerge from her island grave, to float into the Royal Archives and to unearth some dusty, long-forgotten old document listing you as the rightful heir to the British throne and then arrange for you to be crowned at some kind of special fast-track coronation? Did you expect all your adoring subjects to cheer wildly in the background as the sparkling tiara was dutifully placed upon your regal blond head and afterward you would just quietly return to your studies at LSE?"

I nodded earnestly at the computer screen.

Then I caught myself.

I wasn't *that* delusional. Was I?

"Justin," I typed rapidly in reply, "don't be silly. Everyone knows there's no such thing as ghosts."

Eight

~~~

"The most powerful emotion we can experience is the mysti-cal."

—ALBERT EINSTEIN

*L*et's pretend for a second that things were in reverse—that I wasn't a starry-eyed American who had journeyed to London, but an eager young British girl who had moved all by myself to the bright lights of New York City. Would I be able to meet other Americans (male or female) in a place as wonderfully diverse and cosmopolitan as the Big Apple? Even if I was stuck in a miserable dorm?

Of course I would. You can't swing your arms in Manhattan without hitting dozens of Americans—and most would be thrilled to befriend you. Most would happily invite you out to meet their friends, or home to meet their families, and would eventually insist that you join them for Thanksgiving dinner.

But this was clearly not the case in London. I knew English people were slightly more introverted compared to Americans, but come on—they weren't invisible! Yet during those first lonely months, they certainly could have fooled me.

I guess during my House of Commons internship I'd spent so much time within that small Anglicized political bubble, I never stopped to notice how utterly international the U.K. capital actually was. And as a result it never once occurred to me that if

I returned to the U.K., meeting English people would be such a ridiculous challenge. (Granted, I did have the direct numbers for a few Members of Parliament but I couldn't exactly call them up and demand to accompany them to the Queen's Garden Party.) So now, without polo invitations pouring in as previously planned, I had nothing to do but sit in my dungeon of a bedroom, repaint my toenails, recalculate my debt, and die of frustration.

Left to my own devices, the bomb shelter situation was becoming borderline suicidal. The single lightbulb dangling from my bedroom ceiling was so dim I couldn't read or study after dark. I couldn't afford the mandatory TV license[26] so I had no television; due to the aforementioned clock radio disaster, I had no music, and I had been waiting nearly six weeks for my phone to be connected by the Old World powers that be. Unless I subjected myself to Max's endearing yet rather obnoxious ramblings, I felt I had no way to prove that I was alive.

To top it all off, everything in London costs roughly four times more than what it should. I'm not joking. A bottle of water is like eight dollars. Max told me that learning to live with London's ludicrously high prices was kind of like learning to live without an arm or a leg—not ideal or especially pleasant, but eventually you kind of adjust. Well, quite frankly, with his bank balance he could afford to adjust. But with my microscopic student budget and my rapidly dwindling credit card power, shopping and nightlife (normally my most-treasured pastimes) simply weren't options for me. So I'd learned to find my entertainment where I could.

Whenever I'd had enough of the depressingly dark and labyrinthine LSE library, I'd head to Hyde Park and Kensington Gardens. More than 30 percent of London (approximately 5,550

---

26 Paying for a TV license is required by law in the U.K. for all television owners and is used instead of commercial advertising to fund the BBC's public broadcasts.

acres[27]) is made up of sprawling parkland and intricate pleasure gardens like these—and most were originally owned by the British royal family and used as their private hunting grounds, before they were made public.

I'd stroll by myself through the parks' lush winding paths, ignore the swarms of Australian rollerbladers, and try to imagine that Henry VIII and his court were thundering past me on their steeds in pursuit of deer and wild boar. I'd perch myself on the benches near the Italian Gardens or the Peter Pan statue and attempt to study my mind-numbing public policy notes, but I'd always end up people-watching instead.

I suppose it didn't help that I'd recently finished a fantastic new novel[28] set in London, the themes of which were keeping me permanently distracted. Aside from a rather elaborate murder plot, the book was about a girl named Ella (British-born, but American-raised) who'd regularly head to Hyde Park at sunrise to watch the early morning joggers go by. Of course, it wasn't long before she caught the eye of a dashing upper-class English boy who happened to be running past her—and soon the two of them were madly in love. Aside from the getting up at dawn part, I was hoping to see if this approach might work for me.

But no such luck.

I'd patiently sit on *my* park bench for hours upon hours— watching people jog around the duck pond or row along the Serpentine; watching children with their adorable school uniforms clamber around on the Princess Diana Memorial Playground. I knew some of these humans had to be English, but it was as if an invisible glass wall existed between us, keeping our worlds divided.

---

27 That's more green space that any other city of its size in the world.

28 *The Drowning People*, written by nineteen-year-old, floppy-haired Oxford student Richard Mason

And soon I came to realize that meeting people in England simply by "catching their eye" was pure and utter fiction.

You don't strike up casual conversation with strangers in England. You just don't. You could sit next to the same person on the same train for twenty-five years, and you still wouldn't dare speak to them. You could be crossing the Sahara desert all by yourself without a living soul in sight for hundreds of miles and suddenly spot the first human you'd seen in over a decade—but if you were English, and he was English, you'd simply carry on trekking without so much as a nod to each other. Anyone who broke this inherent rule was deemed dangerous at best. Therefore the only appropriate way to meet others was to be introduced to them by someone you already knew and already trusted. For foreigners wanting to make friends, it was an infuriating catch-22—which is why most gave up on the English and ended up mixing only with other foreigners.

But I had no intention of doing this. It was the easy way out. And besides, if I was going to be spending all my time with non-English people, why on earth did I come all the way across the ocean to the U.K.? I might as well give up on my dream, go back to America, be with my real American friends, have a nice American job, meet a nice American guy, and save myself and everyone else the transatlantic hassle.

Still, there I was.

Sitting in Hyde Park. With no friends, no family, and no money (and while we're at it, I might as well add no prince), wondering why I was so miserable in the place I felt certain I would be the happiest.

I tried to visit my favorite royal landmarks as often as I could in an effort to cheer myself up. I went to Buckingham Palace, Kensington Palace, the Tower of London, Hampton Court, Windsor Castle. I was unbelievably lucky to live so close to such incredibly stunning buildings. I'd been inside most of them at least twice already, and couldn't really afford tickets to go inside any of them for a third or fourth time, so instead I'd simply walk around and around them, filling my soul with their beauty and magic. And then, one day it dawned on me that perhaps that was the problem—that all this beauty and magic was actually the root of my new-found misery.

Everywhere I looked in London, I saw the Queen's profile or the Queen's initials—on the lampposts, the mailboxes, sometimes even the rubbish bins. Even the word "Royal" was everywhere: Royal Mail, Royal Air Force, Royal Opera House, Royal Ballet, Royal Shakespeare Company, Royal Albert Hall, Royal Botanic Gardens, Royal Ascot, Royal Regattas, Royal Parks, Royal Societies, Royal Academies, Royal Collections. The elite world I had longed to enter since I was a little girl was now shamelessly dangled in front of me, taunting me on a daily basis.

And as I stood outside those gorgeous royal palaces and stared through the bars of the wrought-iron gates surrounding them—instead of delight and inspiration, I was filled with painful, heart-wrenching frustration. No one seemed to understand that I belonged inside!

Sure, I was closer to my dreams than I was in my hick farm town, closer than I ever was when I had lived in America . . . but suddenly, the few centimeters from one side of the palace gates to the other seemed cruelly impossible. Now that I was so close, I realized how far away I really was.

And always had been.

One afternoon as I sat on the tube on my way home from my morning lecture on urban planning, I did the typically English thing and avoided all eye contact with other humans by pretending to be really interested in the ads above their heads. I halfheartedly read about cold medicines and night school and Indian beer, until I spotted an ad promoting the new tours of Buckingham Palace! To my horror, I saw there were only two days remaining before it would be closed to the public. I didn't even know it was open to the public!

In order to raise money to restore the recent fire damage at Windsor Castle,[29] Buckingham Palace was opening its doors to the public for the first time in history. I knew these plans were in the works—but I thought they were scheduled for next spring, not this fall! How many times had I gazed longingly through those black swirly gates? And this was my first chance to go beyond them. (I'm not going to say it was my *only* chance—because I was inevitably going back one day as a guest instead of a tourist—it's just that I thought it would be nice to familiarize myself with the place before that day arrived.)

I promptly switched lines, got off at St. James's Park, walked past the little lake full of ducks, geese, and pelicans, and took my place in the queue to buy my £12 admission ticket. So what if it meant I couldn't afford to eat the next day? I knew that finally seeing the inside of Buckingham Palace would nourish me in its own way.

I was finally assigned a tour group and was carefully herded though palace security along with twenty or thirty others. I tried to ignore all the fat tourists shouting things like, "So if the Queen lives here, then does the King live in Big Ben?" or "Are we going to see Duke Andrew, the Prince of York?"

At last we were ushered into the richly plastered State Rooms filled with priceless paintings by Rembrandt, Rubens, and Ver-

---

29 In 1992 Windsor Castle (the largest inhabited castle in the world) suffered severe fire damage, which destroyed some of the most historic parts of the building. It was announced that up to 70 percent of the cost of restoration (estimated at approx £50m) was to be met by charging the public admission to Buckingham Palace. Her Majesty The Queen was to personally contribute £2m.

meer, gorgeous sculptures by Canova and Chantrey, piece after exquisite piece of Sèvres porcelain, and some of the finest English and French furniture in the world. But I found myself looking at them with a disturbing indifference. As if I had seen them a thousand times before.

Suddenly, I felt dizzy and light-headed. Everything around me was so familiar I wanted to cry. In a split second, the tour became one of those terrible dreams when you want to run from something but you can't move, or you want to scream but you can't make a sound. But I didn't know what I wanted to run from! Or why I wanted to scream. Or why, despite all the overpowering emotions coursing through me, I didn't ever want to leave.

I should have braced myself. I should have known it would happen again.

I have to admit that this sensation was not new to me. It had happened a few times before during my semester abroad: once on the main staircase of Hampton Court Palace, once in the dining room in Windsor Castle, and once in the Crown Jewels exhibit at the Tower of London. And every time, I had brushed it off, telling myself it was nothing more than my overreaction to finally being in England.

My friend Heather once told me that she loved the Beatles so much that she couldn't bear to listen to their music. And I knew exactly what she meant. To me, looking at anything royal was just like witnessing an astoundingly beautiful sunset or a glittering night sky. It hurt to look and it hurt not to look. And for a long time, I was sure my intense emotional response was part of that.

Whatever the reason, the feelings I experienced in these royal buildings was always exactly the same: Imagine the deepest, most crippling love you've ever been in and mix that with the most painful sadness you've ever felt, then multiply it by a thousand. And then imagine it swoops down on you out of nowhere—so hard that it knocks the wind out of you, and you can barely breathe. That's what it felt like. And I should have known that touring Buckingham Palace would be no different.

I'm not crazy. Really, I'm not. In fact for a long time I tried to approach the whole thing logically because I thought surely it could be rationally explained. So what if I had cried when I saw the Crown Jewels? Wouldn't any girl burst into tears after seeing diamonds and rubies that big?[30] Or maybe after so many years of living in a crazy hippie farmhouse full of purple walls and Guatemalan cushions, being surrounded by all that sumptuous furniture at Windsor Castle had filled me with such ecstasy that I felt faint. Same with Hampton Court. I was probably just being silly and overemotional and letting my royal-obsessed imagination run wild.

But I wanted to be sure.

So during my short backpacking trip through Europe, I'd made a point of visiting as many castles and palaces as possible. I wanted to see if the strange familiarity I had felt in England would come back the minute I entered any vaguely royal setting. But nothing happened in the dozens of castles and chateaus and royal residences I went to in France, Monaco, Spain, Germany, Belgium, and Italy. No heart-swelling achiness, no trapped underwater dizziness, no baffling weepiness. Nothing.

So I knew it *wasn't* just me being girly and teary-eyed and excessively romantic. It was more than that. And on a much,

---

30 Some of the most exceptional and historic jewels in the world can be found in the Tower of London's royal collection, including the Great Star of Africa, the largest top-quality cut diamond in existence (set in the Sovereign's Sceptre with Cross, it boasts 530.2 carats and an estimated worth of $400 million), and the infamous fourteenth-century Black Prince's Ruby, a crimson jewel the size of a chicken egg set within the Imperial state crown.

much deeper level than that. And so far, it only happened in England.

Back in Buckingham Palace, I tried to stay with the group. I slowly filed past the famous Throne Room, and focused on keeping my breathing even. Wasn't Diana's family wedding photo taken here? Upon this dais, against this crimson velvet backdrop? Okay, that's good, I told I myself. Stay calm and focus on Diana.

The tour continued to move forward and in a surreal daze, I went with it. We reached the Corinthian marble columns of the Grand Hall, the sumptuous Grand Staircase with its gilded balustrade, the flock wallpaper and jewel-toned damask of the Drawing Rooms, the arched doors and windows of the Music Room, the lavish coved ceiling and ivory walls of the State Dining Room, and the sprawling, parquet-inlaid baroque Ballroom. I felt detached from everything—like I was in someone else's body and watching myself from above. Every precious object I laid eyes on—every porcelain vase, every prominent painting, every silk tapestry—triggered a tangle of memories so dim and buried so deep inside me that I had no idea how to reach them. My heart was pounding like crazy, bursting with things it used to know, pleading with me to remember them, and I thought I was going to collapse with the force of it. But I kept it together.

Thirty minutes later, the tour ended and I was thrust outside into the rare London sunshine. The feelings left me as quickly as they came, leaving me to wonder if I'd imagined it all.

Exhausted and bewildered, I sat down on the marble steps of the Queen Victoria Memorial[31] and tried to compose myself. I tried to ignore the hot dog vendors who had shamelessly placed

---

31 Built in 1911, the Victoria Memorial is a massive marble structure standing eighty-two feet tall and situated directly in front of Buckingham Palace. Vaguely resembling a giant wedding cake, the memorial features a thirteen-foot statue of Queen Victoria surrounded by three bronze angels representing the classic Victorian virtues of justice, charity, and truth.

their carts in front of the royal gates, and forced myself to look past the swarms of camera-toting tourists. Neither seemed to realize that their very presence ruined the true grandeur of the sight that had brought them there.

I finally managed to block out the noise of the fray and focus my gaze on the elegant front of Buckingham Palace. My God, how I preferred *those* massive gray stones to the ones of the bomb shelter, I laughed softly to myself.

I was calmer now, but no less confused.

Despite what others seemed to believe, I think it's fair to say that my obsession with England wasn't all in my head. Whatever it was, I could actually feel it affecting me physically. And it was a lot more ethereal than I cared to admit.

Were my crazy parents right all along? Did all of this unbearable yearning really have something to do with a past life? Had I really seen these royal furnishings before? Had I really lived in these palaces? Did I even believe in this stuff?

Of course there was no reply. Nothing but the stoic stares of the Queen's Guards in their silly bearskin hats.

Nine

"Eliza, you are to stay here for the next six months learning to speak beautifully. . . . At the end of six months you shall be taken to Buckingham Palace in a carriage, beautifully dressed. If the King finds out you are not a Lady, the police will take you to the Tower of London where your head will be cut off as a warning to other presumptuous flower girls."

—Henry Higgins in the film *My Fair Lady* (1964)

I had to find Rupert.

It was the only way forward. If the only way to meet English people was to be introduced to them by another English person then I figured I had better track down the only English person I knew. And fast. I simply couldn't endure one more night with Max at that god-awful Long Island Iced Tea bar.

But the mobile number I had for Rupert eighteen months ago didn't work anymore and I didn't have an e-mail address. And although it was 1999, London still didn't have White Pages or anything vaguely similar. I couldn't look him up on an online university directory because even if I knew which university he'd decided to go to, those kinds of details (which are so necessary to everyday networking in the U.S.) were considered highly confidential in the U.K. Friendster didn't exist. MySpace didn't exist. Even the MP he used to work for didn't know where he was but finally suggested I write to Rupert's parents and (was there hope at last?) gave me a partial address.

I didn't have a house number, a street name, or a postcode—just a county. It was the American equivalent of mailing a letter with nothing but the person's name and state written on the envelope.

But I didn't care. I was willing to try anything.

I scribbled a desperate note to Rupert, begging him to get in touch and explaining how he simply had to rescue me from this social hell I was currently enduring. Then I dropped the letter into the red cylindrical postbox, putting the future of my English social life in the hands of Her Majesty's Royal Mail.

And what capable royal hands they were! I nearly fainted when Rupert called me a few weeks later. His parents had not only received my letter, but had forwarded it to him at Oxford where he was now studying politics. I was so happy to hear his familiar insouciant voice I could barely contain myself.

"So, Jezza," Rupert teased, "have you moved into Buckingham Palace yet?"

"As a matter of fact, Rupert, I have not," I replied. "It's been a nightmare since I came back to London."

"You mean Princess Anne didn't immediately propose herself for tea when she heard you were back in town?" he persisted.

"Rupert!" I wailed. "I don't know what's going on in this city anymore. Meeting English people is practically impossible. And meeting English people with royal connections is worse than looking for a needle in a haystack! Stop snickering like that! I'm being serious."

"Jezza, what did you expect? Something like a third of Londoners—including you—were not even born in the U.K. Christ, even when *I* lived in London my flatmates were Swedish! And everyone knows the LSE is just a place for wealthy foreigners. Moving back to London was a really stupid plan if you wanted to meet English people."

"I'm realizing that," I whimpered softly.

"Christ, you sound miserable. Why don't you come visit me in Oxford? I'll show you what a night out with a bunch of English students is like and I can show my mates what a completely mad American bird looks like."

"I would love that."

"Why don't you come over tomorrow night?"

"But it's a Thursday. I have a lecture on Friday morning."

"Jezza, no one goes to lectures but foreigners."

Something told me that visiting Rupert was going to do more for my future than any master's degree ever would. So I agreed to take the bus to Oxford the very next day.

It's funny how you never really know why certain people cross your path in life. I'd always thought of Rupert as a rather exasperating office buddy. Little did I know that he would lead me directly to the glittering English people I thought I would never find.

⌒

Growing up, there were only two videos in my household: *Hair* and *My Fair Lady*. (Well, three if you count *The Making of "We Are the World,"* which I don't.) On special occasions (like a good report card or after a visit to the dentist) I was allowed to watch one and you can guess which one I picked.

Hair is based on a Broadway musical about a tribe of flower-power hippies and the drug/music/antiwar/free-love culture of the 1960s. It's mainly famous for being performed with all of the actors naked in some of the scenes. My dad claims the original play broke through the barriers of theater in the same way that the hippies broke through the barriers of society. Fine. All I know is that I wasn't allowed to watch horror movies or swimsuit-clad beauty pageant contestants, but I *could* watch groups of all-nude hippies dancing around Central Park and singing to themselves about the dawning of Aquarius. Gotta love my parents' logic.

Meanwhile, *My Fair Lady* is my favorite film of all time. It was then, it is now, and I'm confident it will maintain this status until the day I die. I'm pretty sure *My Fair Lady* was one of those things my parents naïvely exposed me to (like royal library books, Disney, and refined sugar) that they assumed I'd enjoy but would eventually grow out of—yet are now kicking themselves twenty years later for starting a lifelong obsession.

But can you blame me?

My Fair Lady is the story of an impoverished young girl named Eliza Doolittle (played by Audrey Hepburn) who sells flowers on the dirty streets of London. When a wealthy linguistics professor named Henry Higgins hears her piercingly crass working-class accent (sounds "like chickens cackling in a barn," he says. "I'd rather hear a choir singing flat"), he makes a bet with a friend that a few weeks of speech coaching is all it will take to pass off this "guttersnipe" as a duchess. Eliza agrees to participate in this wager and by the end of the movie everyone at the Embassy Ball is convinced that she is of royal blood. And Henry falls in love with her of course. But the most important part is that everyone thinks she's royal just because her accent changed, when only months ago she was a common ruffian living on the streets.

As you can probably tell, viewings of *Hair* only occurred after every two dozen screenings of *My Fair Lady*. And it's a good thing, too, because *My Fair Lady* proved to be an invaluable education for me when it came to understanding the intricacies of the English class system.

I realize the very concept of a class system is hard for most Americans to comprehend—after all, it's been drummed into our heads since birth that all people are created equal. But in England, class is something that practically permeates the air. House of *Lords* and House of *Commons* only scratches the surface of the class system's grasp.

In America, social divides are primarily about income. But thanks to *My Fair Lady* I knew that the English defined themselves by a bevy of qualities that had nothing to do with raw cash and everything to do with one's language, style, and manners.

If you're English and you speak with upper-class pronunciation and use upper-class vocabulary, you will always be considered and treated as a member of the upper class, even if you're bankrupt, working in a factory, or living on welfare.

Conversely, if you're an English billionaire, complete with private jets and expensive cars and houses all around the world, but you speak with a working-class accent or accidentally use a bit of working-class terminology, you will always be recognized as working class—no matter how much money you have and continue to make.

If you want to know what an upper-class English accent sounds like, just watch any movie starring Hugh Grant or Rupert Everett and listen to their voices. (And I *dare you* not to become weak at the knees.) If you want to know what a working-class accent sounds like, watch something like *The Full Monty*, *Layer Cake*, or *Snatch*. While these three films are all really entertaining movies, no one can tell me that the rough accents of the characters are attractive in any way.

While the English are able to determine one another's class within seconds of hearing another's voice, the U.S. has no equivalent to this. Think about it. Your accent—be it from the Bronx, Texas, Wisconsin, or a tiny mountain town in Colorado—doesn't come with any kind of class label and you're not instantly judged or pigeonholed by the sound of it. You can usually tell *where* in America someone is from, but you can't tell anything about their socioeconomic background. And thank God for that.

I'm no actress and as much as I hoped it would, my fairly neutral American accent wasn't changing anytime soon. (I liked to view this as a sign of strong character rather than a particularly weak ear.) Besides, I can always tell if an American is attempting to fake an affected English accent and it's not at all flattering.

So while my accent was here to stay, I was eternally grateful that it gave very little away. Can you imagine if Rupert's friends could tell that I came from a redneck town the minute I opened my mouth? Can you imagine if nothing more than my *enunciation* revealed that for the two years before I was born my parents didn't believe in money? When it came to hiding my identity in that respect, all I can say is God bless America.

⟶

Oxford University has hundreds of famous alumni, including Lewis Carroll, J.R.R. Tolkien, and Crown Prince Naruhito of Japan,[32]—not to mention the dreamy Tony Blair and Hugh Grant himself. And with its legendary towering spires, sprawling green lawns, and breathtaking eleventh-century architecture, it sure beat the dull gray buildings of the LSE. If you stopped for a second and tried to imagine Oxford without the modern cars parked along its streets, you could easily transport yourself a few hundred years back in time. And I was doing just that when I arrived on Rupert's doorstep just before dark.

"Jezza! I can't believe you're here!" Rupert exclaimed as he kissed me on both cheeks.[33] "Quick! Drop off your rucksack and get in the cab! We're going to a toga party!"

I looked behind me. Sure enough, there was a mini cab[34]

---

32 Husband of the aforementioned Princess Masako

33 Continental-style cheek kissing for both greeting and parting appeared to have been adopted in the U.K. Not sure if this existed only in my particular social community or if it was a more pervasive kissing movement. (*Debrett's Etiquette for Girls* claims that you should aim for the right cheek first.)

34 A mini cab, unlike a black cab, is a taxi that can be arranged only by phone and does not stop to collect passengers in the street.

waiting at the curb with the engine running. But all I had was an overnight bag! How was I ever going to find a suitable outfit for a toga party in less than sixty seconds?

Like a female Clark Kent, I rushed up the ancient staircase of the elegant student house and exchanged my chunky turtleneck sweater[35] for a plum-colored, cleavage-enhancing party top (never leave home without one). Glancing frantically around Rupert's bedroom, I grabbed a white pillowcase off his unmade bed and pinned it diagonally around me into a makeshift toga. I retouched my makeup in the cab and when we stopped to pick up one of Rupert's friends along the way, I hopped out and grabbed some random greenery from a stranger's front yard and wove it through my hair in what I hoped looked like a Greek-style wreath.

When we arrived at the party I thanked my lucky stars again and again that I had made such a superhuman effort. For never in my life had I seen so many good-looking, half-naked Englishmen in one room.

⟶

I honestly couldn't believe my eyes. It's no wonder I couldn't find any Hugh Grant look-alikes in London! They were all at this party! And draped in nothing but flimsy white sheets!

Everywhere I looked I saw rosy cheeks, sharp noses, and golden hair that rose into little cute wings behind their ears. Their rowing and rugby muscles flexed gloriously as they offered me cup after cup of sangria with English accents so marvelously upper-class and cavalier, for a moment I truly thought I might have died and gone to heaven. It was like someone had gone through all of the lusty English fantasies locked away in my brain and magically brought them to life!

---

35 Or "polo neck jumper" as the Brits would say

I was positively swimming in happy delirium. If there were girls at that party, I didn't notice. All I knew was that I was finally surrounded by young, well-spoken English boys. The ones I was afraid I might never meet.

For the first time in months, I was having conversations with English people that didn't involve buying a train ticket or saying thank you for my change. And after roaming around London for weeks—desolate, friendless, and practically invisible—suddenly all kinds of people (*English* people) wanted to meet me.

Rupert seemed to know exactly what effect this party was having on me. And forever amused by my English obsession, every so often he would drop hints to provoke me even further.

I had just finished dancing to "Mambo No. 5" with Hugh Grant look-alike No. 5 when Rupert pulled me aside and nodded to a pair of floppy-haired boys standing across the room.

"You'll like Piers," he whispered to me. "His family owns a castle in Scotland. And I'm sure you'll *love* Giles. He's going to inherit a lordship."

Castles? Lordships? Despite my sangria-enhanced state, I perked up instantly. Just like when a dog hears someone mention its name, my head tilted and my eyes widened.

"Really? A lordship?"

"Jezza!" Rupert laughed. "Don't look so gobsmacked! They're just normal people."

I still couldn't believe this was Rupert's life. He got to hang out with these people every day and seemed totally unfazed by it. What must it be like to be born English? To be able to take all of this magic for granted?

I looked across the room at the two toga-clad boys and sighed happily. They were just as good-looking and half-naked as any of the others. Suddenly, Giles caught me looking at him.

Oh my God. He winked at me!

This was my chance.

I looked right back into that future lord's gorgeous aristocratic eyes and gave him a demure smile. Then I gracefully went upstairs to fasten the leaves more tightly into my hair.

To make a long story short, Giles followed me. And before I knew what was happening, we were in someone's bedroom ravishing each other. This is the problem with being drunk. I was drunk on a toga party full of British Greek gods, and I was most definitely drunk on eight cups of sangria. I didn't exactly stop to analyze that ripping off togas in such a hasty manner was perhaps not the best way to behave with a future lord. I was too caught up in the glorious idea that I was actually kissing a future lord. So caught up, in fact, that I didn't realize that the toga party had become so crowded that it had pushed its way upstairs and into the very bedroom where the ravishing was taking place.

Suddenly, fifteen or twenty people wearing togas realized they had interrupted two people who were not wearing togas. Luckily, I was too drunk to be embarrassed about it. (And even luckier my jeans and bra had not been removed.) I quickly put my pillowcase toga back on, reapplied my lipstick in the bathroom mirror, and reentered the party as if nothing had happened.

See? I was fitting into British aristocratic life just fine.

Ten

"Good party behavior is a breeze for the well-mannered guest."
—Debrett's New Guide to Etiquette and Modern Manners

When I came to my senses—or more accurately, when I sobered up—I wondered if, after the toga incident, I would be able to show my face in English society ever again. I asked Rupert about it and he told me I was overreacting. But Rupert's a guy. Guys always think girls are overreacting.

Despite these worries, I somehow managed to block the scandal between his future lordship and me out of my mind and continued to take the double-decker bus from Victoria Station to Oxford every weekend that I could.[36] I felt slightly guilty about neglecting my lengthy reading lists and tedious seminars at LSE, but a girl's got to think of her royal future.

Before I left Colorado and went off to college, I had tried to host a black-tie summer dinner party to say farewell to all my friends in high school. Held in my backyard, I'd designed the invitations, wrote out the place cards with fake aristocratic titles, bought elegant floral centerpieces and linen napkins, strung fairy lights

---

36 I even tried to transfer to Oxford completely. But the programs weren't equivalent and I was already too far along in the academic year.

through trees, assembled scores of delicate canapés, and cooked an elaborate five-course menu for twenty. I'd even hired my thirteen-year-old brother and his skater-punk friends to be "my staff" and made them wear matching outfits. I had brandy and cigars for the boys, and parlor games ready for the girls. I'd done everything in my power to create the façade of a formal turn-of-the-century English country house–style affair, and everything in my power to make myself forget, if only for an evening, that I lived thousands of miles away from England and a mere mile away from a Super Wal-Mart.

But less than an hour into the party, couples were making out on the lawn, guests were climbing the fairy-light trees in such large numbers that a branch broke and fell onto the dining table, someone had stuck their *entire hand* into the center of my beautifully crafted chocolate-raspberry torte, and my staff were so stoned that they were hanging out with Jasper in his doghouse. Everyone was ignoring my seating chart and the order of the courses and pretty much treated the entire event like any other high-school beer fest—except they were wearing old prom attire instead of khaki shorts and drinking my specially mixed cocktails instead of cans of Bud Light.

This was only my first month or so of drinking (I had decided to start practicing before college), and I wasn't used to the exaggerated effects alcohol had on my emotions. And when I saw my elegant chocolate-raspberry torte being devoured by the handful, I lost it. Stumbling over the hem of my red velvet evening dress, I ran toward the tipi in fits of tears as my perfect party crumbled around me.

I remember that Mike, who was forever begging his provincial buddies to "give the three-piece suit a chance," was the only one that followed me. *He* appreciated what I was trying to create.

"Don't worry, Countess," he soothed as he sipped cognac from his hip flask. "Someday you'll find the civilized debauchery you're looking for."

He was right.

⟿

Unlike most English people I would later meet, Rupert's clique of friends seemed to grasp that being American wasn't entirely my fault, merely my misfortune. And in retrospect, welcoming me into their social circle was probably an act of charity as much as anything else, but I was having way too much fun to dwell on it.

Rupert's crowd all looked and sounded and acted exactly the same. Same accents (upper-class), same fashion sense (the more sloppy and disheveled you looked, the more money you had), same skin (glowingly and annoyingly clear). Keen to be surrounded by guys and girls that spoke and lived exactly as they did, they'd found each other quite quickly once university began and, for the most part, kept to themselves.

The more time I spent with them, the more I realized that it was precisely their extreme privilege, precisely their profound to-the-manner-born self-assurance that had been ingrained in their DNA for centuries, that made them so utterly charming. And I found this inner contentment to be a sharp and refreshing contrast to the arrogance and smugness that existed in so many self-made or new-moneyed Americans.

Still, there were hints of class snobbery that were clearly here to stay. Gold signet rings bearing one's family crest (worn on the pinky for both men and women) were de rigueur and overall, there seemed to be a fanatical preoccupation with genealogy. Unlike the American mind-set, which is primarily about what you can one day *become*, for these kids the focus seemed to be much more about what you had *been*—your family's history, your ancestor's achievements, and so on.

They wouldn't be caught dead at the student union or larger

university parties—darling, those were for the masses, the plebs, the rough working class. (Meaning, those were for the bulk of British students[37] that hadn't attended a private school and didn't speak with perfect BBC English.[38]) Instead, their social life consisted mainly of getting obliterated at each other's houses or dinner parties, and occasionally crashing the local bars and nightclubs.

And then there was me, the token foreigner, who by some cosmic miracle was along for the ride.

⟶

Upon first meeting me, relatively sober English conversations always began with the most important things: where one lives, the people at the party one knows, where one went to boarding school, and one's family background. I couldn't exactly say, "A bomb shelter, no one but Rupert, an American public school full of hillbillies, and was practically raised in a tipi." But luckily, in England you can pretty much get away with talking about nothing but the weather for the rest of your life and still pass as unbelievably witty and well mannered.

New conversations with more intoxicated English people were easier; they simply assumed I wouldn't be at the party in the first place if I weren't a suitable, well-connected, and established guest and therefore moved immediately to more trivial and flirtatious small talk.

It was here that I learned the value of exclamatory exaggeration: the choice of wine is simply brilliant, *riveting*, divine; a broken toaster is ghastly, beastly, *God has struck!*

---

37 All U.K. universities are free (there are no private institutions) and supposedly merit-based. Although Oxford and Cambridge are often accused of elitism, upper-middle-class students account for less than 45 percent of Oxbridge entrants.

38 "BBC English," or the educated spoken English of southeast England used by news anchors on television produced by the British Broadcasting Corporation, is generally considered to be the *prestige* British accent (though it is somewhat politically incorrect to admit it).

And it was here that I learned the importance of understatement: Hurricanes? Middle Eastern conflicts? ("Darling, how *terribly* boring!") Traffic accidents? Broken bones? ("A bit of a bother.")

Both boys and girls seemed to constantly have their arms around each other, were forever kissing each other on both cheeks, and seemed to talk quite openly about almost any subject you can think of. Considering they'd all attended single-sex boarding schools for most for their lives, and university was truly their first time living in mixed company, I was rather taken aback to see that their sexual maturity (at least on a social level) greatly surpassed that of American students of the same age. Their parties and dinner parties weren't full of the juvenile fraternity/sorority antics I was used to; these bashes were straight out of Oscar Wilde. As young twenty-somethings, they seemed to be in total denial that they were living on the cusp of a new millennium, and coped by pretending to be mini nineteenth-century adults. Bearing in mind that I've always pretended to be exactly the same thing, I loved every second of it.

I have to say being the only American in the room was wonderful—it brought me tons of male attention and I basked in it. But there were other times when my very novelty only served to remind me of how different I was from them, and how far I still had to go if I really wanted to blend in. My slightly "wild" London life spiced up their dinner parties ("Can you *believe* the poor girl lives in town?") and perhaps added a touch of mystery or cosmopolitanism to their evenings, but I often wondered if they kept me around in the same way that they might keep an interesting pet.

⌐⌐

I once read a hilarious article[39] about student binge drinking and how it was considered a huge problem among U.S. universities,

---

39 Hassinger, Kris. "Binge drinking problem exaggerated," *CollegiateTimes.com,* Nov 2003.

but oddly, not a problem at all in the U.K. The author, intrigued by the anomaly, had looked into how the U.S. and U.K. officially defined student "binge drinking" and unearthed some very entertaining results: Whereas the puritanical Americans defined binge drinking as "five beers in one sitting for a male, or four for a female," the forever-jovial Brits defined the problem as "an extended period of time, lasting *at least two days*, during which a student repeatedly becomes intoxicated and gives up his or her usual activities and obligations in order to become intoxicated."

Don't get me wrong—I love my cocktails more than anyone, but I also thought part of being a student meant attending the occasional class and setting aside the occasional time to study and I found it rather bizarre that none of Rupert's friends appeared to do either. Their "extended period of intoxication" seemed to be lasting all year.

(Actually, I take that back. Now that I think about it, I *did* witness Rupert and a few of his mates going over their Spanish in a pub one Sunday afternoon. But they were "studying" while drinking pints of beer and watching a rugby match on TV so it hardly counted.)

Needless to say, I was shocked by this British disregard for academics—particularly when I thought back to how much time I spent studying at Rochester. There, everyone around me studied for several hours in the library every single day. Even on weekends.

Were Rupert's friends simply much smarter than me? So much so that they never needed to study? I have to say that for some reason I highly doubted that. Rupert's friends may have been witty raconteurs, but they were hardly closet geniuses.

One day, when I randomly mentioned to Rupert's friend Hugo how my friends in America were killing themselves to get into the top five business schools in the country, he looked horrified.

"You can't be serious," he said. "Surely getting an M.B.A. is because one wants to play golf on the roof of a frat house, or meet a ravishing young oil heiress. You don't mean to tell me that your American friends, as charming as I'm sure they are, are competing purely for *academic standing*! Personally, I can't think of anything worse than being cooped up for two years in the MIT library. To think nothing of the damage it would do to one's CV."[40]

Again, I was genuinely puzzled by this response. Not caring if I momentarily came across as an ignorant American, I asked Hugo to explain further.

"To put it bluntly, my dear," he continued patiently, "in this country, it's considered bad manners to be clever. It implies that your family's history and status aren't enough to get you by in life. Everyone knows only the lower classes feel the need to show off their academic prowess."

Guess I'll keep that LSE scholarship to myself then.

⟶

Now that every weekend I was immersed in English society, I was terrified of wearing the right clothes in the wrong combination, or using the right words in the wrong context. You must say sitting room, not living room; sofa, not couch; loo, not toilet. The list of unwritten rules was endless, and the smallest blunders on my part (apparently you must say, "what a lovely house," and never say, "what a lovely home") would occasionally cause a flurry of barely concealed shudders among my new friends.

English etiquette, especially among the upper-class characters I was mixing with, was a minefield—and I wanted to get it

---

40 CV: curriculum vitae. Used in the U.K. instead of the word résumé. CVs can be several pages long and usually include personal information that is practically illegal to disclose to U.S. employers—including age and marital status.

right. If my hippie parents wouldn't send me to Swiss finishing school to learn such things (and with no Professor Higgins begging to tutor me like in *My Fair Lady*), by God, I would teach myself!

As part of my self-taught assimilation course, I decided to read *Debrett's*[41] *New Guide to Etiquette and Modern Manners* cover to cover. Emily Post may have been the goddess of American etiquette, but Debrett's was the only true authority on proper English behavior and I was determined to encapsulate all of its wise teachings.

Table manners were the real test. (I've actually met an English girl that stopped dating an English guy because he neglected to hold his knife correctly.) But I knew most things already: bread plate on your left, wine and water on your right, spoon your soup away from you, tilt your bowl away from you, fill others' glasses before you fill your own, place your knife and fork side by side on the plate when finished eating, and so on. This stuff was easy, mainly because it's also considered correct form in America.

Not that anyone in my little Colorado town realized this. After driving thirty miles to the nearest fine dining establishment for my much anticipated prom night dinner, I can't tell you the horror that welled up inside me when my date proceeded to use my bread plate throughout the entire meal and then casually tossed his cutlery on the table when he was finished. And I'd thought I'd bagged one of the more refined guys in town!

And I already knew (or thought I knew) the basics of English eating etiquette: fork in your left hand, knife in your right (*never* switch hands), always eat with your fork upside down

---

41 *Debrett's* (founded in 1769) is internationally recognized as the arbiter of etiquette and behavior, as well as the main authority on significant individuals in British society.

(*never* use it to scoop), never cut things with the side of your fork, and so on.

But then there were several English rules that were entirely new to me, and I have to say, when I read about them, their arcane absurdity astounded me. From what I could tell, dozens of invisible, nonfunctional rules existed purely to ostracize those that knew them from those that didn't. (And to allow those in the know to tell terribly amusing anecdotes about those who weren't.)

For example, port must always be passed clockwise. You don't talk about it. It just happens. And if I hadn't happened to read about this universal beverage traffic law the night before, the port's journey would have stopped with me and everyone would have enjoyed being silently aghast at my American ignorance and talked excitedly about the incident among themselves for weeks to come.

Then there's the monstrous challenge of correctly eating something as simple as peas. According to *Debrett's*, the "correct way to consume peas is to squash them on top of the fork." By this they mean using your knife (held in your right hand) to smash the peas violently against the back of your fork (which you are holding in your left hand with the prongs facing down) until they are sufficiently mushy and secure, after which it is safe to bring the fork to your mouth. No piercing of peas is permitted; no scooping of peas is permitted. And under no circumstances are you to turn the fork over and push the peas onto the inside of the fork with your knife. That would be far too easy. And far too working-class.

Sure, I should've been reading my criminal rehabilitation textbook cover to cover instead of attempting to teach myself how to correctly peel an orange with a knife and fork (I dare you to try it), but again, I had a strange sense that mastering

Debrett's would do more for my future than debating the pros and cons of the prison system. (Not that I didn't care deeply about reforming the prison system.)

⁓

Of course everybody in Oxford was blissfully ignorant when it came to my hippie upbringing, and my ongoing regime to mold myself into the perfect royal consort seemed to be working—aside from the small fact that I was still looking for the royal in question. But I remained patient; Peter wasn't going anywhere and my skills still required much honing. And in the meantime, I would continue to test them on Rupert's friends.

"Jerramy, you are the only American I'm actually fond of" was a comment I heard often, and it was music to my ears.

And when someone told me, "Jerramy, you are the only American I know that has true class," I knew things were going very well indeed.

My farm town existence was receding rapidly into oblivion. I was a long, long way from the Hog Back.

Professor Higgins would have been very proud.

Eleven

"I am happy that George calls on my bedchamber less frequently than of old. As is, I now endure but two calls a week, and when I hear his steps outside my door, I lie back on my bed, close my eyes and think of England."

—LADY ALICE HILLINGDON, WIFE OF 2ND BARON HILLINGDON, 1912

Although these Oxford guys may have looked and sounded like Hugh Grant at his sexiest, their behavior was nothing like the shy, dithering stereotype that Hollywood so sweetly portrayed. While in most of his movies, Hugh Grant can barely glance at a girl without stammering and turning bright red, Rupert's foppish friends were unbelievably confident, assertive, and gregarious— *especially* with the opposite sex. When it came to their dealings with girls (or at least when it came to their dealings with me) their elegant charm was as enticing as their staggering audacity. It was pure James Bond–style impudence (cut-glass accent included), and I found it irresistible.

Despite his incessant teasing, Rupert admirably maintained his role as my surrogate brother, allowing me to flirt with as many lords and non-lords as I saw fit. But even with this freedom, I was making a concerted effort to counteract my dreadful behavior at the toga party. Because to tell you the truth, I was not that kind of girl.

In my defense (and in spite of recent evidence to the contrary), I must insist that I've always been quite prudish at heart. Throughout my teens I'd been surrounded by so many goat-roping cow-boys that held no ambition whatsoever other than to get drunk and drive around in pickup trucks[42] until the day they died, that for the majority of high school, my interest in boys was practically nonexistent. I did regard myself as rather inexperienced—but considering the alternatives, quite frankly, I didn't mind.

I was nearly eighteen when I had my first kiss. And my first time wasn't until several years after that (because with college came four years of loud-mouthed New Yorkers like Max). My extended intervals of self-imposed chastity were extremely effortless—mainly because in those surroundings, physical at-traction simply never existed for me.

But meeting Rupert's circle of friends changed everything. I was *shocked* at the heady effect these English boys had on me and became rather frightened by my endless desire to kiss every male within arm's reach that spoke to me with a plummy English accent.

At the turn of the century, respectable Englishwomen used to force themselves to think of their childbearing duty to the British Empire in order to get through any kind of passionate activity with an Englishman. Fast-forward a hundred years and there I was seduced by the mere thought of one day serving the British Empire! Trembling with pleasure at the very idea of any passion-ate activity with an Englishman! And yet some people still had the nerve to accuse me of single-handedly reversing the feminist movement. If anything, I was moving it forward!

Nonetheless, in this new temptation-rich environment, I really had to watch myself. I knew that if I wasn't careful, my personal and unique interpretation of "Lie back and think of England"

---

42 In fact, a popular bumper sticker for many of these pickup trucks was "Get 'er drunk."

could lead to scandals that would make the toga incident pale in comparison.

But I had to wonder, what patrician predicament would my accent-addiction lead me to next?

⌒

Later that month, I received an invitation to Rupert's twenty-first birthday party that was to be held in an ancient windmill somewhere in the east of England. An American friend of mine pointed out that it's a good thing England is stuck in the past because the modern equivalent would be to throw a party in a nuclear reactor, but I ignored him. Americans had no right to lecture me on what was and wasn't an appropriate party. They couldn't even binge drink properly.

As usual, this party had a theme: "Dress as Your Hero." I have to admit, I didn't quite understand this constant English obsession with costume parties. Prior to meeting Rupert, the last time I remember going to a party where a costume was required (other than Halloween) I was in third grade. Now I was attending "fancy dress" parties practically every week.

My real heroine was, without a doubt, the late Princess Diana. She was the epitome of everything I ever dreamed of becoming. She was gorgeous, stylish, an excellent social hostess, and an even better philanthropist. Although she was possibly the last traditionally chosen[43] princess, she proved that her royal role was just as relevant to the public today as it was thousands of years ago.

Two years before I found Peter in the Windsor family tree, I remember watching Diana's fairytale wedding on television. My grandparents had dotingly taped it for me, and as a four-year-old, I sat cross-legged on their floor, watching it over and over—utterly

---

43 Meaning Charles didn't have much say in the matter.

entranced by Diana's magic. In that instant, she became the living link between the fairytale in my heart and the fairytale I knew my life could become.

Diana died three months before I was scheduled to come to England for the first time. I was devastated. After waiting all those years, my milestone trip had suddenly become bittersweet. I knew I would never see Diana in person; I knew I would never get to meet her.

Initially, I refused to believe anyone when they told me the news of her death. It was nearly one in the morning, I (big surprise) was at a college frat party, and I was certain that my friends were playing some vast practical joke on me and my royal obsession. But as the evening wore on, and more and more people came to tell me the heartbreaking news, I realized that the impossible was true.

I remember locking myself in my dorm room with piles of newspapers and crying for hours as I pored over the tragic headlines, staring at the TV as the knee-deep sea of flowers piled higher and higher in front of Kensington Palace. I stayed up by myself to watch the 4 A.M. funeral, as all those who loyally pledged to stay up with me fell asleep soon after midnight.

It felt like some merciless higher power had single-handedly plucked the biggest inspiration out of my life, leaving me to face the world alone. No one could console me. The only person who came close was, quite unexpectedly, my dad—who told me he felt exactly the same way when John Lennon died.

Nearly ten years later, people still laugh and joke and scoff at my heartache, but it is a genuine loss from which I will never recover, and to this day, I still wear black on the 31st of August.

Did I dare dress up as Princess Diana for Rupert's party? When I'd created a Diana costume for my eighth grade honors history class, I'd quickly learned that my long blond hair wasn't particularly conducive to her look. However well intended, I knew any impersonation of mine would never do her justice, and I also knew the Brits would see the entire costume as terribly nouveau and tacky.

So, I resorted to heroine #2: Princess Grace of Monaco, another idyllic princess who was killed tragically in a car crash. Prior to becoming Princess Grace, she was the ultraglamorous screen actress known as Grace Kelly. And yes, she was American. I figured that with this costume, for once my accent might work in my favor. Granted, the real Princess Grace renounced her U.S. citizenship in order to marry her true love Prince Rainier, but I could hardly hold that against her. I would have done the same thing in a heartbeat.

I eventually settled for a black sheath dress with a peach silk cardigan, my highest, most glamorous black heels, a single string of pearls, and a pair of Hollywood cat-eye sunglasses. I coaxed my hair into thick Grace Kelly waves and finished the look with the hard-won tiara from my oh-so-controversial teen beauty pageant. Sadly, the tiara was set with rhinestones instead of diamonds and therefore rather unauthentic, but what could I do? Genuine jewels could only be mine when I was a genuine member of the royal family. I had to have patience.

As I stood in King's Cross train station waiting for my platform to Windmill country to be announced, I got a phone call from Rupert's friend Tigger. (Tigger's real name was Arabella but she insisted on using her boarding school nickname. And thanks to Rupert's incessant whispering, I also happened to know that her father was on *The Times* Rich List.[44]) Tigger was already at the windmill and wanted to know if it wouldn't be terribly inconvenient for me to pick up the latest copy of *Tatler*, an En-

---

44 The annual *Sunday Times* "Rich List" catalogs the thousand wealthiest people in Britain, the richest Britons living abroad, and the richest people in the world.

glish fashion magazine. Apparently the October issue was meant to hit the shelves that day. Of course I agreed and rushed to the newsagent before catching my train.

Once seated, I began to flip through it and saw that it was more than an ordinary women's glossy—it was a society magazine! How on earth had I lived in England this long without looking at one?

I was reprimanding my own stupidity when I stopped dead in my tracks. I was looking at a picture of Rupert. Above him was a picture of Giles. And next to him was a picture of Tigger dancing with Freddy Windsor! For those of you who don't know, allow me to point out that Lord Frederick Windsor[45] is thirty-second in the line of succession to the British throne and a major pal of Prince William.

I knew my circle of English friends was a lucky break. But I had no idea that I was spending my weekends dancing with boys who danced with girls who probably danced with Prince William! I had no idea the entire United Kingdom paid to see pictures of them at parties! I giddily wondered if the windmill party would show up in the next issue.

Rupert picked me up at the train station and we drove through a plethora of fields, farms, and pastures. I knew we were somewhere near Sandringham[46] (a much-loved country retreat of the Queen) so I kept my eyes peeled for glimpses of Her Majesty.

Just before twilight, and right when I had decided we were absolutely in the middle of nowhere, we pulled up to the towering windmill. (I have to say, windmills are much bigger than I ever realized.) Tigger had *Tatler* in her hands and was checking to see if

---

45 Freddy's father is Prince Michael of Kent (the Queen's first cousin).

46 Park House, where Princess Diana was raised, is also located on the Royal Sandringham estate.

she looked suitably photogenic before my bags were even unloaded from the car.

I ducked through the miniature windmill door and entered the loud buzz of the party. The large, circular wooden space was heaving with guests supposedly dressed as their heroes, but from the looks of it, I'm not sure anyone took the theme as literally as I did. A guy dressed as "Hugh Grant" (hardly a stretch!) was opening about ten bottles of red wine and "Alicia Silverstone" was making sangria. I have to say that this bunch were so ridiculously handsome and beautiful to begin with, that visually imitating handsome and beautiful celebrities was annoyingly effortless for them. Despite all my attempts, I never seemed to glow as much and as naturally as they did. Still, I suppose if I'd been blessed with a lifetime of guaranteed privilege, I'd glow from within too.[47]

I went upstairs to change into my costume and found about six bedrooms filled with wooden bunk beds. It reminded me of the summer when I worked as a camp counselor. Who knew that a windmill could easily sleep fifty people? I quickly made the finishing touches required to transform myself into Princess Grace, then descended the ancient staircase, and officially joined the party.

As ever, I was the only American and loving it. I drank my red wine and happily drifted from one charming character to the next. In a surreal haze, I flirted with Groucho Marx, had a deep conversation with one of the Spice Girls, and batted my eyelashes at several Hugh Grants. I was downing perhaps my third or fourth Jell-O shot (or "vodka jelly" as the Brits call it) when I saw him come in through the tiny windmill door.

Did I know him from somewhere?

He had broken his leg (skiing in Switzerland, of course) but

---

47 As Oscar Wilde once said, "All charming people are spoiled. It is the secret of their attraction." In this context, I couldn't agree more.

hadn't let his giant cast[48] stop him from dressing up as Superman. And what a glorious Superman he was! He had one of those cute, dimpled baby faces that I adored, and perfectly formed muscles that bulged rather authentically beneath his blue Superman T-shirt. He had the requisite upper-class glow, the requisite disheveled hair, and the requisite rosy cheeks. Just by looking at him, I knew his requisite accent would be to die for.

I racked my wine-soaked brain trying to remember where we might have met. I mean, how could I have possibly forgotten a creature that was half superhero, half aristocrat? As I watched him hop toward a chair on his crutches, he caught me staring at him and smiled shyly, his blue eyes twinkling.

In a flash, I realized why he looked so familiar. I had just been looking at his picture in *Tatler*!

That does it. I was officially a girl on a mission. I focused intently on his blue Superman T-shirt, and without letting my eyes stray from that red and yellow Superman symbol, I began to make my way through the crowd.

I was just about to tap Superman on his muscley shoulder and confess something similar to undying love, when a guy dressed as Captain Hook stepped directly in front of me, blocking my path.

First of all, I always thought Captain Hook was a villain, not a hero. But I had to admit that the pirate rags flattered his broad shoulders in a very regal, very sexy kind of way. I smiled politely and tried to wriggle toward my original love interest, but the tall, burly pirate simply wouldn't let me.

So we just stood there. Eyes locked, hearts pounding. The

48 Or "plaster," as the Brits would say

chemistry between us was undeniable and it kind of threw me. Finally, I broke the sexually charged silence.

"I am Princess Grace of Monaco," I said, extending my hand. "I don't believe we have met." Because of all the wine (and also because of his dark hair, and his perfectly chiseled, tanned face), I had to make an effort not to slur my words.

Seriously, this constant temptation just wasn't fair! There were simply too many of them. And they were simply too good-looking. How was I supposed to cope?

"The pleasure is all mine, Your Serene Highness," he answered, kissing my fingertips. "I am Captain Hook."

For one, he actually knew my official title. For two, his accent was so well-bred that for a split second I wondered if my heart was still beating.

"Would you like to tour the machinery of the windmill?" the pirate continued, still grasping my tiny hand in his own.

"Yes," I breathed. "I mean, um . . . how terribly kind of you, Captain. I would like nothing more."

I truly think that perhaps I have some sort of rare medical disorder. I truly think I must have been suffering from some sort of mysterious condition that caused all brain activity to shut down in the presence of any cut-glass English accent. It was the only explanation. Why else would I have agreed to climb dozens of rickety ladders in my best three-inch heels through some ramshackle windmill with some random guy dressed as Captain Hook whom I'd known for all of thirty seconds?

⟋

After quite a precarious journey up quite a few precarious ladders (a journey not at all conducive to those wearing skirts or those who had recently consumed four to five glasses of wine), we finally reached our glamorous goal: "the machinery of the windmill."

Honestly, it was nothing but a bunch of giant rusty gears and deteriorating wooden boards. Hardly worth a tour, but I suppose guys like dull mechanical stuff like this. Still, I had to acknowledge that the view of the moonlit sea from so far above was positively breathtaking. And before I knew what was happening, the pirate and I were kissing.

Don't get me wrong; the pirate was *hot*, and kissing him was fantastic. But even in my highly inebriated state, rolling about passionately on those crumbling, termite-infested floorboards at least ten stories above the ground didn't seem like the safest idea, and I tried desperately to communicate this to him. But the pirate showed no signs of coming up for air and it occurred to me that this was one situation where my knowledge of *Debrett's* wasn't going to help.

So I lay there—hopelessly and deliciously pinned beneath his ruffly pirate shirt and wonderful pirate kisses—waiting to plummet through the floor to my death, and thought of England.

⌐

Eventually, the rather risky kissing marathon came to an end. The pirate disappeared toward the bar and I was able to return to the party's significantly more stable ground-floor footing. And just I was tottering down the last rungs of the last ladder, I found myself face to face with a smirking Rupert.

"Jerramy, you are aware that Captain Hook is the Queen's second cousin?"

God help me. What had I tangled myself up in this time?

My head was spinning with the possible ramifications of my quasi-royal conquest, so I ran away from Rupert and headed to the safety of the food table. My cheeks were flushed, my arms were tingling, and I could literally feel the alcohol coursing through my veins. I knew food might be a good precautionary measure to prevent myself from accidentally making out with any more royal relatives.

I was helping myself to some grapes, a slice of bread, and a piece of brie, when Charles, dressed as James Dean, sauntered up to the buffet. Charles. He tormented me at every party in Oxford. And he *would* dress as James Dean, wouldn't he? Who else would he possibly dress as?

The truth is Charles belonged on the cover of *GQ* magazine. He was agonizingly attractive. His every movement was an unconsciously graceful, pantherlike pose. His bone structure was flawless. And you could probably get a paper cut on his cheekbones. Silently, he poured a cup of sangria and handed it to me.

"Charles," I heard myself saying, "did you know you have perfect bone structure?"

For the love of God. What was I doing? Why did I insist on playing with fire?

"Jerramy, you are too kind," Charles said absently, his lazy, insouciant accent piercing my very soul.

He always did this. He always put himself directly in my path but refused to pay me the slightest bit of attention. Like right then he was busy looking at an antique map on the wall, and looking unbearably like a Burberry model while doing so.

"It says here," Charles murmured, "that there is a herb[49] garden on the grounds of this windmill."

Then he turned to me as if only just remembering that I was standing there and said, "Let's go see if we can find it."

He held his hand out behind him and didn't even look to see if I would take it. My God, he was arrogant. And my God, did I love it.

Our fingers entwined and we walked out the front door of the windmill into the crisp autumn night. Everything was bathed in moonlight and covered in drops of dew. And I was deliciously

---

49 Bizarrely, in England the *h* in *herb* is not silent.

drunk. And as I tried to come to terms with the sight of his bone structure in the moonlight, my heel caught in a cobblestone crevice and I went tumbling down into the wet grass, pulling Charles with me. As we landed, our lips came together and the whole thing accidentally slipped lusciously out of my control.

For those few minutes, I was transported to another universe, aware of nothing but me and this English Burberry model rolling around in the grass and locked together in the darkness. If someone had come up to me in that moment with a clipboard and asked me what my name was, I'm not sure I could have answered. It was a truly an incredible kiss. Then, as fast as we had fallen down, Charles pulled me up and we retreated to the warm chaos of the windmill.

⟶

The party was still going strong. People were dancing on the furniture and childishly pelting each other with wine corks and bread rolls. When I saw that I was *covered* in grass and mud, I hurried to the bathroom. I had to remove all evidence that the two of us had done anything other than gone for an innocent walk! I was hardly the type of girl to make out with more than one boy in a single evening. I rarely made out with more than one boy in a single year!

I closed the rickety bathroom door behind me and switched on the light, only to find myself nose to nose with Captain Hook, who switched it right off again, pinned me against the tiny sink (boy, did he love to pin), and started kissing me again. What was going on here? One minute I was trying to find my superhero soulmate and the next minute half of the windmill was trying to kiss me!

Not that I was complaining. The pirate was a pretty good kisser himself. And he *was* related to the Queen.

Suddenly, a loud knock snapped me out of my royal fantasy.

"Grace Kelly. Let me in. I have mud all over me." It was Charles.

Again, I had to wonder why *Debrett's* didn't think to write one measly paragraph on the correct etiquette to extract oneself from a pirate.

"Listen, Captain Hook," I whispered frantically, "I can't let Charles see you in here with me!"

I was telling the truth. I had no intention of becoming known as the American girl who kisses two guys in less than five minutes. Even if I had.

"Okay," he whispered back. "I'll just climb out the window."

Right. Of course. He'll just climb out the window. He said it as if he climbed out of bathroom windows every day. There would probably be a photo of me covered in mud, standing on a toilet, and pushing the Queen's second cousin out of a window in next month's *Tatler*. I could see it now:

Unknown American social climber and Grace Kelly wanna-be shoves The Honourable Something Something-Something out of a windmill window as society birthday party spins dangerously out of control. . . .

I tried not to think about it. With Captain Hook safely evacuated, I slowly opened the bathroom door. Charles smiled at me politely as if I were a stranger, then squeezed past me toward the sink. His entire demeanor was so indifferent toward me, I was forced to wonder if I had actually imagined the whole amazing kiss-in-the-grass episode. Except for the small fact that we were both still covered in grass.

Back in the main room of the windmill, I heard Rupert calling for me.

"Jezza! There you are!" He was very drunk. But he was also sitting very close to Superman. Oh how I'd strayed from my first love of the evening!

Rupert pulled me onto his lap as I walked by, raised his pint glass, and slurred, "Jezza, you're a top bird!" before spilling most of it over my grass-stained Princess Grace cardigan.

But then, true to his costume, Superman saved the day.

He lifted me off Rupert's lap and safely onto his own, turned to me with his big round Superman eyes, and in a husky English accent that made my stomach flip, he said, "Are you tired?"

I nodded dreamily and rested my head on his muscley shoulder.

"Me too," he said quietly. "Let's find ourselves a bunk bed."

⟶

The next morning, a bunch of us headed to Superman's parents' house, which happened to be five minutes down the road, and cooked ourselves a full English breakfast—which is quite possibly the world's best cure for a hangover. Over platefuls of fried toast, fried bacon, fried sausages, fried tomatoes, fried mushrooms, and fried eggs sunny-side up, I tried to pretend that the night before I hadn't made out with three out of the seven guys sitting at the breakfast table.

Twelve

"Be patient toward all that is unresolved in your heart."

—RAINER MARIA RILKE

I rushed to the newsagent every day, earnestly awaiting the next issue of *Tatler*. When it finally appeared, I handed over my three pounds and quickly flipped to the society pages. No sign of the windmill party. I breathed a sigh of relief. That party would not have been an idyllic social debut.

Still, I vigilantly scanned the party photographs searching for faces I might recognize—and what do you know, there was Superman! And another of Giles! I closed the magazine and smiled with satisfaction. It was only a matter of time before my face appeared in those pages as well. First, aristocratic social circles. Next stop: royal circles.

Nevertheless, after the windmill party, I had to admit to a certain trend. Costume parties full of aristocratic boys with aristocratic accents were not really helping me with my prince search and I was really starting to worry if they were actually having an adverse effect.

I mean, what if Captain Hook knew Peter? Let's face it, as the Queen's second cousin, he must know at least *some* of the royal family. With that connection alone, gossip could easily reach my future husband, warning him to stay clear of this flighty new American girl that kisses any costumed Englishman placed in front of her. Not the best reputation to precede me.

I knew that I had been deprived of aristocratic boys for so long that my subconscious was merely making up for lost time. And I knew that, quite frankly, I had been unfairly subjected to a nonstop stream of temptation. But I also knew that no matter how many times Rupert insisted I had nothing to worry about, my wanton behavior *had to stop* before it became borderline promiscuous. No matter how sexy his toga, or how lovely his accent, or how many times he was pictured in a magazine—I had to stop.

So, right then and there, I decided to grab ahold of myself and date English guys properly. Make them call me, send me flowers, and take me to dinner. My days of ripping off togas and tangling myself up with pirates were over. Over! I was going to cut down on the cocktails and sangria and play hard to get. Forget the *back* pages of *Tatler*—I had to save myself for the front cover.

⌒

The next day I received a phone call from a boy I met at the windmill. Oddly enough, it wasn't a boy I had kissed, not that that would have narrowed it down for you. It was from a boy who had dressed up as the Pope. His name was Andrew and he needed a date to an upcoming London reception.

Clearly, Andrew was not a Pope in real life. Far from it. He was a young gentleman of leisure who enjoyed partaking in more than his fair share of tennis and debauchery. And it seemed this reception would be involving both of his favorite pastimes. We were to attend a black-tie gala to mark the finale of a series of U.S./U.K. singles and doubles championships that had been held all week at The Queen's Club[50]—the most prestigious tennis club in the country, if not the world.

"However," Andrew drawled to me over the phone in his dev-astatingly upper-crust accent, "I'm afraid that this invitation must be purely platonic. It's going to be quite a party, and I think it best if you and I keep our options open. As long you as arrive on my arm, the rest of the evening is your oyster."

Andrew's oyster terms suited me just fine and I happily agreed to be his transatlantic arm-candy. But seriously—how was I sup-posed to concentrate on my social exclusion paper that was due that week? All I could think about were swarms of world-class British athletes dressed in tuxedos![51]

Andrew and I arrived during the final game of the tourna-ment. But it wasn't normal tennis like I was expecting. It was a spin-off game called "racquets" that is only taught at exclusive British boarding schools. Apparently it started off in the eigh-teenth century as a game played in English prison yards yet some-how morphed into a game for the wealthy aristocracy. Don't ask. All I know is that only a dozen or so courts on the planet can even facilitate racquets and Queen's Club has two of them.

Anyway, as Andrew whispered all the club gossip in my ear, I sipped my champagne and tried to make sense of it all. To be hon-est I had never been one for spectator sports. I would have rather done just about anything than watch baseball or football or almost any game involving a ball. I just can't focus on any of it. I might as well sit and watch fish swim back and forth in a fish tank.

But racquets was different. It all moved so fast and the players moved with such amazing, inhuman skill that my heart was ac-

---

50 As seen in the Woody Allen movie *Match Point* (2005)

51 Or "dinner jackets" as the Brits would say, also known as "DJs." Most boarding school boys have owned one since their teens.

tually pumping as I watched the last minutes of the tournament. The game we watched was between the #3- and #4-ranked racquets players in the world within the under-twenty-four age group. And I was particularly transfixed by #3. When he was declared the winner, I clapped as loudly as I could without spilling champagne over my little black dress.

The reception that followed was terribly civilized. Then again, for me it was all relative. At that point, any party that didn't involve shoving pirates out of bathroom windows seemed civilized. As always, I kept my farm town upbringing to myself and dazzled everyone with my charming *Debrett's* manners. No pirate-esque episodes that night, that's for sure. I was so over that silly stage in my life.

The American businessmen had turned out in massive numbers and all seemed to have conveniently left their wives at home. Andrew was nowhere to be found so I was left to fend for myself in a banquet room full of black-tie testosterone. I was attempting to converse with four drunken Chicago tycoons, when I felt a tap on my arm.

I turned around and let out a tiny gasp, for there, standing right next to me, was #3! He was freshly showered and his blond hair was still wet and poked off his head in perfect little spikes. Up close, he was absolutely stunning. Like one of those soap-opera actors whose good looks can't possibly be real. Also, I know you should never judge a guy wearing a tux because tuxes always make guys look better than they do in real life, but the black wool of his double-breasted dinner jacket made #3 look more preposterously handsome than ever. His jaw was so square, his shoulders so broad, and his skin so tanned, I felt as if I was standing next to a life-sized Malibu Ken doll.

I stood there dumbfounded as the Ken doll took the champagne glass out of my hand and replaced it with another glass flute filled with something pink and bubbly. And then, in an Etonian[52] accent that took my breath away, he said, "I thought you might prefer a Kir Royale instead of plain champagne."

I don't think I'd ever heard a more beautiful pick-up line in my entire life.

It sure did make a change from America. I think the best pick-up line I ever heard there was from a guy in Daytona Beach who zoomed past me in his flashy red convertible shouting, "Take your shorts off, baby!"

Everything seemed to be moving in slow motion and I could barely speak. I just couldn't believe that this gorgeous Ken doll was actually talking to me. His name was James St. John[53] Carrington-MacCarthey.[54] How soap opera is that?

We chatted for a while, but to be fair, he did most of the talking—I was too tongue-tied to do anything more than giggle and bat my eyelids. After a while it became clear that I was keeping him from all the important sports people who wanted to congratulate him on winning the tournament, and as ever, there was a gaggle of overaged businessmen waiting to talk to me, so we went our separate ways.

For the next few hours, the party went on around me and I floated through it, refusing to drink anything but Kir Royales. Around 1 A.M., those who were still standing retired to the clubhouse lounge to watch highlights from some sort of horse race.

---

52 The elite Eton College, located right next to Windsor Castle, is a private boys' boarding school (ages thirteen to eighteen) founded by King Henry VI in 1440. Tuition is approximately $46,500 per year and up until recently, one had to be registered at birth to even be considered for a placement. Famous alumni include Prince William, Prince Harry, Prince Michael of Kent, The Duke of Kent, George Orwell, Ian Fleming (creator of James Bond), and eighteen British prime ministers.

53 Pronounced "Sinjin"

54 Hyphenated last names—or "double-barrelled surnames" as they are called in the U.K.—are common among the British upper classes. They were originally created to ensure that property and titles would be inherited from both sides of the family upon marriage.

Andrew kissed me graciously on the cheek, said good-bye, and disappeared into the night, and I collapsed into an overstuffed leather sofa in the back of the room, asking myself for the millionth time why I insisted on wearing such ridiculously high heels.

Most of the people around me were focused on the big screen television and the noise of the commentators filled the room. I was so warm and happy in my comfy sofa that I began to nod off until I felt a familiar tap on my arm. I looked up and there was my beautiful Ken doll.

He sat down next to me on the sofa, leaned over, and began to whisper something to me in French. Due to Colorado's close proximity to Mexico, my parents had made me take Spanish in high school instead of French, ignoring my insistence that one day I'd be living much closer to France. As result of this, I had no idea what the Ken doll was saying to me. All I know is that I didn't want him to stop. His hand was on my leg and inching slowly up the skirt of my little black dress. Quite frankly, I didn't want that to stop either.

Suddenly he switched from French to his exquisite Etonian English and whispered, "I want to take you on a tour of Queen's Club."

Wait a minute. Let's pause for one tiny second. Did Eton and Harrow[55] and all those other prestigious boys' boarding schools teach all their students that if you like a girl, you invite them on a tour? Regardless of the venue? What if I had been in my own house? Would he have invited me on a tour of my own room? What if we were in a grocery store? Would it be a tour of the produce section?

---

55 Harrow is another elite (and expensive) boys' boarding school that was attended by at least half of Rupert's friends. Famous old Harrovians include seven British prime ministers (most notably Winston Churchill), Cary Elwes (the prince in the movie *The Princess Bride*), and Lord Nicholas Windsor (youngest son of the Duke and Duchess of Kent).

I quickly snapped out of it and before I knew what was happening, James St. John Carrington-MacCarthey and I were lying on the floor of an actual racquets court and making out in the dark. I decided to start playing hard to get next week.

At the latest.

⸏

Luckily, I was removed from temptation for a while. My first semester at LSE was coming to an end and I busied myself with frantic paper-writing. Also, in case you hadn't heard, New Year's Eve 1999 was kind of a big one. To save money, I wasn't going home for Christmas (Oh, no! My first Christmas away from my family and the naked hot springs—how was I ever going to get through it?), but whenever people started talking about their elaborate party arrangements for the millennium, I have to say that the sheer splendor and scope of *my* plans outshined everyone else's by far.

⸏

It was the last semester of my senior year of college, and my superstylish friend Natalie, who lived across the hall from me, had started seriously dating a boy who lived next door to me. His name was Krishna and everyone, including me, thought he and Natalie were perfect for each other.

One day, Krishna came into my room to chat while he was waiting for Natalie to finish getting ready. (She always took hours to choose an outfit.) As we laughed about drunken stories from last night's party, Krishna began to take a closer look at all the royal posters adorning my walls.

"Did I ever tell you that back in India, my mom is a princess?" Krishna said casually in his contagiously cheerful way.

What??? Krishna's mom was a princess?

"Hurry up, baby doll!" he called to Natalie. "The movie starts in ten minutes!"

Natalie came rushing out of her room, looking unbelievably stunning as usual, and they were off—leaving me to wonder how Krishna, my beer-loving, tennis-playing, all-American neighbor with his backward baseball cap, could possibly be connected to an Indian royal family.

But he was. In fact, he was the nephew of His Highness the Maharaja of Rajasthan.[56] And I had been invited by Krishna and Natalie to spend the millennium with them and the rest of the royal family at their Royal Palace in India.

⟶

There were odd times (including that absurd TV/book chart phase) when the free-love hippie parents became positively fascist. This was another one of those times.

"I don't think you should go," my mom told me. "I'm really worried you might be caught up in the Y2K."

"What better place to get stuck than in a palace?" I countered.

This conversation was getting ridiculous. It wasn't like I was asking her to fund my plane ticket to Mumbai; I was merely doing the daughterly thing and kindly informing her of my plans. I mean, I was already in London—which was practically *halfway* to India. (And quietly dipping into my new student loan money would easily cover the cost of the flight.)

"I don't think it's safe for you to travel as a woman on your own. You might be forced into a harem or something," she continued.

"I won't be alone! Besides, didn't you try to hitchhike to Woodstock by yourself?" She didn't like being reminded of that one.

"That was different."

---

56 Out of respect to the family, the exact region will not be named.

·"Not really."

"Jerramy, you can't fly around the world on a whim like some spoiled trust-fund kid! You can barely afford to be in London! Every penny you have should be going toward LSE, not wasted on one crazy party after another! You can go to India some other time. It's not like this is a once-in-a-lifetime opportunity."

"Mom! I'm being invited to party with *a royal family* on the eve of *the millennium*. If that's not a once-in-a-lifetime opportunity, *what is?!*"

"What if you get malaria?"

I was tempted to hang up on her. "I won't get malaria." Seriously, what happened to all the usual do-what-makes-you-happy hippie talk?

"Jerramy, if you go to India, I'll be very disappointed in you." I'm surprised she tried this one. I've never responded to any kind of guilt-related discipline and she knew it.

"Mom, don't worry about me. I'll be perfectly safe. And I'll send you a postcard from the palace." And with that, I said good-bye, called up the London travel agent, and bought my once-in-a-lifetime ticket.

To my horror, Air India was hijacked the night before I was scheduled to leave. Luckily I was taking a different airline, but it made me wonder if maybe my mom was right to be worried about me sometimes. But nothing, not even terrorists, was going to stop me from missing this party.

⟍

After the gray gloom of London, stepping into the glorious Bombay sunshine was pure bliss. Krishna had his driver pick me up at the airport and drive me to his family's apartment where I could freshen up and wait for my connecting flight to Rajasthan.

On Christmas Eve, my mom used to drive my brother and me through the poorer neighborhoods to remind us of how lucky we were. Because of this exposure, I genuinely thought I knew what poverty was. And as a smug masters student of social policy, I definitely thought I knew what poverty was.

But I didn't.

Only during that short car ride through the backstreets of Mumbai did I learn.

People, millions of people, literally living in piles of dirt. People literally going to the bathroom on top of each other—along with the cows, dogs, and monkeys that were living in the dirt with them. There were dozens of people with freakish birth defects crawling around on shriveled limbs. I saw a leper, I saw a girl with feet as big as watermelons with about ten toes on each, I saw people without legs rolling around on boards. They'd surround the car and paw at me through the windows with crazed, deranged eyes. It was like stepping inside that picture of Dante's Inferno that appeared in one of my high school textbooks. It was like what hell must honestly look like.

I'd seen homeless people on the streets of New York and London, huddled in doorways under heaps of filthy blankets, but here there were entire families sleeping on the roadside! Scores and scores of children living like animals and peeking desperately out of cardboard boxes—and the horrors stretched as far as I could see.

And there I was, in the plush, air-conditioned luxury of my chauffeured car, separated from my fellow human beings by this unbearable, mind-boggling gulf of fate. Life's unfairness cut through me like a dagger. What had I done to deserve my spoiled lifestyle? Why had I been spared such a dreadful existence and not them? The sheer scale and hopelessness of it all pummeled my heart and I was nearly crying by the time we reached Krishna's apartment.

What on earth was I doing at LSE studying first-world policy? Studying how to help people who *already had* floors and toilets? It all seemed so decadent and so useless next to the grinding poverty I'd just witnessed. How could I possibly stay in a palace after this?

As the car drove on, I suddenly remembered the night my dad had told me, "You're lucky you have feet."

And for the first time, I actually understood what he meant.

Thirteen

"Where life is possible at all, a right life is possible;
Life in a palace is possible;
Therefore even in a palace a right life is possible."

—Marcus Aurelius Antoninus,
Roman emperor (121 a.d.–180 a.d.)

The astonishingly beautiful sandstone palace, which had been partly converted to a five-star hotel after India claimed independence, had 347 rooms and was probably twice as big as the U.S. Capitol building.

Due to the long-haul flight and various stopovers, by the time I arrived at the palace, I hadn't slept in nearly forty-eight hours. Jet-lagged and delirious, I allowed myself to be escorted through the private royal wing filled with gilt furniture and elegant artwork and into the lavish suite I was to share with Natalie and Heather. I saw them, we screamed, we hugged, and although we had tons to catch up on since we hadn't seen each other since graduation, they told me to get dressed immediately because we were going to a party with *the princes* in five minutes. My hands were shaking so much from nerves and lack of sleep I could barely put my lipstick on straight.

The first prince was short, nothing special. The second prince (the Crown Prince) was strikingly beautiful. Amazing eyes, shiny black hair, perfect white teeth, perfect build, perfect square jaw. Perfect. And he had gone to Eton so you can guess what his accent sounded like. All hope for my behaving coherently for the remainder of the trip was gone as I began to star in my own Indian fairytale.

⌒

The cocktail party (mind you, this is only a pre-millennium-party cocktail party) was just as I knew it would be. There were glowing fires, Persian rugs, silk pillows, live music, and dozens of uniformed servants handing us drinks—all under the most amazingly clear stars I'd seen since Colorado. (That's one thing I missed about living in the middle of nowhere—no light pollution means you can always see the Milky Way.)

Still, I had trouble comprehending how all this modern affluence could exist so close to such mind-numbing poverty. Heather and I were pondering these ethical questions as best we could over our constantly flowing gin-and-tonics, when the Crown Prince appeared and pulled me onto the dance floor.

And as I danced under the dazzling Rajasthan stars with a real-live handsome prince, I had to remind myself that I started my day drinking a mug of instant coffee in the bomb shelter.

⌒

We partied until nearly 6 A.M. I saw royals and their guests dance on tables, fall down stairs, and order full-course meals to be served in the formal dining room at 4 A.M. and basically run around the palace like a bunch of crazy little kids. I loved every minute of it. Drunk, sleep-deprived, and jet-lagged beyond all comprehension, when I was finally getting ready for bed, I accidentally brushed my teeth in the tap water and panicked. What if I got malaria? I could already hear my mom saying, "I told you so."

At 10 A.M., the phone rang. "Your ladies' presence is requested in the prince's quarters for brunch. Be there in twenty minutes. Dress smartly." Just what three hungover girls that require at least one hour of primping minimum—much less primping for a prince—want to hear after close to zero hours of sleep. As you can imagine, it was a crisis of huge proportions.

Brunch was served in the garden, which might as well have been Jasmine's garden from Disney's *Aladdin*—complete with pillars, fountains, and the occasional peacock. I half expected a tiger to come prowling around the corner at any moment! I adore Indian food in general, but this was Indian food literally fit for a king—and compared to the cottage cheese rolls served at the bomb shelter, it was heaven.

I was introduced to the rest of the royal family and they were wonderful. From the Queen Mother to the Princess Royal to the various royal cousins to the Maharaja himself—all of them were genuinely kind, surprisingly open, and incredibly welcoming. Within days, I felt I had known them for years.

To my delight, after brunch we were invited to attend a royal polo match. My first invitation to a polo match had finally arrived!

Remember when I said racquets was the only interesting sport I'd ever seen? Well, I take that back. Polo is the sexiest sport on the planet: gorgeous, strapping players (including the princes) on horseback in hot pursuit of the ball, thundering hooves, bits of grass, clouds of dust, the loud smack of the mallet . . . the entire event was the epitome of sportsmanship, equestrian skill, and valor. And as I sat with the elegantly dressed spectators and applauded the princes between sips of champagne, I understood completely why polo had been the royal sport of choice for so many centuries.[57]

⌁

Next, the girls and I hit the palace pool. This was the life! And my mom was worried I'd be forced into a harem? Please. I don't think I'd ever felt safer.

---

57 *"Let other people play at other things. The King of Games still remains the Game of Kings."*—phrase carved beside an ancient polo ground in South Asia.

Still, I was begging for sleep and we headed back to our room under the impression that we'd have time to nap and prepare for dinner. How wrong we were.

"There's a cocktail party for the American ambassador to India," said the voice on the telephone. "Please be on the veranda in fifteen minutes. Dress smartly."

Another epic primping crisis. But if I know anything, it's that one can't say no to royal invitations. Even if your curling iron doesn't work with Indian electricity and your hair is still dripping wet from the swimming pool.

Cocktails began at six and continued until 11 P.M. Natalie is from an extremely wealthy American family (in fact, she and Krishna used to compare funny stories about their servants). And as I consumed ever more gin and tonics, and bantered with a seemingly endless string of royal cousins, I watched as she charmed everyone with her perfect finishing-school posture and giant sapphire earrings; I observed how gracefully she smiled when she realized the ambassador was a personal friend of her grandmother. She blended into that crowd better than any of us and it was painfully obvious to me. Captivating a room full of British politicians or upper-class Oxford students was one thing, holding my own with real royals was quite another. And with a sharp pang, I realized how much further I still had to go, and how much more I still had to learn.

Dinner was served close to midnight and I was seated next to the Maharaja. After five hours of cocktails, I wondered how I was going to make sparkling conversation with a royal patriarch through an eight-course formal dinner—all while making sure I was sipping my soup in the right direction. Thank God for *Debrett's*. And thank God for those cocktails. Still, the Maharaja had held his title since he was four years old and I was sure he'd had far loonier dinner companions than me in his time, so I tried not to worry. As expected, His Highness was amazingly friendly and his superb social skills made it incredibly easy for me. He even knew one of my professors at LSE!

Dinner ended at 1 A.M., after which young and old alike headed straight to another rooftop party. Did anyone ever sleep in this country? We fell into bed at 7 A.M. until three hours later when our presence was requested in the prince's quarters for brunch. It was like Groundhog Day. With the help of no sleep and far too much alcohol, I repeated this heavenly schedule for nearly a week. Cocktails weren't always with the ambassador, and watching the princes play polo sometimes became watching the princes play tennis, but other than that, the days in the palace floated by and I felt like I was living in some kind of hologram-generated dream world.

Still, behind the scenes, my heart and I were locked in a constant moral battle. I was perpetually torn between enjoying the sumptuous luxury around me and feeling incredibly guilty for participating in any of it when I knew what existed outside the palace walls.

⟶

New Year's Eve arrived.

The party was not to be held in the palace, but on the roof of a fifteenth-century royal fortress located at the top of a lofty 125-meter hill. Although we were scheduled to leave for the fortress at 7 P.M., we didn't get back from polo until after six. A primping crisis ensued like you have never seen. Nightmarish proportions.

Natalie wore a stunning fuchsia ball gown, Heather was in elegant black velvet, and I wore silver satin with a magenta pashmina. All the guys wore black or white single-breasted formal jackets[58] with gold or bejeweled buttons. We're talking real gold and real rubies. No costume jewelry in sight.

There were several hundred guests invited to this party and we all drove caravan-style up the mountain to reach the fortress. The royals, as they do, rode in convertible Rolls-Royces and as we followed behind them in normal cars I saw that the entire village, many dressed in rags, had lined up on the side of the road to wave to us.

When we reached the gates of the towering fortress, the Maharaja promptly got on an elephant and began to lead the twenty-minute procession up the ramparts to the rooftop. Again it was straight out of Disney. Picture a real-life version of *Aladdin*'s song "Prince Ali, Fabulous He, Ali Ababwa" complete with music, horses, camels, dancers, fireworks, snake charmers, and girls throwing rose petals and wrapping garlands around our necks. (And of course, servants galore handing you drinks.)

I watched in awe as villagers clasped their hands into the prayer position[59] and dropped to their knees in the presence of the Crown Prince. They truly respected him and his historical significance and seemed to be genuinely at peace with his privileged position. I suppose that's the thing about India; the concept of karma is quite powerful there. Perhaps they believed that royal families have earned their position in life through good deeds accumulated in past lives; and likewise, they believe that those cursed with poverty and suffering are enduring it as a result of past-life mistakes. What goes around truly comes around, and while you may be a pauper in this life, you could easily be a prince in the next. Is that why no one was especially disturbed by the massive gap between the rich and the poor?

---

58 Called "Sherwanis"

59 "Namaste" for those of you who do yoga. The direct translation of Namaste is: "The god in me sees the god in you."

As we entered the final doorway to the party, a servant holding a giant silver container reached in and handed me a small piece of opium.

"It's like a party favor!" laughed Natalie.

My poor parents. They were missing all the fun.

Of course I graciously declined and then watched in amusement as the young English diplomat standing behind me carefully broke his opium pellet into two halves.

"Would anyone like to share this with me?" he asked politely.

He turned toward the glamorous English magazine editor who had brought along her eighty-year-old mother.

"What about you?" he asked. "Would your mum like half an opium?"

I know *my* mum would, I thought to myself.

⟶

The roof of the fortress overlooked the sparkling lights of the city and the stars were out in their millions. Servants were everywhere; handing out cocktails and mouthwatering appetizers. There were rooms filled with soft cushions and mellow music, a dance floor open to the stars, and another room filled with exactly 1,999 flickering candles—the 2000th to be lit by the Maharaja at the stroke of midnight. Then there was dinner (which was more like a giant medieval Indian feast), which you could help yourself to at any time.

The hours sped by. I could have been at a pretentious London nightclub with other pretentious twentysomethings. Instead, I was on a fifteenth-century dance floor with four-year-olds and eighty-year-olds, students and diplomats, natives and expats, royals and commoners, new friends and old. You could literally feel the love and hope in the air. And as we chanted the countdown to midnight, and a dazzling fireworks display filled the sky, I knew I couldn't have asked for a better way to embark on a new millennium.

                 ⌒

We partied far into the night and didn't make it back to our bedroom until around eight or nine in the morning. Still, we shouldn't have been surprised to hear the phone ring before noon.

"What is it?" I asked Heather as soon as she hung up.

"You're never going to believe this," she groaned, flopping back onto her bed and covering her throbbing head with a pillow.

"What?"

"We're going *camping* today. And we have to be ready in twenty minutes."

Visions of the dense Colorado forest flashed before my eyes: trying to assemble that stupid tent, digging a hole to go to the bathroom, bug spray, canned soup, no running water, no mirror to do my hair, my mother droning on and on about survival skills and sacred Native American land . . . Quite frankly, family camping excursions made up some of my worst childhood memories. Was this really how New Year's Day was going to be spent?

We drove for an hour through the desert before reaching our campsite. Overlooking a shimmering lake and a sprinkling of palm trees stood twenty tents made of spotless cream-colored canvas. Our tent was heated, carpeted, had three single beds, a mosquito net, a working sink, and a flushing toilet. For some reason, I didn't think my mother's camping survival skills were going to be needed. Lunch was catered by the palace, served on linen tablecloths beneath the shade of a giant marquee, and let's just say it had nothing to do with canned soup.

Afterward, all the royal men mounted their horses and all the girls, including me, were given a camel. Mine had the most adorable face in the world—large expressive eyes and big furry lips; I

wanted to take him home with me! I climbed between his massive camel humps, and as servants handed us cold bottles of Tiger
beer, our hoofed convoy rode through the gorgeous sands of the
Rajasthan desert until sunset. It was the perfect cure for my first
hangover of the century.

On the long flight back to London, I sat back in my seat and
thought about how last New Year's Eve I was stuck in a Colorado
blizzard and forced to watch amateur line-dancing competitions
to a song called "Boot Scootin' Boogie" in a place called the Big
Barn.

And this New Year's Eve, I had literally danced with a
prince.

Admittedly, he wasn't an English prince. But a girl's got to
start somewhere.

Fourteen

"The unique, the complex, the extraordinary and irreplaceable Diana, whose beauty, both internal and external, will never be extinguished from our minds."

—Charles, ninth Earl Spencer

"No meetings are accidental."

—Marianne Williamson

Springtime arrived and Britain was abloom with daffodils, tulips, delphiniums, and all those other pastel-colored, fairyland-looking flowers. The newspapers were printing recipes for hot cross buns and things at LSE were slowly winding down. It looked like I might actually graduate—with honors no less!

Meanwhile, Princess Diana's birthday was also approaching,[60] as was the third anniversary of her death. Other than occasionally visiting the cluttered and overcrowded gates of Kensington Palace, I had yet to formally pay my final respects to Diana. And now that her resting place was open to the public, I knew the time was right to make my pilgrimage to Althorp.

Needless to say, no one else I knew was interested in spending a Saturday afternoon mourning the lost life of a fallen princess, so I boarded the train to Northampton by myself and braced myself for the sad, soul-cleansing trip that would follow.

---

60 On July 1st, 2000, Diana would have been thirty-nine years old.

When Diana's father became the eighth Earl Spencer in the mid 1970s, Diana and her two older sisters became ladies, her younger brother Charles became a viscount, and all of them moved to Althorp—the traditional, ancestral home of the Spencer family. (Diana's family has lived at Althorp for nearly five centuries, spanning twenty generations.)

Althorp (pronounced "Althrup") boasts 121 rooms, is surrounded by a 600-acre park, and is set within a 13,000-acre country estate. Although Diana was technically considered a commoner, as you can see, she wasn't exactly penniless when she married Charles. But that doesn't make me love her any less. No one can help the life he or she is born into. I, of all people, know that.

To prevent distasteful crowds running rampant through the grounds (as unfortunately happens at so many of my favorite royal sites in England), Althorp strictly limits the number of visitors to the estate each day. Also, unlike Buckingham Palace, there is not a hot dog cart in sight. As a result, the extensive gardens of the stately, historic house were strangely quiet—exuding a calm, peaceful atmosphere of serenity and respect.

How ironic that Diana met Charles on these very grounds. Little did she know that a simple pheasant shoot in 1977 would change the course of her entire life.

I proceeded to slowly make my way through the converted stable block that held the Diana exhibition. The stylish exhibit tastefully depicted the life and times of Diana, but to be honest, I found nothing there that I didn't already know.

In fact, college friends used to amuse themselves by testing me on my innate Diana knowledge. Late at night, whenever we were bored of studying, they'd Google her biography then quiz me.

"How many diamonds surround the sapphire on Diana's engagement ring?"

"Fourteen."

"What was her cat's name?"

"Marmalade."

"What was Diana's nickname for William?"

"Wombat."

"What is her shoe size?"

"U.S. or U.K.?"

"Um, U.S."

"Size nine."

They could rarely stump me. I'd been reading about her for nearly twenty years and the answers just flew off my tongue. If only I had the same capacity for things I was actually meant to be studying!

Still, I found the entire exhibit to be very emotional. I drifted through the displays of old letters, old passports, and old family photo albums; I peered into glass cases filled with her old school reports and well-loved stuffed toys; and I watched countless screens showing never-before-seen video footage from her childhood. It was heartbreaking.

I eventually reached a large room that held dozens of Diana's celebrated dresses and suits—many of which I had seen before when they first went on display in Kensington Palace. What always struck me about seeing her clothes on mannequins instead of in photographs was how very ordinary the pieces actually were. It instantly becomes clear to anyone standing before her empty dresses that it was Diana, not the designers, who filled the garments with such magic and vibrancy; it was Diana, and Diana alone, who made them worthy of the catwalk.

Toward the end of the exhibition stood Diana's famously beautiful wedding dress. I hadn't expected it and I nearly cried when I saw it.

People make fun of that dress and its 1980s meringue-style puffiness, but when I was a little girl I thought that ivory silk taffeta with its big bow, giant puffball sleeves, sparkly embroidery, never-ending layers of tulle, and its magnificent twenty-five-foot train was the most magical, most romantic fairytale dress I had ever seen. (Even now, I secretly kind of want those very same puffball sleeves when I get married. I don't care if sleek wedding gowns are all the rage.)

As a dreamy four-year-old watching Diana's royal wedding for the first time, never in a million years did I think I would one day get to see that storybook wedding dress in person. And then with a sad twinge it occurred to me that the only reason this wonderful exhibition existed was because Diana no longer did.

Finally, I entered a special area devoted to Diana's groundbreaking charity work. The walls were covered with enlarged photographs of the tireless and eternally beautiful Diana engaged in her endless work with land mines, palliative care, families of prisoners, refugees, and asylum seekers. There were also colorful displays detailing the ongoing efforts of the newly established Diana, Princess of Wales Memorial Fund[61] and all the ways that the fund continues to champion the causes she held most dear.

I stood for a long time in that section. For this was the thing I loved about Diana more than anything else. More than her stunning beauty and more than her royal title, I loved that Diana genuinely understood the importance of utilizing the unique and far-reaching power of being a princess.

Wherever she went, for better or for worse, Diana knew the press would follow—yet she had the principles and the courage to use this incredible power to draw the world's attention away from herself and toward those that needed it most. I often thought that

---

61 I recommend visiting www.theworkcontinues.org for more info about the memorial fund. When I first heard the news of Diana's death, donating to this fund was instrumental to my healing process.

if I were blessed with the same dazzling status, I could only pray to also be blessed with the same selfless courage.

⟿

Somewhat shaken, I left the exhibition and headed to the house itself. With its stark Corinthian columns and classic façade, the exterior of Althorp was slightly imposing, so I was surprised to discover the inside of the house to be so warm and welcoming.

I shuffled in behind the few other visitors, and began to marvel at the antique furniture, marble busts, crystal chandeliers, and the unbelievable collection of paintings—Rubens, Van Dyck, Reynolds, and Gainsborough, to name just a few. But despite all its grandeur, Althorp felt very much like a real family residence, almost like a real home.

Eventually, I plucked up the nerve to venture outside through the Pleasure Gardens and toward Diana's grave. Diana is buried on an island in the center of an ornamental lake known as the Oval. A path lined with thirty-six oak trees (marking each year of Diana's life) leads you to it and nearby is a small arboretum containing trees once planted by Prince William and Prince Harry. It's been reported that Earl Spencer once had a dream in which four black swans swam in the lake, acting as sentinels and guarding the island, but I didn't see any black swans that day so I don't know if he ever followed through on that vision.

Amazingly, I was the only visitor near the Oval at that time. I sat on a bench at the edge of the lake and gazed at the water lilies surrounding Diana's sacred, wooded island. It was a very sad and very surreal moment. And in retrospect, I'm glad I had it all to myself. Diana's presence is what had balanced my personal universe. She had always been there, in my mind's peripheral vision, for me to turn to when I began to question my own goals. And as I sat there, meters away from her resting place, the heartache I felt was overwhelming.

I thought back to the first time I saw her walk down the aisle of St. Paul's Cathedral to the first fairytale kiss she shared with Charles on the balcony of Buckingham Palace to the evening my silly college keg party was interrupted by the shocking news of a car crash in Paris. I thought about the fierce devotion she held for her two sons, and how she effortlessly mixed the glory of motherhood with sexual glamour—knowing that, as a woman, there was no need to downplay either one. I thought about her endless quest to alert the world to the plight of those infected with HIV and to the suffering of the homeless, and how she was at her most radiant when she was reaching out to those in need.

The poverty I witnessed in India still plagued me and I often wondered what she would have done in that situation. Would she have stopped her chauffeured car to comfort all those children living in their cardboard homes? Would she have hugged that leper? Would she have postponed her New Year's Eve celebrations to talk with the ragged villagers? I think she would have. And again, as I sat there, I made a silent plea that one day I might achieve Diana's maturity, Diana's grace, and Diana's unearthly ability to look beyond herself in every situation.

I thought about the tragic night of her funeral, the silent mournful crowds that filled Hyde Park, Tony Blair's poignant reading, Elton John's unprecedented performance in Westminster Abbey, and the wonderful, comforting words of Earl Spencer's perfectly crafted eulogy. And slowly, as I watched the lake ripple and sparkle in the early summer sunshine, I began to feel at peace. And on some bizarre synaptic level, I knew that Diana was too.

I'd been at Althorp for nearly four hours, and emotionally, I was exhausted. I was also famished. I decided to grab something to eat at the little teahouse, quickly wander around the gift shop and bookstore, then begin my two-hour trek back to London.

And so I began to meander leisurely back through the Pleasure Gardens, not really wanting to leave such a spiritually peaceful place, but knowing that I should.

As I inched toward the stable block, I saw a tall, sandy-haired figure talking to one of the gardeners. I didn't take much notice at first, but as I moved closer, I couldn't believe my eyes. It was Earl Spencer himself! Diana's own brother!

Without thinking, I walked right up to him, introduced myself and began to tell him how much I admired his tribute to Diana. As we walked along the path, I told him how I had once written a paper for my speech writing class on how wonderful it was, how his words were so in tune with his grieving global audience, how it was perhaps the only thing that comforted me during that terrible time and how it has become a piece of writing that I have turned to repeatedly ever since.

Then I caught my breath. What on earth had I just done? With all my royal research and supposed training, you'd think I'd be slightly more calm and collected when it came to impromptu meetings like these. But to his credit, Earl Spencer had listened politely to the entirety of my frantic American ramblings and never once made a move to escape.

"Thank you," he said graciously. "That's very kind of you to say."

I breathed a sigh of relief. You really had to admire him for not having me escorted off the premises by security.

We had reached the entrance of the bookshop by then and he was instantly greeted by a retail-manager-type person who clearly needed to speak to him about something.

"Lovely meeting you, Miss . . ."

"Fine," I answered.

"Indeed. Lovely to meet you, Miss Fine." And he disappeared into the back office.

I floated around the bookstore in a daze. I had just spoken with Peter's aunt's brother. Coincidence? I think not.

My trip to India had left me practically bankrupt, but I decided that I simply had to buy a bound copy of Earl Spencer's speech. The tattered newspaper copy that had been taped to my makeup mirror for the last three years was hardly going to last forever.

As I brought the speech up to the register, Earl Spencer appeared again.

"Would you like me to sign that for you?" he asked. The cashier looked surprised.

"I would love that," I replied, more awestruck than ever.

"What is your first name?" he asked, grabbing a blue felt-tip pen off the counter and turning to the first page of his speech.

"Jerramy," I answered, elated that we were already on a first name basis.

"Jeremy?" he asked incredulously.

"Yes," I said patiently, "like the boy's name. But spelled J-E-double-R-A-M-Y." (Thanks again, Mom and Dad, for making so many moments in my life more awkward than they need to be.)

To Jerramy, he scrawled, *from Charles Spencer, 22nd July 2000*
It was proof.

Proof in writing that I was moving ever closer to my royal destiny.

And proof that perhaps Diana's ghost was watching over me after all.

⌒

Before catching my train back to London, I stopped at the newsstand and bought the latest issue of *Vogue* and a copy of *Hello* magazine. I really couldn't afford such literary luxuries, but this day was Diana's day and I knew she would have approved.

The train began to move; I sat back in my seat, and with Earl Spencer's autographed speech tucked safely in my shoulder bag, I began to casually flip though the pages of *Hello*. After all those months in the bomb shelter, I could always count on *Hello* to bring me a much-needed glimpse of civilization. There was something about seeing celebrities showing off their fabulous clothes and houses that instantly put me in the best of moods.

Oh my God.

I stared at the headline.

PETER PHILLIPS GRADUATES UNIVERSITY. GIRLFRIEND ATTENDS.

Girlfriend? Girlfriend? I quickly closed the magazine. I couldn't handle it. Not then. And definitely not in public.

What was going on here? What was it with me finding all this life-changing information in random magazines while sitting on trains?

Still, I didn't dare open that *Hello* for another three hours. I waited until I was sitting safely within the walls of my bombshelter bedroom. I locked the heavy dungeon door behind me and sat down gingerly on the bed. Then, ever so slowly, I opened to the article and made myself look at the photos.

There he was—as handsome as ever in his black cap and gown.[62] Just seeing his wide smile was enough to send my heart racing.

Then I took a deep breath and willed myself to look at the girlfriend.

This can't be right.

I looked again. I must have stared at her for a full minute.

Then I started to smile. This was no stick-thin supermodel.

---

62 Peter graduated from Exeter University with a degree in sports science.

This was no glowingly gorgeous blueblood that I couldn't possibly compete with. *Not at all.*

As I began to read the article, I found there was even more cause to rejoice. The girlfriend was *American*! He likes Americans!

I was overjoyed. Not only did I not have to be ultrabeautiful to turn Peter's eye (or "uberhot" for that matter, as Max predicted), I didn't have to be an aristocrat! I didn't even have to be English! It was the best royal news I'd read in years.

Apparently, Peter and the American met at an English horse-jumping competition—the kind of civilized equestrian event where giant belt buckles and garish cowboy hats are nowhere to be found. And might I point out that if my parents hadn't raised me in a town full of rodeo kings and queens, if they hadn't raised me in a town where people put bumper stickers on their pickup trucks that said, "Save a Horse, Ride a Cowgirl," if they hadn't raised me in a town where young cowboys actually lassoed passing *cars* for fun—I might not have rejected horse riding entirely. Instead I might have taken a keen interest in the sport. I might have excelled at it. I even might have attended the very same horse-jumping show and met Peter Phillips there myself—saving everyone a great deal of time.

⌒

The next day, I hurried to the LSE computer lab, scanned the photo and e-mailed it to my friend Charlotte in the U.S. We had met during my summer in D.C. and even with the five-hour time difference, she replied instantly.

"Jerramy," her e-mail read, "I'm in SHOCK."

(Charlotte had a thing about block capitals.)

"The photo you sent me is UNSPEAKABLE. GRACELESS in every way."

You can say that again, I thought.

"But no need to be upset with Peter," she continued. "Don't

forget, he hasn't met you (yet). He doesn't know what he doesn't know. Love, Char."

A whole ocean away, I sat and stared at her words on the computer screen.

She was *so right*.

He doesn't know what he doesn't know.

Fifteen

"Follow your bliss and the universe will open doors for you."

—Joseph Campbell

My gazillion-page dissertation on funding higher education (a subject quite close to my heart considering the size of my student debt) was finally finished and I found it quite comical that I, the least scientific person on the planet, was about to be awarded with a masters of science.[63]

Neither Max nor I bothered to attend our formal graduation ceremony, but when our LSE degrees were finally delivered to the bomb shelter, Max was irate.

"They call this a diploma?" he bellowed. "It looks like it was done on a dot-matrix printer. And frankly, I've seen better seals at the Bronx Zoo!"

I laughed. As usual, he kind of had a point.

Max was returning to America that afternoon and it was harder for me to say good-bye to him than I expected. In a weird way, I'd come to rely on all his brutal and twisted insights.

"Jerramy," he said, as he hugged me in the bomb-shelter lobby, "I'm gonna miss you. But I'm sure as hell not gonna miss anything

---

63 Admittedly, my social policy degree was categorized as *social* science but I found this highly entertaining nonetheless.

about this backward country. Call me if you're ever on the Upper West Side, because you won't find me back in London ever again."

And so far, he has been true to his word.

⌐

Tragically, I had to face the fact that my extended stint as a professional student had ended and that the time had come for me to find some sort of a grown-up job. I had kind of hoped I'd be married to Peter by now and wouldn't have to worry about such things, but alas, things were moving slightly slower on that front than previously expected.

Granted, I had several flattering offers to work on Capitol Hill—but as much as I adored the thrilling world of American politics, my English adventure was far from over.

As usual, everyone told me I was crazy. No British company was ever going to jump through all the legal hoops required to hire some twenty-three-year-old American girl fresh out of college. But as usual, when faced with such closed-minded pessimism, I was hardly deterred.

With only two months left on my student visa, I turned that bomb-shelter bedroom of mine into a bonafide cover letter factory, and by the time I was finished I had sent my CV to nearly four hundred U.K.-based companies. (I know this because I paid for the postage.)

Remember when I mentioned that one of the key princess criteria was a brilliant career? Well, with immigration rules being what they were, that criterion was going to have to be prioritized toward the bottom of my Princess To-Do list. Because at that point, *any* career would do as long as it meant I could stay in England.

Much to my surprise, within days of blanketing Great Britain with my résumé, the calls for interviews came pouring in. I interviewed at banks, technology firms, consultancies, magazines. I even happily maxed out one of my remaining credit cards with all the shopping I did for interview suits. But the instant prospective employers discovered that I needed a U.K. work permit, the interview was cut short and I was politely asked to leave.

Then I tried a new strategy: I wouldn't tell them I needed a work permit until the very last second. This worked well in the beginning. If they didn't ask for the information, I simply wouldn't offer it. And a week later I had two London job offers! I could choose to work as a public relations assistant or for a company that organized academic conferences. I was ecstatic. England and I would be together forever, just like I knew we'd be! I decided PR was more my style and the next day I was assigned a desk, met everyone in my department, and was told to come back the next day to sign my contract.

All was going swimmingly until my phone rang that same evening. It was a woman from the PR company. "Jerramy, I have some bad news. HR has decided that pursuing your work permit is too difficult. . . . I'm sorry, but I have to revoke your job offer. Believe me, I'm as upset as you are . . . but you know what the Home Office[64] is like. . . . Really, I am sorry. . . . If only you were English . . ."

I couldn't believe my ears. If only I were English? I was more English than 90 percent of English people! I understood the rules of hereditary titles! I knew why some family crests had unicorns and some had lions! I could tell you who was tenth in line to the throne! I could name the Home Counties! I could name the former colonies! I could quote Churchill and Shakespeare and Austen and Brontë until I went blue! I actually knew the lyrics to "God Save the Queen"! I liked milky tea with sugar, I enjoyed wearing tweed, and I even understood[65] the rules of cricket!

---

64 The Home Office is the British governmental department responsible for immigration, justice, and security.

65 Well, sort of.

Didn't the Home Office realize this? Didn't they realize how much I loved England? Didn't they realize how much I *belonged* on English soil?

Finally, after days of ranting and raving on the state of global immigration, I decided to grab a hold of myself and do something rational. I decided to seek legal advice. So I made an appointment with one of the best immigration law firms in the city, marched into their distinguished offices, and explained my dilemma.

The instant I met my white-haired solicitor and saw the weary look in his eye, I knew he had counseled one hysterical American too many.

He sighed loudly and said, "Miss Fine, as you are an American citizen with no known links to the Commonwealth or to the EU, you have three possible options if you wish to become legally employed in the U.K."

Three options! See? Things were looking up!

"Miss Fine, were any of your grandparents born in Ireland, Scotland, or England?"

I was about to mention how it was highly likely that I was switched at birth and wasn't entirely sure about the answer to that question, but I decided against it.

"No," I squeaked. "My grandparents were second and third generation American."

"Well, Miss Fine, that's unfortunate. Otherwise you would have been granted an ancestral visa."

I sat there thinking of all the young people I knew who had Irish or Scottish grandparents. Most of them did nothing all day long but sit around and watch MTV. Most of them probably couldn't even find London on a map. And there I was being told that *they* were allowed to work in the U.K.? Was there any justice?

I tried to stay calm. "Well, what's my second option?"

"Your second option, Miss Fine, is to become a missionary."

"A missionary? Like a Mormon or a Jehovah's Witness?"

"That is correct. Do you see yourself partaking in full-time missionary work before your visa expires?"

Was he really asking me this question?

"Um, no," I answered. "I'm pretty sure that's not a possibility."

"Then, Miss Fine, that brings us to our final option."

Please, please, please let option three be the one. I looked at him expectantly. "Go on," I said.

"Miss Fine, do you have a boyfriend here in England? Or maybe a fiancé?"

For godsake, must we talk about the tragedy of my love life right now?

"Well . . . at the moment I don't. But believe me, it's not for lack of trying!" I laughed. But the solicitor didn't laugh with me.

"Well, Miss Fine, I suggest you try harder, because unless you find yourself a British husband in the next three weeks, I'm afraid you have exhausted your options."

And with that, he handed me a bill for 190 pounds.

I began to panic. I began to wonder if I should become a Mormon. I was still going to interviews, but now that I was being upfront about my work permit situation I was having zero luck. I was running out of strength and according to the date stamped onto my passport, I was running out of time. I had thirty days until deportation.

⟶

It wasn't until the end of my last term at LSE that I actually met a real-live English person that actually lived in London. Two things shocked me about this meeting: a) Max introduced us; and b) the meeting took place in a dingy LSE pub filled with rowdy Americans. Nevertheless, this was indeed a genuine English specimen.

His name was Adam, and although he wasn't an aristocrat, he was insanely charming (not to mention quite good-looking). His contagious humor and biting wit made him the center of every party and people positively flocked to him. I certainly was no exception. It had taken me nearly a year to find someone like Adam in London, and now that I had, I wasn't about to let a jewel like him go. So whenever I couldn't make it out to Oxford, I would do my very best to spend the weekends at his side.

Late one evening, Adam and I were drinking the night away in a trendy Covent Garden nightclub, when he mysteriously pulled me away from his entourage and into a more secluded corner of the bar.

"What's up?" I asked him.

Adam was so adorable—tall and blond with big blue eyes. For an English guy, he was unusually loud, but he was so charismatic and lovable it was maddening. LSE was filled with arrogant students who thought they were going to rule the world one day, but Adam's intelligence was eons above them. When Adam and I first met and he told me that he planned to be prime minister, I didn't doubt him for a second. It was so refreshing to meet someone else who had fully surrendered to the power of their passion (political or otherwise) and the two of us had clicked instantly. And as I looked up at him that Friday night in the dark corner of bar, I wondered for the millionth time why there was no spark between us.

"Jerramy, I'm sure you have probably guessed by now, but I'm gay."

Oh. That's why.

"Adam! Why didn't you tell me before?"

"Well, telling everyone is probably not the best idea for my political career right now." He looked over his shoulder to make sure no one was listening. "However, what *would* be good for my image right now is a girlfriend—and not just any girlfriend. An up-and-coming politician of my caliber could have nothing less than a blond Jackie O like you on his arm!"

"Adam!" I laughed. "What are you talking about? Do you want me to pretend to be your girlfriend?"

"No, Jerramy. I want you to be my wife."

I stared at him. Maybe I had misheard him with all the blaring techno music. "What did you say?"

"I said I want you to be my wife. I know you are having a work permit crisis, but if we get married, you would be allowed to stay in the U.K. Not to mention you would be great for my image! We both win. Think about it." And with that, he pulled me onto the dance floor.

Like a certifiable mental patient, I actually started to consider Adam's ludicrous proposal. After all, aside from the royal part, Adam was pretty much everything I was looking for. He was cute, he was English, he was smart, he was funny, not to mention he would probably be prime minister in my lifetime. Not to mention that I would love to be a political wife. If he were straight, I actually might have stopped holding out for Peter Phillips and married Adam the very next day.

But are perfect men with such a perfect set of perfect qualities ever straight? Of course not. And do they ever stop befriending me? Don't be silly.

My mom tells me this is because I am intelligent and glamorous and that gay guys are drawn to these qualities. This makes me wonder exactly which qualities of mine straight guys are drawn to, but I have learned to take this explanation as a compliment. Besides, wasn't Princess Diana forever on the arm of Elton John and Gianni Versace?

Still, try tossing around the pros and cons of marrying a gay guy over a few glasses of white wine and see how insane your world becomes.

We'd have to be married for four years. After the divorce, I'd have instant U.K. resident status and could live and work anywhere in the country. Simple. Easy. Painless. Pass the Sauvignon Blanc.

I just couldn't believe I was at a point in my life where I had to make such a ridiculous decision. This had never once entered into my carefully calculated live-in-England-and-meet-English-royalty-and-live-happily-ever-after-plan.

I decided I had better seek nonlegal advice on this one and I began with girls.

Before I even broached the subject with my wacky friend Amy, I knew what she was going to say. Talking to Amy is like listening to a professional motivational speaker. She can take any set of circumstances, no matter how hopeless or absurd, and make you think that it is the ideal situation.

"Marry him!" she said.

"Really?" I asked.

"No question," she said confidently. "When you finally meet the man of your dreams, he will love you so much that he won't care about you and Adam."

"You mean when I meet Peter Phillips the fact that I am a twenty-seven-year-old American divorcée who married a homosexual to stay in England will be totally irrelevant?"

"*Totally* irrelevant," she insisted.

I understood what she was saying, but somehow I didn't think the phrase "love conquers all" was created with the above scenario in mind. But still, maybe I was just being old-fashioned.

All the girls I talked to had similar modern idealism. So, I sought opinions on the matter from guys. Who, of course, advised me to do exactly the opposite.

"Don't do it," Mike said firmly when I called him up.

"But why?" I whimpered. "Isn't it true that when I finally meet the man of my dreams, he will love me so much that he won't care about me and Adam?"

"Jerramy, no man will ever trust a woman who has married for convenience, no matter how much he loves her."

The more wine I drank and the more advice I received about my potential gay marriage, the more I didn't know which way was up.

I found myself at a sappy American dinner party and the beautiful, young, ultra-Christian hostess said to me in a chirpy voice, "Jerramy, if you don't believe that marriage is a contract between you, your spouse, and God, go ahead and marry Adam." It occurred to me that maybe I should have gone to her for advice on missionary work instead.

Meanwhile, the parental advice was equally as baffling. My dad was barely ruffled by the idea. "Jerramy, just marry the kid if you need to." I think he found it faintly amusing that his daughter could be married to England's first gay prime minister.

My mother was just as useless: "Jerramy," she said, "I want you to think really hard before you marry this gay guy." Thanks, Mom. But I will also try to think really hard before I marry a straight guy.

In the end, I didn't accept Adam's kind proposal. Prime minister or not, gay or not, marriage is about true love. And I knew my handsome, charming, English, royal, *straight* husband named Peter was out there waiting for me, and deep down I knew he would appreciate such a decision.

⟶

I won't bore you with the painful details, but eventually the gods intervened (as they always do) and a London company hired me and gave me a work permit before I succumbed to the lure of gay marriage. It was rather predictable, really. Like most intelligent but innumerate blondes in London, I ended up in publishing.

They say that when it comes to your career, you should always do what you love and never, ever do it for the money. Well, I'll tell you right now I wasn't doing it for the money. (I think I actually had a better standard of living as a student.) In fact the minute I accepted the position, several city-dwelling relatives accused me of wasting my expensive education and selling myself short. But I didn't care. Being in England made my heart soar, and in that way, I was genuinely doing it for love.

I think the problem with a lot of people out there is that they tend to confuse their career with their calling, their earning power with their success, and where they work with *where they belong*—and there was no way I was going to fall into that real-world trap. Besides, I tended to be extremely traditional when it came to such things and I had a strong feeling that—regardless of my future salary level or corporate rank—meeting my true love, being his perfect royal wife, and experiencing the miracle of giving birth to our royal children were probably going to be slightly more rewarding than sending faxes, faffing with press releases, and delivering quarterly reports.

Thankfully, weekends in Oxford helped keep everything in perspective. I quickly realized that enthusiasm of any kind about one's job was terribly un-English. As you might have guessed, one's career is not nearly as important as one's family background, where one lives, where one went to boarding school, and the people at the party one knows.

Sixteen

"My greatest happiness is to serve my gracious King and Country."

—Horatio Nelson

"Expectation is the root of all heartache."

—William Shakespeare

When I was in ninth grade, a new family moved down the road from us and as ever, I was recommended to them as a good local babysitter. I went to visit the mother, Madeline, for my "babysitter interview" and I was delighted to see that this grown woman seemed to be as obsessed with Disney princesses as I was!

Disney figurines made of porcelain filled the shelves in her house—and I found out later that she even had figurines of Cinderella and Prince Charming on her wedding cake! Not to mention that I'd been there less than ten minutes when her four-year-old son told me that I looked like Aurora from *Sleeping Beauty*. Now, *this* was a family after my own heart!

Not only that, Madeline was a successful romance novelist—unheard of in our small town! (And unbelievably impressive and exotic to me at the time.) Madeline and I talked for hours that afternoon, and sensing that she might understand, I decided to tell her about my letter to Peter and the devastating response I had received from Buckingham Palace.

I was right. She did understand. And in her southern accent, she told me it was the most romantic thing she had ever heard in her whole life. She quickly ran into her bedroom and brought out a copy of *W* magazine. I had never seen *W* magazine before and was amazed that an American society magazine even existed, much less was delivered monthly to a house in my cowpoke town!

Inside Madeline's *W* was an enormous full-color, double-page spread on Peter Phillips, which she promptly tore out and handed to me. As I began to scan the article, she took off her rhinestone-rimmed glasses and looked at me very seriously.

"Darlin,'" she drawled, "Of course this boy didn't write you back straight away! That's not how fairytales work!"

"It isn't?" I whimpered.

"Of course not! Where's the fun if you find your prince so easily? That isn't a story! There has to be *drama*! There has to be *heartache*! You're too young to live happily ever after so soon! Give it time, darlin.'"

Although I was never quite sure if Madeline was able to separate me from any of the fictional characters in her novels, her words never left me. And lately I seemed to be following her literary instructions to the letter. Drama and heartache? Boy, would she be proud. I was becoming a certified expert in both.

⟶

I had fantasized about leaving the bomb shelter since the first day I walked through its doors, so once all the paperwork for my new job was secure, I embarked on a widespread search for the perfect English flatshare[66] in which my nearly perfect English life could officially begin.

---

66 Because accommodations in London are so insanely expensive, most young professionals live in "flatshares" made up of two to six people. See the movie *Shallow Grave* (1994) for a better idea of how these viewings and flatmate interviews work.

Adam wanted to live in a giant house in a terrible London neighborhood (it was "edgy," he insisted) with five other closeted gay guys, and although I was invited to join them, I kindly declined. Everyone at Oxford still had one more year to go before they graduated and I obviously couldn't afford to live by myself. So basically, when it came to London accommodation, my only choice was to find myself a flatmate.

My plan was to go over every "flatmate wanted" ad with a fine-toothed comb until I found an English girl to live with who was as well versed in *Debrett's* as I was; someone who was equally as silly, romantic, and bold; and someone who would be my partner-in-crime as I continued to scour the U.K. for my destiny. But shopping for the perfect flatmate is not like shopping for the perfect pair of shoes. You actually have to *live* with the person. One minute you're introducing yourselves and the next minute you're sharing a bathroom every morning. When you think about it, it's very weird. Still, I'd lived with perfect strangers in college and they turned out to be my best friends, so I knew there was at least *a chance* that moving in with a complete stranger wouldn't be a total disaster.

I can't even tell you how many flats I looked at during that time. I would get up at 6 A.M., buy the paper, circle all the promising ads, and call them up before breakfast. For a nocturnal person like me it was not at all enjoyable, but it was absolutely necessary because most of the flats were taken, usually sight unseen, before 6:15 A.M. Clearly I wasn't the only person in the city desperate to live with strangers.

As I've mentioned before, I firmly believed that living with non-English people defeated the purpose of living in England in the first place—so I wouldn't even go to the flat viewing if the person on the other end of the phone didn't speak with an English accent. This meant I had to make about fifteen to twenty phone calls for every one viewing appointment, but I knew it would be worth it in the long run.

I scheduled about four or five appointments per day, and spent weeks trekking around the city, knocking on doors, and wondering if the flat inside would become my new home. But usually I was so appalled by the level of squalor I encountered, and the nerve these people had to charge for it, that I didn't even bother to determine their knowledge of *Debrett's*. After two days of this, it became depressingly clear that I would have to *double* the amount I was willing to pay for rent if I wanted anything close to first-world living conditions.

With my new, completely irrational budget, things improved and the building I finally chose to reside in was located in St. John's Wood—one of the smartest neighborhoods in London! It was just minutes away from the infamous Abbey Road, was a short tube ride to work, had a friendly concierge, and the lobby was impeccably clean. Yet as I rang the bell to meet the flat's occupant, I still braced myself for the worst.

When the door finally opened I was shocked to see someone standing there who looked relatively normal—presentable even.

"My name is Rebecca," she smiled, gesturing me inside. Dainty and dark-haired, she was quite pretty, well dressed (in a Laura Ashley sort of way), and her accent wasn't bad either.

"I'm twenty-seven years old," she continued, "and I'm a manager at [a major investment bank]. I work very long hours and am hardly ever home, so if you moved in you'd have the place to yourself most of the time."

I told her a little about myself. I didn't mention anything about royalty, of course, but I did mention my quest for the perfect English guy.

"Well," she said, "I've recently broken up with my boyfriend, but I'm almost ready to get back on the London dating circuit myself. Perhaps the two of us could go out together occasionally."

Maybe this was the partner in crime I'd been looking for! Oh, how wonderful would it be to have a real female friend again!

The flat itself was tiny but gorgeously furnished. A big bay window, glass tables, white sofas. There was no dryer, and the washing machine (which was in the kitchen) was the size of a mixing bowl—but that had been the case in every London flat I'd seen so far. So other than the dreadful laundry facilities, it was perfect. And very grown-up.

"I have a good feeling about you," said Rebecca. "If you want the room, it's yours."

I was told my whole life that I shouldn't make impulse purchases, but in this situation I had to!

"I'll take it," I said. And less than fifteen minutes after meeting her, I handed Rebecca a check for the deposit and a full month's rent, and tried to ignore that I probably could have rented a huge five-bedroom house in America for exactly the same amount.

Sounds sane so far, right? Miss Laura Ashley and I sipping Earl Grey and gossiping wildly in our glamorous flat overlooking Lord's Cricket Ground. Well, for a while that's exactly what it was like. But soon things started to get a little creepy.

⟶

It was fairly subtle at first. . . . One day Rebecca told me that she never watches R-rated movies. A week or so later, she asked me to explain the difference between marijuana and cocaine. (As if I looked like someone who might know!)

Granted, I'm not a fan of horror movies, and much to my parents' disappointment I'm anything but a drug connoisseur—but still, these comments struck me as exceptionally odd for someone her age.

Then things started to get weirder. I noticed that her side of the shelf in the bathroom began to fill up with exactly the same makeup and hair products that I used. If Rupert or Adam called, she wouldn't tell me and she was obsessed with trying to get me a job at her bank. (Like I had any skills that would be even vaguely useful to a bank.) It was all very disturbing.

Adam suggested that I rent *Single White Female* and watch it with her to see her reaction. But it was an R-rated movie so that plan never would have worked and I don't think she would have made the connection anyway.

When I told Rupert about my flatmate predicament, he grinned immediately. "I bet she's a lesbian," he said. "She must be in love with you! Can I move in and watch the two of you snog?"[67]

But I really don't think Rebecca was a lesbian. I think she just really wanted to *be me.* Or even worse, really wanted me to be her best friend.

Like clockwork, Rebecca e-mailed me every Thursday afternoon to see if I would join her and her banking friends for after-work drinks. And in the beginning, I agreed. (Hey, I'm not one to turn down a chance to meet handsome English bankers!) But each time I took the tube all the way to Canary Wharf[68] to meet up with her near her office, these so-called banking friends never materialized. Instead, Rebecca would corner me in the least so-cial part of the bar, and then talk to me for hours about herself and how wonderful she was. How skinny she was, how clever she

---

67 *To snog*: British slang meaning "to kiss passionately."

68 Canary Wharf is a modern business development, boasting three of London's tallest buildings. It's located in the London Docklands and rivals London's traditional financial center.

was, how rich she was, and so on. If I tried to change the subject, she would look at me blankly and then go right back to talking about herself.

On top of it all, bars in Canary Wharf were the first I'd seen in London that resembled anything close to the friendly, relaxed atmosphere found at a typical American happy hour. I was shocked to see that these cute English banker guys (albeit only when suitably drunk) actually approached girls they didn't know! However, if any cute English banker guys ever dared to approach the two of us, Rebecca would quickly shoo them away. "You're really not *our* type," she would tell them and then she would turn her undivided attention back to me.

I quickly learned to come up with excuses every time she invited me out for a drink—which was, as time went on, beginning to happen almost daily.

One evening Rebecca and I were busy cooking dinner in the kitchen (actually I was the only one doing any cooking because did I mention she eats nothing but rice cakes? That's right. Nothing. But. Rice cakes.) when she said to me, "I have been invited to two *amazing* parties this Friday night. One is at my vice president's huge house and the other is at this fantastically trendy club in Notting Hill. There are going to be some *amazing* guys. You must come along!"

The parties did sound like they had potential, so against my better judgment, I agreed.

On Friday night, I came home from work early and got all glitzed up for our big night out on the town. I was applying the finishing touches to my eye makeup when Rebecca poked her head into my room and said, "Jerramy, let's not go to those parties tonight . . . let's just go out by ourselves."

I was livid. And spent the next five hours trapped in the corner of a quiet bar listening to how wonderful she was. I learned my lesson that night, and after that I turned down Rebecca's invitation for drinks every single time without an ounce of guilt.

⌐

I continued to flee to Oxford on the weekends (considering I was sharing my apartment with a borderline stalker, I kind of had to) and one Saturday night I found myself at a Moroccan-themed bar with Rupert and the usual suspects, all of whom I may or may not have kissed on previous occasions.

The bar was dark and loud and crowded and as I was making my way back from the ladies room, I suddenly realized that I had lost my group. Just as I was beginning to wonder if they had accidentally left without me, I noticed that another one of Oxford's many Hugh Grant look-alikes was standing across the room and staring at me. On closer inspection, I realized that I recognized this particular look-alike but I couldn't place him. Had I seen him in *Tatler* recently?

I'd been downing gin-and-tonics for several hours and all inhibitions had been thoroughly erased long ago, so I walked right up to him.

"Forgive me for being forward," I began, "but you look very familiar. Do I know you?"

"Jerramy, how you trample on my heart. We met at a dinner party last year."

I still couldn't remember. (But might I take a moment to mention that he also *sounded* like Hugh Grant?)

"You sat next to Rupert, you wore a lovely black skirt and a tiny bright blue top, and if I recall correctly, you brought a superb bottle of Chilean Sauvignon Blanc."

Wow. It doesn't surprise me that he remembered the alcohol, but to remember what a girl was wearing? That requires superhuman concentration for a guy. I was impressed.

"We never got a chance to talk properly," he continued, "because the whole thing turned into some wild, drunken, orgy-style party."

I laughed. "Why doesn't that surprise me? They seem to happen so easily in Oxford."

"Oh, but Oxford does them so well." His accent was *killing* me.

He told me his name was Fergus and before I knew what was happening, the two of us were seated in a dark, Moroccan corner and chatting away.

"Tell me, Jerramy. Do you think it is Britney Spears's wholesome sexiness or sexy wholesomeness that is so sadly underrated?" Fergus was so silly and so serious at the same time and the combination was agonizingly attractive.

"Sexy wholesomeness—definitely,"[69] I replied.

Right then, a girl of about eighteen wearing a slinky black dress walked unsteadily over to our table. She was visibly distraught, visibly drunk, and looked like she was trying not to cry.

Instinctively, I grabbed her hand. "Are you alright?"

"My boyfriend just broke up with me," she stammered. She was shaking really hard now and I squeezed her hand. She knelt down beside our table, talking between hiccups.

"You two look like such a happy couple," she sobbed. "I thought if I came over here it would give me hope . . . that I might be happy someday . . . and a couple . . . and that things might turn out okay . . ." Her words dissolved into tears.

"It *will* turn out okay," I whispered. Fergus looked utterly perplexed, trying desperately to comprehend this strange female-language.

---

69 Please note that this was back in 2000—Britney Spears had yet to enter her trailer-trash phase and was still generally considered to be wholesome and sexy.

The girl looked up, wiped her eyes, and gave an embarrassed smile, "I'm sorry to intrude on your evening."

"Not at all," said Fergus. "It was our pleasure to give you hope."

As the girl walked away, Fergus said, "Now that was depressing, wasn't it? Let's leave this place before someone else tries to sponge hope off of us!"

I laughed and followed him outside. Somehow, it had become 2:30 A.M. Rupert was still nowhere to be found. "Fergus, what am I going to do? Rupert has my wallet, and my phone, and I'm supposed to be sleeping on his sofa tonight!"

Fergus seemed unworried. "My wholesome and sexy Jerramy, don't fret. I'll take care of you tonight. After all, apparently when I'm with you, people get the odd impression that there is hope for me! So much hope for me that I can share it freely with others!"

We found his friends, who were standing in a taxi queue of at least a hundred people. "Come on, chaps!" Fergus bellowed. "Forget taxis! We are young! We are strong! We have hope on our side! Let us walk home!"

No one could resist his swaggering confidence, so we drunkenly linked arms and began our journey home. Five minutes later, the sky opened and it began to pour. All the boys started to run and suddenly I realized I was the only girl in the group, not to mention the only one wearing high heels. Normally I don't run unless there is a fire or someone is chasing me, but the thought of my perfect Barbie curls frizzing into a Medusa-style nightmare compelled me to run as fast as my heels would carry me.

Finally, finally, finally we got to the house. But it was locked! All of its occupants were still out clubbing! My clothes were soaked and water was still gushing down from the sky. I had to get inside before the damage to my hair became irrevocable!

"I know," said one of the boys (I think his name was Tom). "I'll climb onto the roof and break in through a window."

Genius. Let's get arrested while we're at it. But Tom seemed impressively adept at such criminal activity and minutes later, I was in a warm, dry house and quite certain that the owners would forgive me once I met them. And as we dried off and put on dry clothes belonging to the owners, I prayed that someone in this group actually knew them.

We settled on the sofas, cracked open the wine, and began talking utter nonsense—the kind of poetic, circular nonsense that can only be produced by drunk, arrogant young people at 4 A.M. Through it all, I tried to work Fergus out. Just like Hugh Grant, he was so subtle and proper that I couldn't tell if he was actually flirting with me or just being polite and friendly. I tried to subtly flirt back, but by 5 A.M., I gave up. He was just being polite.

I said good night to the boys and found myself a spare bed. As I lay there, it dawned on me that I had drunkenly followed six male strangers through the broken window of a temporarily abandoned house—possibly everything my mother had warned me never to do. But still, I felt perfectly safe.

Just then, Fergus came stumbling into the room looking for blankets. He kept tripping over things in the dark and his adorable clumsiness made him seem more like Hugh Grant than ever.

"The rest of the chaps have selfishly claimed the other beds for themselves," he whispered through the darkness. "Would you mind terribly if I slept in here on the floor?"

I whispered back, "Don't be ridiculous. This bed is huge. We can share."

"Are you sure? I don't want you to think I am being inappropriate."

"Fergus! Don't be silly! Get in here!"

He got in next to me, making sure to keep as far away from me as possible. I am so bad at reading signals. He really, truly was just being polite and friendly. He didn't like me in that way at all.

Suddenly, the watch on Fergus's wrist began to beep and flash. He sat up and looked at it, frantically pressing buttons to make it stop. "Jerramy! It's daylight savings time! We have gained a whole extra hour to talk rubbish!"

And so we had. So we lay there, side by side, staring at the ceiling and talking into the darkness.

"I just had déjà vu," Fergus said.

"Really?" I asked. "I never know what to think when that happens to me. What do you think it means?"

"I like to think it means my life is going exactly as it should. And that the moment is so meant to be, it was already preprogrammed into my mind."

Okay, it was 5 A.M. (again.) Time to be brave. "So, you think lying in this bed with me, right now, was meant to be?"

He was silent. All I could hear was our breathing. We had both turned our heads and our lips were millimeters apart.

I was used to guys that pulled me aside and pinned me to things and started kissing me without even knowing my name! But with Fergus, I was so nervous, I was shaking. This had never happened to me before. Finally, after an eternity of anticipation, we kissed. It was sweet, tender, innocent. Like your first teenage kiss—without any of the awkwardness.

"I've been wanting to do that all night," he whispered. "But I thought for sure you weren't interested."

"What?" I whispered. "I thought *you* weren't interested!"

"Allow me to prove you wrong." And we began making out like teenagers. Later, Rupert told me that Fergus lived off a huge trust fund. But at the moment, I didn't care if he was a pauper.

In the midst of our fumble, Fergus stopped. "Let's make one thing clear. I let you get away at that dinner party, but I am not going to let you get away again."

"Clear!" I giggled. And we carried on kissing. He was adorably shy at first, but it wasn't long before his hands landed firmly on my bottom.

"What have we here? By George! I believe I have discovered America's greatest export."

I giggled again. "I do what I can for Queen and Country."

Fergus stopped and looked straight into my eyes. Dawn was beginning to filter through the darkness of the room. "Jerramy, you are a dream. We are going to have a splendid relationship."

Still wearing our borrowed/stolen clothes, eventually we fell asleep. In the morning when I tried to take a cab to Rupert's house, the cabbie told me to save my money because he lived across the street. Rupert laughed hysterically when I called to tell him where I was.

I never did meet the owners of the abandoned house, but Fergus carefully entered my phone number into his mobile and kissed me good-bye at Rupert's doorstep.

"I shall ring you tomorrow, Miss Fine. And I shall take you to my favorite pub in London." We kissed again. "And then I will take you away for the weekend." We kissed again and I closed the door.

That was the last time I saw Fergus.

Seventeen

*"What allows us, as human beings, to psychologically survive
life on earth, with all of its drama, is a sense of purpose and
meaning."*

—Barbara De Angelis

*S*plendid relationship, indeed.

The Fergus episode affected me deeply and I decided to take
a break from Oxford for a while. But back in London, Rebecca
remained relentless. I was literally running out of excuses and
about a month later, I finally caved in.

I figured one more drink couldn't hurt. Besides, I'd been feeling
under the weather that week so I would force myself to make it an
early night. That Friday evening, I took the Jubilee Line to Rebecca's
offices and as I ascended the enormously tall escalator into Canary
Wharf, I marveled again at London's incredible diversity. It was like
fifty mini cities all crammed into one, each beautifully unique.
Compared to the ancient buildings and winding streets found in the
rest of London, Canary Wharf was ultramodern and its giant sky-
scrapers sparkled gorgeously along the river. It was the beginning of
November and the air was so icy I could see my breath.

Rebecca came running toward me as soon as I came out of the
station. "Jerramy! There you are!"

I could see the hem of her floral Laura Ashley skirt poking
out under her long black coat. Just one drink, I told myself. Then
I'm out of here.

"We are meeting a bunch of my banking friends tonight," she said.

Yeah, right. Unlike me, those imaginary banking friends are smart. They never show up. I mentally braced myself for the tedious evening ahead.

"Actually," she continued excitedly, "We are meeting a few members of my staff. You'll love them. They are such partiers!"

Yeah, right.

We arrived at the bar, and what do you know, banking friends and banking staff were nowhere to be found. I ordered a double gin-and-tonic to dull the pain. The bar was packed with lively young professionals, but not surprisingly, Rebecca managed to inch me into an isolated corner.

"Jerramy, I'm sorry to keep bringing this up, but why do you think my boyfriend broke up with me?"

For the love of God. Do we have to talk about this again? Maybe he realized you were a lunatic! Maybe he realized you had no personality! Maybe he realized you ate nothing but rice cakes and watched only PG movies!

I smiled at her sympathetically. "Rebecca, *I've told you*. It has nothing to do with you. It was *him*. He just wasn't ready for a relationship."

She nodded vigorously. "You're absolutely right. Because you know what? He used to tell me how beautiful I was all the time!"

Oh God. Please make it stop.

Apparently, my prayer was heard. Just then, the double doors of the bar swung open and about half a dozen young male bankers bounded over to us bringing a gust of cold air with them.

I was in shock. Rebecca had actually told the truth about her staff coming out for drinks. And they were cute! And they were English! And they *did* look like partiers! Oh God. Did I look okay? I quickly scanned my outfit: black trousers, rose cashmere V-neck, kitten-heel boots, adequate hair day. Could be worse.

"Jerramy, this is my boss," said Rebecca, acting as if she had just introduced me to the Prince of Wales. I have no idea why she was batting her eyelashes at him like that. The boss was quite a forgettable guy in his fifties and even though he probably made heaps of money, he was wearing a cheap leather jacket.

Rebecca made a big sweeping gesture to the younger members of the group and announced, "And these . . . are my staff."

She might as well have said, "And these are my servants."

The girl simply couldn't get any more condescending, and I instantly felt sorry for the servants. Their perfect English complexions were still red from the cold and they looked so happy to be out of university, so eager to please. It wasn't their fault that they landed their first banking job under Rebecca's crazy command. How on earth did they cope?

Rebecca continued to beam at her boss, reveling in his attention. Strangely, he seemed to enjoy her company, or maybe he was just keeping her on his good side so she would continue doing most of his work for him. Whatever the reason, the point is that I was no longer talking to her. Instead, I was talking to . . .

"I'm Alex. Can I buy you a drink?"

"Gin and tonic, please," I said.

This was more like it! Broad shoulders, rosy cheeks, twinkly eyes. And he was wearing a tweed hunting jacket. (Why couldn't all those hunters in Colorado wear tweed instead of day-glow orange? And why couldn't they have accents like Alex's?)

He smiled at me and right away, I felt I had always known him.

"So, Jerramy. How did a sweet girl like you end up living with

Rebecca?" His manner was so kind and confident and calming, I knew I could tell him anything and he wouldn't judge me.

I glanced behind me to make sure she wasn't listening. "To be honest, Alex, I'm looking for a new flatmate. Rebecca and I . . . are . . . very different."

He laughed. A deep, gorgeous laugh. "Do you think I would buy a drink for a girl that was anything *like* Rebecca?"

Now it was my turn to laugh. This guy was not one of Rebecca's brainwashed disciples! He was totally on my wavelength.

Alex lowered his voice and continued, "Not only is she a horrendous boss, she drives me absolutely mad! She *begs* me to have a drink with her every day after work. Every single day! I finally ran out of excuses. So did everyone else. Why do you think we're all here?"

"Why do you think *I'm* here?" I giggled. "I ran out of excuses too!" We clinked glasses to our newfound kinship and slowly eased away from the crowd.

"But I'm glad I came tonight," Alex said quietly. "Otherwise I wouldn't have met you." He looked straight into my eyes and my insides melted. Not just because of his accent. It was something else. Something much more powerful.

Alex was intelligent, compassionate, and funny. He was also irresistibly English and as we talked, Rebecca was the furthest thing from my mind. With beguiling nineteenth-century finesse, Alex told me about his boarding school, his love of fox hunting, and his passion for the Scottish countryside. Within minutes, a scene from our future flashed before my eyes: Alex sitting at the head of our antique dining table, the perfect father to our two adorable children, and winking across at me, his adoring wife.

"Last call!" the barman shouted.

Damn London and its 11 P.M. closing time![70] As the bell of last orders clanged loudly, my fantasy vanished and I realized Rebecca was standing in front of me.

"My boss wants to continue drinking in Soho!" she said in her fake happy voice. "Do you want to come?"

If it meant more time with Alex, I'd follow Rebecca anywhere.

The two of us hopped in a cab and said we'd meet the boys at Mezzo. Once in the cab, Rebecca turned to me and smiled mischievously, "Do you fancy Alex?"

I smiled giddily and nodded. I couldn't help myself. And oddly, Rebecca genuinely seemed happy for me.

Mezzo was *the* place to be in 1985—the décor makes that perfectly clear. But because of its unusually late hours and central location, it's still amazingly popular with London's partying professionals. If you're looking for a drunken banker to buy you a drink after midnight, Mezzo is the place to go.

Once inside, Alex and I picked up right where we left off. The gin-and-tonics flowed and so did our conversation. He laughed at all of my Rebecca stories and I laughed at all of his Rebecca stories. I couldn't remember ever having such a good time. Simply being near him made me happy.

Less than an hour later, Rebecca already had her coat and gloves on when she interrupted us. "Jerramy. It's midnight. Let's go home." She barked her orders at me like bullet points on one of her banking memos.

"I'm going to stay," I told her. "But have a good night. Make sure your boss gets you into a cab safely."

I turned back to Alex and then realized she was still standing

---

70 By law, almost all bars in England must stop serving alcohol at 11 P.M. Only nightclubs and members bars have special late licenses.

there. And glaring at me as if I had murdered someone. What was the big deal? Aren't people allowed to go home at different times?

Apparently not.

"Jerramy! We came together, we leave together!" She was practically shaking with rage. I think she was close to throwing a tantrum.

Somehow, I managed to stay calm. I wasn't going to let her and her little fits ruin this perfect night.

Very steadily, I said, "Actually, I'm going to stay a little bit longer if that's alright." Behind my back, I squeezed Alex's hand for support. And he didn't fail me.

"Listen!" he shouted. "George Michael is playing! Let's go dance!" He was pretending to be far drunker than he was and I watched in awe as he pulled the whole group of us, including Rebecca and her boss, onto the dance floor. Instantly, everyone was happy again and distracted by the music. He defused the Rebecca situation so quickly and with such skill, I could have kissed him. But I didn't.

A few eighties songs later, Alex and I took a break from dancing and went to the bar. Rebecca was fast on our heels, her boss standing helplessly at her side.

"Jerramy," she commanded, "it's time to go home!"

I took a deep breath. "Rebecca," I said calmly, "I really think I am going to stay."

Rebecca stepped closer to Alex and pointed her gloved finger at him. "*You* are a member of my staff!" she shouted. Then she whirled around and pointed at me, "And *you* are my flatmate!" Then she looked at both of us and in the most spine-chilling tone I have ever heard she said, "Don't. Even. *Think* about it."

And then, as an evil afterthought, she said coldly, "Alex, your annual review is next week. Don't forget that."

I reeled in horror. It was one thing for her to treat *me* terribly, but to *blackmail* Alex just because he was *talking to me*??? The eight gin-and-tonics circling through my bloodstream suddenly kicked in all at once. My vision blurred. I bolted to the ladies room before anyone could see my drunken tears.

The bathroom was swarming with girls slaving away under the fluorescent lights, trying to salvage what was left of their 1 A.M. makeup. The fat Jamaican bathroom attendant stared at me blankly as I ran past her. I threw myself into a cubicle and sobbed uncontrollably against the wall. How could this be happening? How could Rebecca be so mean to me? How could she be so mean to Alex? What if Alex's job suffers because of me? As the cubicle walls spun faster and faster around me, my tears streamed harder until I couldn't catch my breath.

"Jerramy, are you in here?" I heard Rebecca's condescending voice shouting across the massive bathroom. I could hear her heels clicking toward me. Oh my God. She was in the cubicle with me! She slammed the metal door behind her and locked it. I was trapped! And she looked like she was about to punch me. I wouldn't put it past her. As far as I was concerned, the girl was capable of anything.

"Jerramy! What is the matter with you?" she screamed.

I was crying too hard into my handful of toilet paper to answer her coherently. Even though she was shorter than me, she was so scary. Like a tiny Cruella de Vil.

"Jerramy! Why are you crying? Is this about Fergus? Answer me!"

"Stop . . . try . . . ing . . . to . . . control me," I said between hiccups. My head was spinning and I could barely breathe. Let me tell you, cocktails and nervous breakdowns don't mix.

"How dare you say that!" She was inches away from my face. I thought surely she was going to hit me. "How dare you! You are the one that is putting my career on the line! When I go back to the office on Monday morning, everyone will be whispering about how I have a slapper[71] for a flatmate!"

Slapper for a flatmate? Visions of all those Oxford parties began to whirl through my brain. All those boys. All that kissing. All those tours. Oh God. She was right! I *was* a slapper!

I put my forehead against the wall and sobbed. Rebecca continued to scream at me. "How dare you risk my career? How dare you! Jerramy, answer me!"

"But I only just met him," I whispered.

I felt certain that my life was going to end in that cubicle. I was going to die of alcohol poisoning and a broken heart and Rebecca's punches all at once. Right there in the Mezzo bathroom.

Just then, there was a loud knock on the cubicle door and we both jumped.

"Is there a Jerramy in there?" asked the bathroom attendant in her Jamaican accent. "There's a man out here askin' for you."

I slowly unlocked the door and poked my head out. An entire crowd had gathered around the cubicle door listening to Rebecca yell at me and they gasped when they saw me. I don't blame them. I caught a glimpse of myself in the mirror and I looked like I had been beaten up in an alleyway. My eyes were red and swollen, my face was flushed and wet, and my mascara was smudged in black, cakey streaks all over my face. I looked hideous.

And then I saw him. Standing there in the doorway to the ladies bathroom was Alex. My tears stopped and my heart soared. He had come to rescue me!

Seeing me in such a state, Alex's smile instantly changed to concern.

---

71 *slapper*: a U.K. word meaning "slut"

"Are you okay?" he mouthed.

"Wait one second," I mouthed back.

I quickly ducked back inside the cubicle. With confidence and strength I never knew I had, I said, "Rebecca, Alex is outside and I'm going with him. You are twenty-seven years old. You have lived in London for five years. It's about time you try taking a cab by yourself."

Rebecca was taken aback by my sudden poise and began to panic.

"You can't go out there looking like this!" She began rummaging furiously through her handbag. "Here! Quick! Take some of my lipstick!"

Clearly worried that Alex might see what she had done to me, she began offering me every cosmetic she had. And between her makeup and mine, we rushed to put my face back together. The finished result was by no means perfect, but at least I no longer looked like a used-up crack whore, merely a very drunk girl who had cried her eyes out. But still Rebecca refused to let me out of the cubicle.

"Jerramy, you look miserable," Rebecca said. "What can I do to make you laugh?"

I stared at her in disbelief. This girl was crazier than I ever imagined. One minute she's yelling abuse at me and on the verge of beating me up, the next she's lending me mascara and offering to tell me jokes?

Leaving Rebecca behind, I dashed out of the ladies room. Alex was waiting outside the door and I ran straight into his arms. He hugged me so tightly and with such tenderness and concern that I began to cry again. Drinking makes me so emotional! I pulled away and looked into his eyes. I didn't even care that my makeup was washing away again; I didn't even care that I looked terrible. In Alex's presence, everything was okay.

"Another gin-and-tonic?" he joked.

I smiled through my tears and shook my head.

"Okay," he whispered in my ear. "Let's get out of here."

And he took my hand and led me into the bustling insanity and amazing beauty that is London at night.

⟿

We walked through the dark debauchery of Soho into the bright lights of Chinatown and emerged into the buzzing madness of Leicester Square. It was nearly 3 A.M. and crowds were still gathering around street performers and lining up for nightclubs. Alex and I shared a hot dog in front of a neon advertisement for *Les Miserables* and he surprised me by singing some of the lyrics.

"I love that show!" I squealed. I'd seen it four times and had every word memorized.

"So do I," he said, then he lowered his voice. "But don't tell anyone or they might think I'm gay. And I *promise* you, I am not gay!"

Our eyes locked. And for the hundredth time that evening, I felt like I was home.

Hand in hand, we wandered out of Leicester Square and past the National Portrait Gallery. A homeless man was shivering on the sidewalk, hopelessly holding a cardboard sign asking for help. It was not an uncommon sight in London and I assumed we'd just keep walking. But Alex stopped and said hello and gave the man a few pounds, and then linked arms with me again and continued walking as if it was the most natural thing in the world. It was all I could do not to break into tears again.

I don't think I'd ever felt so many strong emotions in such quick succession as I had in those few hours. I had sipped cocktails and danced without a care in the world, I had been yelled at and threatened, I had cried until I couldn't breathe, and now I was holding hands with the most kind and compassionate English guy I had ever met—a guy who had already seen me at my smeared-mascara crack-whore worst and didn't care.

Eventually, we reached Trafalgar Square. The splashing fountains glowed in the moonlight and Nelson's column towered above the four gigantic bronze lions. It was one of my favorite spots in the whole city. Especially at night.

You need to understand that the Trafalgar lions are huge. (The top of Alex's head barely reached the tips of their paws.) But their commanding presence has always brought me a certain comfort—they remind me of a dream I used to have when I was a little girl, a dream about two lions that loyally guarded the entrance to my house. Later, during my self-imposed studies on heraldry, the dream made perfect sense, for I discovered that the lion symbolizes the English Throne.

Alex must have noticed the faraway sparkle in my eyes as I gazed up at the lions, or maybe he read my mind. "Let's climb onto his back," he whispered in my ear.

It was absolutely freezing outside and our gloves kept slipping against the smooth metal. And as ever, my heels certainly weren't helping matters. But after several false starts, Alex hoisted me onto the lion's graceful back, and then pulled himself up next to me.

I know I say it constantly, but I don't think I have ever seen London look more beautiful. Or the full moon more radiant. With the regal lion below me, the gleaming moon above me, and Alex at my side, my heart was ready to overflow.

I tore my glistening eyes away from the moon to find Alex looking at me. "You have the longest eyelashes I have ever seen," he said. I turned to him slowly, afraid to let myself believe that he was actually here with me on this lion, afraid to ruin such a dreamlike moment.

"Where is that dazzling smile I first saw in the bar?" he asked.

I tried to smile, but my mind had suddenly switched to

Rebecca, and I couldn't manage it. Instead I quietly gazed into Alex's eyes, wanting to climb into them and envelop myself in their kindness.

"Jerramy, I know you want to tell me all the awful things Rebecca must have said to you tonight. But please don't. I can't bear to hear how she hurt you. As is, I can barely trust myself to be civil with her at work on Monday. And she is my boss, so I have to be civil."

"It's okay," I said softly. "I understand."

I knew Rebecca would already be less than civil to him on Monday, and I felt physically sick knowing it was all my fault. A tear escaped the corner of my eye and slid slowly down my cheek. I might as well face it. I was going to be crying all night.

"Jerramy, you will get through this." Alex continued, "Your eyelashes and smile are only the beginning of your qualities."

My God. Was he really saying this to me? I was used to togas and windmills and bathroom windows. This was . . . What *was* this?

He was still talking. "Your cheerfulness is contagious. Tonight I saw how you made everyone around you feel comfortable and welcome. Even the people you secretly didn't like! I have never seen such a happy person deflated so quickly."

I just stared at him. Maybe I was still crying. I couldn't tell anymore. It was so cold. And I was so exhausted. And so overwhelmed by the beauty around me. And still in total shock that this perfect boy was saying such nice things about me.

I looked down Whitehall toward Big Ben. Sure enough, there it was—golden and gorgeous against the night sky. "I don't understand how something as silly as a clock can move me," I whispered to myself.

Alex heard me. "She speaks! If the lady needs to see the silly clock, by George, she shall see it!"

He helped me off the lion and we headed toward Big Ben. He sang show tunes and we danced down the abandoned streets. He twirled me around and around to keep me warm until we were on Lambeth Bridge and the Houses of Parliament sparkled in the distance. His arms were around me as we stared across the river at my silly clock tower.

It was the exact same scene that had stared back at me so many years ago from the poster on my bedroom wall. But it was real. And right as I turned my head toward Alex to tell him, he kissed me.

My head spun. My surroundings vanished. There was only Alex and me inside an untouchable bubble. As our lips parted, I looked at him, and realized those few seconds were the closest to heaven my soul had ever been.

⟶

Alex and I wandered around London until sunrise. Finally, we could take the numbing cold no longer, and he hailed me a cab.

"If I come home with you, I'm sacked for sure!" he laughed. Then he took my hand, carefully helped me into the taxi, and kissed me good-bye.

"I will call you tomorrow," he said. "I promise."

The door closed and I waved at him as the cab drove off into the misty London morning.

I never heard from Alex again.

Eighteen

~

*"Don't assume that because obstacles have arisen in your path,
that your path is flawed."*

—RICK JAROW

$\mathcal{S}$ee what I mean about drama and heartache?

And I haven't even mentioned the fact that when I got home
the morning after meeting Alex, part of my building was on fire
and they wouldn't let me in—so I had to sit outside on the curb in
the bitter cold for another four hours, still wearing my smeared
crack-whore makeup, while Rebecca chatted inanely beside me as
if the whole cubicle incident had never happened.

If Madeline's wise guidance was to be believed, then surely my
life had become enough of "a story" by now. Surely, I (the brave
young heroine) had endured enough drama and heartache, and
therefore my prince was bound to show up on the scene any second. Right?

I just didn't get it. I'd spent months caught up in a passionate
hurricane of fiery embraces with pirates and racquets players and
God knows who else—yet suddenly I'd allowed myself to be
completely pulled in by much weaker waves. It's amazing to me
how courageous my heart was back then—how freely it loved
before it knew there was anything to be afraid of.

Sure, I'd kissed quite a few English boys that year. But I was
young. I was in England. I couldn't help it. But rarely in my

entire life had I found boys that I actually *liked*. Yet, in that month, I had met two. And unless I was imagining things, both of them gave me the distinct impression that they liked me back. And then both of them promptly fell off the face of the earth.

I know Fergus and Alex weren't even royal, but if I could barely keep the attention of a normal English guy, how on earth would I be able to keep the attention of Peter Phillips?

Maybe both Fergus and Alex had suddenly dropped dead before they had a chance to contact me. Maybe they had been abducted by aliens. (Frankly, I liked pretending they dropped dead.) I just didn't understand. One guy acting like a bastard, I could handle. But two in row? Why did *both* of them feel the need to lie to me? Why did *both* of them put on this incredible act that made them seem like the kindest, most caring, most romantic guys in the world when they knew all along that they had absolutely no intention of ever seeing me again?

Was it possible that all of that sweet talk was simply to make sure they could kiss me? For godsake, I didn't need sweet talk! I didn't need a complicated charade. All they had to do was let me hear their boarding-school accents, pin me against something, kiss me as hard as they could, and then walk away. Don't tell me moments are "meant to be." Don't tell me I'm "a dream." Don't climb on moonlit lions with me or rescue me from nightclub cubicles. Just kiss me and then walk away before my heart has a chance to feel anything.

I cried on and off for weeks. I played Britney Spears and sobbed. I played the soundtrack to *Les Misérables* and sobbed harder. Fergus and Alex were discussed and analyzed in excruciating detail with dozens of female friends via dozens of transatlantic phone calls. We searched endlessly for evidence that might explain such heartbreaking behavior. All actions, all dialogue, all nuances were examined repeatedly. Countless theories were formed, but not a single conclusion.

What on earth was I doing with my life? Is this why I'd gotten a master's degree? Did I truly think I was going to find a prince and then everything would fall into place? Was I really that stupid and naïve? How could I go on believing in true love when I of all people had the least evidence that it existed?

To make matters worse, my boss casually informed me that according to the Home Office, there was a significant chance my work permit could not be renewed and that I might have to return to the U.S. in less than three months. Excellent.

My living space was a nightmare, my love life was in shambles, and my very ability to legally exist in the U.K. was hanging on by a tiny bureaucratic thread. Was there anything else the universe wanted to throw at me? Was this a test? Or was this a forthright cosmic message that I should catch the first flight back to America?

It was spitting icy rain as I walked to the tube station after work. The sky was dark gray and everyone who brushed past me looked angry or suicidal. Under the dark shadow of my umbrella, my beloved England suddenly seemed cold and vicious. Just like a boy, it had turned on me without warning and for no reason. A double-decker bus drove by and splashed muddy water over my favorite white coat. I felt the familiar tears welling up in my eyes— they were getting to be a pretty permanent fixture these days.

My God. When had my dreamland started making me this miserable?

As if I were following some sort of internal beacon, I changed directions on the tube, and instead of heading back to my flat, I found myself wandering through the damp grass of Green Park. It had finally stopped raining and as I approached the towering sculpture of the Victoria Memorial, its carefully chiseled white marble glowed softly in the last light of the evening sun.

It was still absolutely freezing outside but I didn't care. I sat down on one of the cold, frosty steps of the memorial, pulled the collar of my coat closer around me, and gazed at the tall, regal stones of Buckingham Palace.

The Palace would listen. The Palace would understand. And like a little girl who had finally come home to a warm house after a terrible day at school, I began to sob.

"Dear God," I whispered, "please tell England to let go of me! Please get rid of that little voice inside of my heart that keeps telling me to stay here! Please make that voice just go away!"

A few people looked at me strangely, and then looked away. Seeing someone cry their eyes out in public was not that unusual. (That was the thing about this crazy city. Everyone seemed to be crying or making out. Nothing in between.)

I buried my face in my gloved hands, not caring that I was making a scene.

"I'm a smart girl," I whispered to myself. "Why do I let a little voice control everything that I do? Why can't I just do what makes sense? Why do I insist on following my stupid heart? I'm not even sure my heart is on my side anymore!"

Hot tears streamed down my face. I put my head in my hands and prayed. Prayed that someone would cut the ball and chain that linked my heart so tightly and so inexplicably to England.

⟶

I'm not sure how long I sat there, crying helplessly into my hands to any entity that might be listening. But my sleeve was soaked with tears when I finally looked up.

I checked to see if anyone was still around.

Nope. It was still just me and the Palace.

We gazed at each other silently for a long, long time.

Then, out of nowhere, I was enveloped by an overwhelming wave of strength. I don't mean to get all mystical on you, but it was almost as if the Palace walls had heard me.

Something out there had heard me. And whatever it was, it filled my wailing heart with a magnificent sense of peace. Everything would be okay. Everything *was* okay.

I had already beaten the odds with so many things! My LSE acceptance, my wonderful Oxford friends, and (as precarious as it was) even my work permit! Was I still living in that vacuum of a farm town with my nutty hippie parents in the middle of western Colorado? No, I most certainly was not. I was living and working and partying in *London*! I was a million times closer to my dream than I was even two years ago! A billion times closer than I was ten years ago! All I had to do was stop second-guessing myself and stay patient.

Sure, I was pretty miserable. But you know what? This was a battle. A battle for my destiny. And like all battles, all fights, and all wars—there was going to be some pain. But I could take it. I *would* take it. Because I had a job to do, a calling to enact—and when it came to that bossy little voice in my heart, surrender just wasn't an option.

So I dried my tears, sat up straight, and with my eyes locked on that mystical Palace, I began to plan my engagement party to Peter Phillips.

⁓

I was contemplating the protocol of the guest list when I felt a tap on my shoulder. Startled, I was surprised to see a Palace guard staring down at me. Not one of the guards with the big bearskin hats who aren't allowed to move or smile, but one of the guards who works outside the gates who are allowed to speak.

"Miss," he said kindly, "are you alright? It's not safe for a young lady like you to be sitting here on your own so late at night."

I looked at my watch. It was 10 P.M.! I hadn't even realized how dark it had become!

"I'm sorry," I said. "I've completely lost track of the time. I'm leaving right now." I shivered as I stood up, then quickly tried to wipe away any remnants of tears.

"Are you sure you'll be okay walking through the park by yourself, miss? Would you like me to get a policeman to walk with you?"

"No, thank you. I'll be fine."

"Miss?"

I turned around. "Yes?"

"Life is never as bad as it seems."

I smiled at him. "I know."

"Good night, miss."

"Good night."

⟶

Adam called me the next day. "Wow. You seem to be in a better mood. Last time we talked I thought you were going to throw yourself off the top of Big Ben. What's prompted the big change? Did you finally meet your prince?"

"No, I've just gained some badly needed perspective." I told him about my late-night date with Buckingham Palace and how it had magically restored my spirits.

"Jerramy, do you mean to tell me that you were physically re-moved from the royal premises by a Palace guard?"

"Adam! Don't be so dramatic! It wasn't like that!"

"Sure, it wasn't. Jerramy, this is the kind of stuff that gets re-corded in secret Palace files. And I'm willing to bet that wasn't the first time you've sat on those steps staring longingly at the Palace like a lunatic. Am I right?"

I was silent.

"See? I knew it! Jerramy, if you don't stop all this stalkerlike behavior, if you ever do meet your prince, the powers that be will take one look at your stalker file and deport you faster than you can blink!"

"Adam, what do you mean *if* I meet my prince? I am going to meet him."

Adam sighed. "Oh, Jerramy. I'm sorry. Of course you will meet him. And you will marry him. And when I'm the first gay prime minister, you, your prince husband, and I are going to throw fabulous dinner parties."

"We certainly will!" I laughed.

And I meant it.

As soon as I hung up, my mother called. She was very excited.

"Jerramy, I've finally figured you out!"

Not again.

"What is it this time?" I asked. "Does this mean that I'm no longer a Self-existing World-bridger?"

"No, that's still true. But this has nothing to do with your galactic signature."

"It doesn't?"

"No! This is something else! But it's just as important. I've done a lot of reading on this recently, and I'm pretty confident about it."

"About what?"

"About the fact that you're an Indigo Child."

Of course. That explained everything.

"Thanks, Mom, now everything in my life is crystal clear."

It was good to know than when times were tough, I could always count on her to bring me a bit of clarity.

My mom wasted no time in sending me all the new age literature on Indigo Children to help me come to terms with this recent diagnosis. And admittedly, as crazy as my mom is, I actually read some of it. Even though some of the essays had worrying titles like "Gifted or Troubled?" and mentioned things like "inter-planetary Indigos," I couldn't help myself. At the end of the day, I wanted to figure myself out as much anyone else.

According to the authors,[72] Indigo Children are highly advanced souls with a strong sense of purpose. In addition to robust independence and a memory of other lifetimes (both of which I arguably possess), their unique psychological attributes include:

1. Coming into the world with a feeling of royalty and acting like it
2. Having no issues with self-worth—Indigo Children often tell their parents "who they are"
3. Never shy in letting parents know what they need
4. Never responding to guilt-based discipline
5. Feeling they "deserve" to be somewhere and are surprised when others don't recognize it

Oh my God.

For possibly the first time ever, I could actually see my mother's point!

Fine. So I had to concede that I was officially an Indigo Child. Now what precisely was I supposed to do with this information?

You see this was where my mother's book kind of let me down. Almost all of it was about parenting young Indigo Children while "respecting their Indigo journey." Nothing much was mentioned about what to do if you're a twenty-four-year-old Indigo. Nothing much was mentioned about what to do if you're a twenty-four-year-old Indigo wandering around London trying to reconcile that "feeling of royalty" that you came into the world with.

---

72 Lee Carroll and Jan Tober, *The Indigo Children*, Hay House, 1999.

Nineteen

"I can resist everything except temptation."

—OSCAR WILDE

Determined to make the most of my unique Indigo Child wisdom, I decided to do everything in my power to diminish the various insanities that were quickly taking over what was supposed to be my blissful twentysomething existence.

I obviously couldn't make Fergus, Alex, or Peter Phillips call and ask me out, and the fate of my work permit was still very much out of my hands, but the one thing I *could* change was my ludicrous living situation. I'd only been sharing a flat with the lovely Rebecca for less than six months, but I couldn't stay in that building with her a moment longer. My mental stability was at stake, not to mention my dating life.

And if that wasn't motivation enough, I'd also discovered that according to Rupert's friends, St. John's Wood, as smart and tidy as it was, was not an acceptable London postcode[73] in which to live. I was mortified when Hugo pointed out my fundamental error.

"Firstly," he explained, "St. John's Wood is the neighborhood

---

73 Postcodes are like zip codes, except they also contain letters. London postcodes begin with N (for north), S (south), SW (southwest), and so on. In snobby London social circles, only several areas (primarily SW1, SW3, and only barely SW6) are deemed acceptable.

of choice for London's plethora of wealthy American diplomats."

(No *wonder* it was so smart and tidy!)

"Not to mention the area also contains that ghastly American School."

(*That's* why there seemed to be so many American kids running around!)

"Jerramy, my dear, for these reasons alone" (I assume he meant the large population of Americans), "you should move immediately."

I loved that Rupert's friends seemed to forget there was an actual American present when dispensing such advice.

"Secondly," Hugo continued, "St. John's Wood is in *north* London." The word "north" was said with a mix of fear and bewilderment. "North London is a place one knows *of*, but not a place one ever visits or fully comprehends."

"But why?" I asked, genuinely curious. "It's not like it's another planet."

"Oh, my darling Jerramy. But that's exactly what it is! North London is full of those dreadful lefties, those baffling intelligentsia types. *Arty, media* people live in north London. *Not*, Jerramy, nice girls like you."

Ah. I guess I never got around to telling Hugo that I used to work for Tony Blair's (left-wing) Labour Party.

"Jerramy, ideally a nice girl like you—if you wish to be surrounded by the right kind of English people—should be living somewhere north of the River Thames and south of Hyde Park."

This, incidentally, was the most expensive ten square miles in all of London. It was also the area where the tube trains were the oldest, the most dilapidated, the farthest apart, and broke down the most frequently. If I moved to an SW postcode as suggested, rent would cost me 25 percent more and it would take me 75 percent longer to get to work.

But if that's where I had to go, that's where I had to go. God forbid anyone in London mistake me for a member of the intelligentsia.

⌒

Adam later told me that he liked living on another planet. But Piers and Rupert strongly concurred with Hugo's shrewd advice, as did several girls at work, and hence my search for the perfect flatshare began for the second time. The only thing that got me through the dreaded routine of waking up at 6 A.M. to buy the paper and make appointments for viewings was the thought of what Rebecca would do to Peter Phillips if I ever brought him to the flat, and what Peter himself would think if he found out I lived near arty media types.

As ever, my specifications were simple: I was looking for a friendly English household full of young, nonmarried nobility begging to adopt an American. Easier said than done, I know, but three weeks and twenty viewings later, I hit the jackpot.

It was 11 A.M. on a Saturday morning when I rang the bell of yet another four-bedroom flat. I was tired, I was hungover, and as usual, I was doubting that the place I was about to see would be worth the insane amount of money they were asking. But as the front door opened, my jaw dropped.

Jude Law's identical twin brother was standing before me with a tiny white towel wrapped around his waist. Square jaw, dark hair, startling blue eyes, tanned muscles, razor-sharp cheekbones. They just don't make guys like this in America.

"Hello! You must be Jerramy. Sorry, I just got out of the shower. I'm George. Come on in." His accent was as fatal as his looks—not quite nobility, but certainly upper class.

George led me into the sitting room, which looked like a normal twentysomething sitting room with newspapers, DVDs, and wine glasses strewn about—quite a change from the sterile hotel lobby look Rebecca insisted on maintaining.

"Can I get you a cup of tea?" George asked.

I could barely speak in the presence of such Adonis-like beauty.

"Yes, please," I squeaked.

George brought me some Earl Grey and then disappeared into his bedroom to get dressed. "Oliver will be out in a minute," he said. "Apologies for the chaos. Saturday mornings tend to move a bit slowly around here." Then he winked!

My heart was still fluttering when a bare-chested Oliver appeared, still wearing his pajama bottoms.

This was ridiculous. Were these guys fashion models or something? Oliver was brawny and blond and his green eyes twinkled with that devilish boarding-school charisma that never failed to make my insides melt.

He swaggered toward me, we quickly introduced ourselves, and despite my attempts to stay cool and collected, I blushed furiously.

"George didn't tell me you were a Yank," Oliver said, looking me over with suspicion. "It was originally our goal to fill the two upstairs bedrooms with proper Chelsea girls . . . but I guess as long as you're pretty it doesn't matter."

I didn't know if I should have been insulted or flattered by those remarks, but I didn't care. The boy was gorgeous.

"Oliver!" George shouted from his bedroom. "Go wake up Sophie so she can meet our prospective flatmate."

A few minutes passed and Sophie, a tall, willowy brunette, came stumbling sleepily down the stairs, still wearing her night-shirt. "Sorry," she grinned sheepishly, "I'm terribly hungover."

I had a feeling that the people in this flat might enjoy the kind of nightlife that didn't involve eating rice cakes and watching PG movies.

At last everyone was assembled, and we went through the

usual rigmarole of interviewing one another. I told them all about me and then they told me all about them. We had a natural rapport and seemed to get along brilliantly.

"What do you guys do?" I asked.

"Well," answered George, who was clearly the unofficial leader of the house, "Sophie works for a dot-com, and Oliver and I work in the exciting world of property."

"I thought for sure you were going to say you were fashion models!" I teased. I figured a bit of minor flirting couldn't hurt.

George didn't skip a beat. "Well, it's funny you say that," he said casually, "Oliver and I *do* do a bit of modeling on the side. Nothing big, though. Just small fashion shows, catalogs, that sort of thing."

"It's the only way George can afford to live in this neighborhood!" Oliver chuckled.

You've got to be kidding me. They were *actually* models?

Ignoring Oliver and ignoring the awestruck look on my face, George continued, "Jerramy, at the end of the day, we're looking for a friend, someone to join our social circle, not just a body to pay the rent and fill the room."

I can't tell you how refreshing it was to hear this! It was completely the opposite attitude of every other flat I had been to!

"That's exactly what I'm looking for too," I smiled.

"Well, Jerramy, I'm delighted to inform you that you have passed the first audition. Round two involves drinks with Duncan—our landlord. If you pass that test, you can move in next weekend. Are you free for drinks on Thursday night?"

"Yes!" I answered breathlessly.

⟶

Now that I was working full time, it was getting more and more difficult to pop to Oxford for Tuesday night cocktails or for a midweek fancy-dress dinner. With the way that bunch liked to party, how was I ever supposed to make it back to London the next morning, much less into the office on time?

Adam kept me company when he could, but he was intensely busy building his political career or secretly rendezvousing with his latest gay crush. I didn't mind spending hours stuffing envelopes for Adam (I wanted him to be prime minister more than anyone), but joining him on his clandestine dinner dates—where I would share a table in the best restaurants[74] with him and yet another good-looking, ambitious gay guy and pretend I had no idea that both men were blatantly flirting with each other—grew rather tiresome. I desperately needed some normal London friends. And thus, I was more determined than ever to pass the second audition.

I'd painstakingly dressed for the occasion: my bright salmon cashmere from Pringle,[75] gray pencil skirt, Jackie O coat, and killer heels. I'd even stayed up extra late the night before to give myself a French manicure. When I entered the trendy King's Road bar at 7 P.M. on the dot, I was a picture of youth, style, and responsibility. There was no way that boring old landlord could fail to be impressed.

Several large glasses of Pinot Grigio later, I knew I was in trouble.

Not only was the landlord my age (his father had lent him several properties to "practice with"), he was hot, he was English, and, get this, *he played polo*. At the very same polo club as Prince Charles!

"Stand up please, Jerramy," ordered Duncan when he first arrived at our table. "I have to make sure that none of my tenants are taller than me."

---

74 The extravagant dinner bill was always picked up by Adam's inevitably wealthy boyfriend-of-the-moment, otherwise neither Adam nor I could afford so much as a single round of drinks.

75 That's Pringle as in the royal purveyor of knitwear for Her Majesty The Queen, *not* the potato chips.

I did as I was told and passed the test. (I'm only 5'6" in heels; and although Duncan was extremely handsome, he was only about 5'10".)

"Right, second order of business, Jerramy, is this: I know that you are American and we will try not to hold that against you, but I have to ask, what are your thoughts on dating? Have English men been to your liking?"

Seated between Oliver and George, I saw Sophie roll her eyes. She'd clearly seen Duncan's absurd interrogation techniques before.

"Oh, yes," I gushed. "I love English boys! Especially ones that have been to boarding school." I was obviously drunk.

"Excellent!" and he raised his glass to me. "Because, let me be clear about this: If I find out that you're dating any guy who has attended this country's *state* school system—you're evicted. No plebs in my house. Do you understand me?"

"Not a problem!" I laughed. (Little did I know he was dead serious.)

"Unless of course," Duncan continued with an arrogant smirk, "the pleb in question is a girl. Lesbianism is vastly encouraged amongst my female tenants."

"Duncan! Enough!" scolded Sophie. "We like her. She's normal. Let her live with us!" The two beautiful boys at her sides nodded in agreement.

Duncan possessed the kind of Napoleonic charm that bordered on cruelty, but I was smitten. And that night, I happily and knowingly agreed to move into his flat for all the wrong reasons.

Male models, polo invitations, and possible royal connections to name just a few.

～

I didn't want to tell Rebecca that I was moving out purely because of her (and risk her setting fire to all of my possessions or something equally deranged). So in order to escape, I ended up concocting a lie about moving back to the U.S. As I left her gorgeous Abbey Road apartment building for the last time, both the doorman and concierge rushed to say good-bye to me.

"We were wondering how long you'd last," the doorman said sweetly. "Girls never stay more than a few months in that flat." (They could have told me that before I moved in.)

No longer living in fear of Rebecca and her evil ways, I was deliriously happy in my new SW home. It was so wonderful to feel part of a close-knit group, and I bragged constantly to my friends in America about George and Oliver's supermodel looks. Even Adam couldn't wait to meet them, thinking surely after their time in the fashion industry they might swing both ways. But I wasn't sure about Duncan's views on gay friends and not wanting to risk immediate eviction, I managed to keep Adam at bay.

It was obvious to anyone with a brain that Duncan was a bastard, but he was a bastard that played polo (and more importantly, a bastard that might *invite* me to polo), so I was willing to put up with it for the time being. But when it came to George and Oliver, I'm not quite sure when it began to dawn on me that they weren't nearly as angelic as they looked.

Every morning George and Oliver did five hundred sit-ups to tighten their perfectly tanned washboard stomachs, and every night after work they insisted on watching one of their two favorite films: *American Psycho* or *Wall Street*. Their unhealthy obsession with movies that contained such similar and disturbing themes should have been enough to set off alarm bells in my head—but I was so enamored by their beauty and charm, in my eyes they could do no wrong.

One lazy Sunday morning, I staggered downstairs a little before noon. As usual, I was hungover—this time from a long, debaucherous dinner with Adam and his latest mystery man at one of the most expensive restaurants in town (our trio's behavior was so rowdy that we were actually asked to leave the Michelin star restaurant toward the end of the night). And as I groggily carried my giant mug of coffee into the sitting room that morning, I wanted nothing more than to spend the next few hours watching mindless television and getting rid of my headache.

George was already sitting in the massive armchair and gazing at the cricket match on TV. As I sat down across from him, I saw that he was wearing a bright green mud mask.

I burst out laughing. I couldn't help it. I'd never seen a guy in a mud mask before! Even girls did them in private!

"Okay," I giggled, "I know you guys love your tanning beds, but is a mud mask really necessary?"

George spoke slowly so the dried mud on his face wouldn't crack. "Just like you, I have to look after my skin," he shrugged.

"Our looks are our money," piped in Oliver, who was also sporting a late-morning mud mask. I watched Oliver as he stopped to admire his biceps in the mirror and then strolled into the room wearing nothing but his boxers. I swear, I don't think I ever saw that boy with more than one item of clothing on at a time. Not that I was complaining.

At first I thought the weekend mud mask routine was funny. Until I discovered that the mud mask George and Oliver used so religiously was actually *mine*. One evening, I had unscrewed the lid of a brand new jar to find it practically empty!

I showed Sophie and she was appalled. We were the only ones who used the upstairs bathroom so together we removed the contents of our entire bathroom cabinet for further investigation. To our horror, we saw that dozens and dozens of our beauty products showed signs of manhandling: giant, bear-paw-sized scoops were missing from pots of expensive moisturizer and cold cream; my bottles of luxury shampoo and conditioner that I had bought in America had only drops left, and Sophie's costly bubble bath set was gone completely.

The whole thing would have been infuriating if it weren't so funny. And as we sifted through the remnants of our cosmetics, Sophie and I were laughing so hard we could barely speak. We knew the boys were oddly meticulous (they were *obsessed* with ironing their Thomas Pink shirts and polishing their Church's shoes), and we also knew they were strangely in touch with their feminine sides (they *loved* shopping at Harvey Nicks[76] and going for brunch afterward), but come on, this was ridiculous.

"I cannot believe I'm funding George's entire beauty regime!" exclaimed Sophie, tears of laughter streaming down her face. "How did I end up moving in with such narcissistic ponces[77]?"

"Because they're cute?" I suggested.

"Oh, yeah." Sophie conceded with a smile. "*That.*"

Of course the boys denied everything. Their beauty always disqualified them from censure and they were so stupidly cute in their denials that we let them get away with it. But in order to monitor any future thieving behavior, Sophie and I smoothed out all of our creams and secretly marked all liquid levels with a pencil.

Just as suspected, within days, my eye cream, face wash, and hair gel had been tampered with again! And so had Sophie's Crème de la Mer moisturizer!

After that, we started hiding everything in our bedrooms. When it comes to her beauty products, a girl can't take any chances.

~~~

That same month, Oliver invited his Scottish rugby buddies to stay with us for the weekend—meaning for two whole nights there

---

76 Harvey Nichols is an extremely upscale London department store; the U.K. equivalent of Neiman Marcus or Barneys.

77 *Ponce*: a person who is ostentatious, snobbish, or effeminate

were five burly guys with chests like barrels, legs like tree trunks, ears like cauliflower, and manners like wildebeests camped out in the sitting room. Not ideal, but it was only for a short while. I could cope.

At Oliver's insistence, Sophie and I joined them for drinks on Saturday night. The wildebeests were sweet, but their Scottish accents were so thick, and they were so incessantly drunk, we couldn't understand a word any of them said. Tired of being mindlessly groped and playfully pawed at, we left the bar early and went to bed.

Sophie's bedroom was right next to mine, and around 2 A.M. I heard voices in the hallway outside our doors.

"Which bird do you fancy?" slurred Oliver in a loud whisper. "English or American?"

Was I hearing things? *Was Oliver offering Sophie and me to his drunken friends?* I held my breath. Please don't let those inebriated buffoons come into my bedroom!

"English," one of them grunted.

Thank God for that! (But *poor Sophie!*)

Cringing, I listened as three or four beefy Scotsmen tumbled onto Sophie's bed. Luckily, she was much meaner than I could ever be. I silently cheered her on as she fought them off and angrily shooed them away. In the meantime, I had moved my desk firmly against my bedroom door. I found out later that Sophie had done the same.

The next day, as the hungover rugby players made themselves breakfast, I noticed a large stain in the middle of our beige carpet.

"What is this?" I asked them, pointing to the offending spot in the center of the sitting room.

"Oh, that? That's just water," one of the wildebeests replied.

"It's definitely not water." I know I sounded like a mother, but

I didn't care. "Oliver? What is it really? What did you guys spill?"

"Oh, we didn't spill anything," explained Oliver calmly. "It's just that Alistair had to take a piss and didn't make it the loo on time. But don't worry! We ironed it."

"What? You *ironed* the urine into the carpet?" I asked incredulously.

"Aye!" exclaimed Alistair proudly. "We tried to dry it with a wee hair dryer, but then we thought the iron would be faster."

For the love of God.

I went upstairs and finished my coffee in the comfort and sanity of Sophie's bedroom. After telling her about the master-mind ironing that had taken place downstairs, I told her how I had heard Oliver whispering the night before about "English or American" and how he had basically tried to prostitute us. She was livid.

"We could have been gang-raped!" she screamed.

Hadn't thought about it that way, but I guess she was right. Both extremely disturbed by the thought, we called Duncan and insisted that he install locks on our bedroom doors.

"What do you mean we are overreacting?" Sophie shouted into the phone. "Duncan! We shouldn't have to use our own bedroom furniture as a barricade in order to feel safe!"

Duncan never did give us those locks. And despite multiple attempts, we never did get that urine out of the carpet. But a few days later, a very embarrassed Oliver sent flowers to my office. If only I could've convinced him to buy me a new mud mask.

⟿

As the days wore on in my new anti-intelligentsia neighborhood, I realized that George and Oliver's wild obsession with looks and appearances was rapidly giving me a complex.

Every outfit Sophie and I wore was scrutinized and commented upon ("Jerramy, are you *sure* you want to wear those cheap shoes with that skirt? You really ought to get yourself some Gucci heels."), as was every guest we dared to bring through the doors of the flat ("Sophie, I say—that mate of yours seemed a bit common. What school did she go to?"). But when the boys started describing to us what they believed to be the ideal female body, I really started to doubt myself.

To give you an idea of what I went through, I urge you to attempt the following fitness test: Make two fists with your palms facing down, extend your thumbs so the tips are touching and then extend your pinky fingers to form a semi-square. According to George and Oliver, the ultimate female "bum" fits within this space.

Let's just say that my size 6 butt (size 12 in the U.K.) failed miserably. I tired to tell them that only a four-year-old's bottom would fit into such a ridiculously small gap, but they were insistent.

"Jerramy, I hate to break it to you," said George earnestly, "but maybe you should join a gym and work off some of that excess puppy fat. You too, Sophie."

Puppy fat? Sophie was a beanpole! And my nickname in high school was Skinny Minnie!

Nevertheless, we both joined a gym the very next day.

How could guys that cute be wrong?

⌒

One morning before we left for work, Sophie and I were sitting at the dining table, hastily eating our breakfast while George and Oliver did their customary five hundred sit-ups.

"Jerramy, can you remind me to pay my Amnesty dues tonight?" Sophie asked absently as she flipped though last night's evening paper.

"Sure," I answered.

George sat down with a plateful of toast. "What dues? Sophie, what the devil are you talking about?"

Sophie looked up at George and rolled her eyes. "I'm a member of Amnesty International. Ever heard of it?"

"Of course I have. It's one of those smart new members' clubs near Sloane Square. I'm planning on applying for membership myself. Dues aren't terribly expensive if I recall."

"George," Sophie spoke slowly and sternly, as if talking to a child, "Amnesty is *not* a members' club. It's a human rights charity."

"Human rights? Christ!"

Oliver stopped doing his sit-ups and turned toward Sophie. "You better not let Duncan know that you're mixing with that kind of crowd."

"You two are ridiculous!" Sophie exclaimed. "It's not like I'm mixing with neo-Nazis or something! And I told you last week that I've started dating a human rights lawyer."

"Better not let Duncan know that either," Oliver said.

"Don't worry, Soph," George said kindly. "I'll cover for you. I'll tell Duncan that your new beau is a *corporate* lawyer." He looked very pleased with himself.

Sophie shook her head in bewilderment. "Thanks George, you're ever so kind."

It was that moment—the moment that George turned his attention back to his breakfast, that I noticed the first trickle of powdery white stuff dripping out of his nose.

And in a flash, I saw my new flat for what it was: Not good. But highly addictive.

Twenty

I may have been living in the appropriate postcode as per Hugo's advice, but what good was it doing me? I was hardly meeting "the right kind" of English people on the street.

Sophie was always with her boyfriend, Duncan was full of empty promises and had yet to invite me anywhere (was I *ever* going to make it to an English polo match?), and every time I went clubbing with George and Oliver, they seemed to spend most of their time in the bathroom.

I once read in the newspaper that cocaine use in London was so high that large traces of the drug could actually be found in the River Thames[78] and let me tell you, after a few months on the London party circuit, I wasn't the least bit surprised. Before moving to the U.K., I never saw cocaine *in my life*—and now it seemed to be everywhere that I went.

Including my own breakfast table.

Just like everything else my endearing male flatmates loved to indulge in, cocaine was expensive, exclusive, and glamorous—and

---

78 Goswami, Nina and Orr, James. "The Thames: Awash with Cocaine." *The Sunday Telegraph*, November 5, 2005.

probably made them feel like they were high-flying bankers or minor aristocrats instead of two ordinary London guys with posh accents and astonishing good looks. Still, George's habit worried me incessantly and I held onto the hope that eventually his vanity would take over and he'd stop snorting before his modelesque beauty was permanently damaged.

I was entirely naïve to it at first, but it wasn't long before I could tell immediately if he had recently "sniffed up." Normally quite relaxed, George suddenly became ultrahyper; his quiet confidence turned to unbelievable arrogance and his polite conversation became a nonstop stream of increasingly implausible and fantastical stories. (I thought his description of jetting to a private island for Elton John's birthday party was particularly creative. But what do I know—maybe he was telling the truth.)

Was I tempted to partake in the powdery fun? Not in the slightest. Despite my mother's amusing suggestion that I might want to experiment, I remained resolute that nothing mind-altering would enter my body other than good old-fashioned alcohol.

Anyway, the point is that I hadn't bargained for all this strange urban hedonism. If anything, I thought Duncan would have introduced me to Prince Charles by now—who in turn would have introduced me to his dearest nephew Peter—and my London life would finally be back on track.

Why did nothing ever go according to plan?

To top it off, there had been some devastating news. So devastating, I couldn't bring myself to read it more than once. Apparently Peter had *moved in* with the American girlfriend! They were living together! In some swanky three-bedroom flat in *north* London— home of the dreaded intelligentsia! (Believe me, I planned on having some stern words with Hugo next time we met.)

I had to meet Peter soon. Time was running out.

⟋

I have no idea what made me think that a British TV appearance (on a dating game show no less!) would be the answer to my woes. Still, I went to the open casting and when the letter arrived from the TV studio informing me that I had been put through to the final audition of *Love Is Blind*, I have to admit I was flattered and ever so slightly excited. Perhaps Peter would see me on TV and fall in love!

Sound crazy? It was.

But I did live rather close to the Thames. I blame all that cocaine evaporating out of the river.

⟋

The first round of auditions wasn't so bad. It was held in a giant London ballroom and it was buzzing with hundreds of famethirsty singles from across the country. I saw right away that while I was dying for a romantic English date (preferably with a royal), this crowd was dying to be on English TV. I didn't want it nearly as much as they did, which is perhaps why initially I did so well.

We sat in groups of twenty while several charming and mediasavvy interviewers asked us lots of questions. And it soon became clear that they were loving my oddball name and candid Anglophilia. (Apparently I am a walking bundle of TV talking points—or so I was told.)

Toward the end they asked us if we had any party tricks to share. I declined, but the girl next to me proudly demonstrated how she could run like E.T. Looking back, I probably should have seen that as a warning sign. But I didn't.

I had seen Peter in a magazine and it was love at first sight. I was certain he would see me on TV and feel the same.

⟋

The day of the final audition, I wore a sparkly vintage blouse, a black circle skirt, pearls, and the most gorgeous patent-leather peep-toe heels you have ever seen. I was the spitting image of a 1950s Hollywood starlet. (Think Grace Kelly in *Rear Window*.) There was no way they could fail to put me on their show.

Unfortunately, somehow I got lost on the way to the studio and ended up trotting frantically through the backstreets of London for nearly half an hour, terrified I was going to be late. I hadn't taken the time to break in my glamorous new footwear, and by the time I arrived, blood was practically pouring out of my shoes.

But it was 2 P.M. on the dot as I walked into the building. Just in time.

"Can I help you?" asked the woman at the reception desk.

"Yes," I replied proudly, ignoring the pain searing through the raw skin of my heels. "I'm here for my two o'clock *Love Is Blind* audition."

The woman looked confused. "I'm sorry," she said, "but are you sure you have the right place? The girls' audition isn't until four thirty. And it's being held in the studio next door."

Well, guess which audition *my* letter told me to go to?

That's right. The *boys'* audition.

Isn't life hard enough without nonstop gender-related mix-ups? (To all future parents reading this book, think about this before you name your baby, okay?)

The receptionist directed me to the neighboring waiting room and I proceeded to sit there for over two hours. I got up once to limp to the coffee machine, but my blisters were too painful to move any more than absolutely necessary.

Finally, I was called into the *girls'* audition with about ten other girls. That's when I realized I was probably the only one over eighteen, and aside from one girl dressed as a gothic vampire, I was the only one not wearing some kind of skin-tight, low-cut, midrift-baring Jennifer Lopez outfit.

The audition began, and I was surprised to see that it consisted of nothing vaguely relevant to what would take place on the actual television show. Instead of interacting with prospective male contestants or reading out practice questions, the whole thing turned into one tortuous hour of improv drama. I was asked to "Pretend you're a chicken laying an egg," "Pretend you're Michael Jackson reading the news," and (you'll see why this one particularly bothered me) "Pretend you're Prince Charles buying condoms."

Now, I am a lot of things, but I am no actress. I'm even quite awful at charades. Needless to say, my attempt to squawk like a chicken, do the moonwalk, or emulate the plummy pronunciation of HRH did not amuse me. Nor, I'm afraid, did it amuse the casting directors.

Next, I received a small screen test during which a giant camera lens was positioned inches away from my face.

"Okay, Miss Fine," said one of the trendy media executives, "I need you to make love to the camera for about thirty seconds."

"Excuse me?" I couldn't possibly have heard her correctly.

"Make love to the camera. You know—just try to be as sexy and as provocative as possible."

I stared at her blankly.

The woman sighed with exasperation and looked at her clipboard. "Okay," she said, "let me put it this way. It says on your questionnaire that your ideal man is Hugh Grant.[79] I need you to pretend that the camera is Hugh Grant and you want him to shag[80] you immediately."

This was ridiculous. And definitely not what I'd planned for my television debut. What if this audition video ever got leaked to Buckingham Palace?

---

79 Of course my ideal man was Peter Phillips. But I felt when it came to national TV, it was best to leave the royal family out of it.

80 *To shag*: U.K. slang meaning "to have sex with"

"Um, I'm going to pass on this if that's okay," I said.

"Fine," she said curtly. "Who's next? How about you, Tracy? Can *you* manage to make love to the camera?"

"Sure!" squealed young Tracy, who was wearing a rather snug spandex jumpsuit. "I'll show you what I do at uni[81] when I'm down the pub and want to get laid!"

"Excellent," smiled the woman, making notes on her clipboard.

After Tracy's antics came Caroline, who began her screen test by reminding everyone (in a piercing cockney accent) that she was a professional lap dancer. I kind of stopped paying attention after that. I mean honestly, what was I thinking? This was hardly the way to Peter's heart.

When the screen tests were finished, the "interview" began. A casting director turned to me and asked the following: "When was the last time you pulled?[82] And what technique did you use?"

That's it. I'd had enough. These people were clearly looking for a girl that could act like a chicken and talk endlessly about sex and that girl wasn't me.

"I'm going to pass on that too," I said politely.

"Miss Fine, you do realize that by passing on this segment as well as the screen test, you will be forgoing the whole audition?"

"Yes," I nodded happily. And with that, I tottered out of the studio as fast as those excruciating peep-toe heels would carry me.

Live-in girlfriend or no live-in girlfriend, surely Peter would agree that television is for watching. Not for appearing on.

---

81 *Uni*: U.K. informal meaning "college"

82 *To pull*: U.K. informal meaning "to succeed in starting a sexual relationship"

⟶

Like any girl in my situation would do, I bandaged my heels and hit the bars. Adam and I stayed out late, downing caipirinhas, celebrating my lucky escape from TV, and commiserating over the loveless Valentine's Day we'd doubtlessly be having later that week. By the time I got home that Thursday evening, it was nearly midnight. Oliver was out, but George was in.

I was in the tiny kitchen getting myself a glass of water when George pulled me aside. I could see right away that he was in one of his extra-hyper, extra-giddy, chemically induced moods.

"Jerramy!" he whispered loudly. "Thank *God* you're here! You're never going to *believe* who's sitting on our sofa this very second!"

He was so pleased with himself he looked ready to burst.

"Prince Charles?" I guessed.

"No, you silly Yank! A stripper! A real-live *stripper!*" He was practically giggling in delight. "I met her tonight at Spearmint Rhinos. And when I asked if I could take her home with me, she *agreed*! Isn't it fantastic? Anyway, why don't you be a lamb and make her a cup of tea? I have to tidy my room so Mandy—or is it Candy?—and I can get down to business." And then he disappeared.

Why did I always do everything George asked? Wasn't I over his hypnotic good looks by now?

I switched on the kettle and walked gingerly toward the sitting room. I'd never had a stripper in my house before, so I can't say I knew what to expect. But judging from the caliber of girls at today's audition, perhaps I'd already met her.

I hid in the hallway and peered into the sitting room. Sure enough, a pretty blonde was curled up on the sofa, quietly flicking through a celebrity magazine. Thankfully, I didn't recognize her.

The stripper had a great figure (obviously), a fake tan (only slightly more orange than George's), and really glittery eye shadow that extended beyond her brows. Other than that, she seemed perfectly normal. Poor girl. Little did she know that George was hardly the gentleman he pretended to be. I took a deep breath and entered the room.

"Hi," I said warmly, extending my hand, "I'm Jerramy. George's flatmate."

"I'm Amanda," she smiled gratefully. In her line of work, I'm sure most women didn't treat her especially kindly and she seemed visibly relieved that I wasn't snubbing her immediately.

I brought out two mugs of tea and settled into the surreal task of keeping the stripper company until George decided he was ready to join us.

"Oh, isn't Prince William lovely!" Amanda cooed, holding up a glossy magazine picture. It was my absolute favorite photo of William, taken during his first year at St. Andrew's University. His blue jeans and navy sweater hung perfectly off his stunning swimmer's physique and he looked breathtakingly handsome. Oh, if I were but five years younger!

"Yes," I nodded eagerly. "George thinks William looks like Bugs Bunny, but I think he's gorgeous."

"Well, I'd take William over George any day!" Amanda laughed.

"I think most girls would," I agreed, "but George doesn't believe me when I tell him so!"

"Well, George is adorable," continued Amanda, getting rather dreamy, "and *so polite*. He really knows how to treat a girl."

I stayed silent.

"And besides," Amanda went on, tossing William's photo aside with her lengthy false nails, "at the end of the day, Prince

William is out of my league. Girls like us don't have a chance with royalty!"

Speak for yourself, I thought.

~

At 8 A.M., my mobile rang.

"Jerramy. Good morning." It was George, brisk and business-like as ever. "Quick favor to ask you."

I was still getting ready for work and looking frantically for my pearl earrings. "Let me guess," I said. "Don't tell Duncan that you officially let a pleb into the flat."

"Well, yes. That goes without saying. But I'm not ringing you about that."

"Make it quick, George. I'm going to be late."

"Yes, yes of course. You see, well, quite regrettably I was called into the office rather early this morning."

"And?"

"And, well, I was hoping you'd be so kind as to peek into my bedroom and see if the stripper is still there. I just don't feel right leaving her there alone in the flat. She is terribly common and I'm afraid she might nick[83] something."

It seemed his hypnotic charm also worked over the phone and like a lunatic, I did as I was told.

As suspected, Amanda was hardly stealing George's designer cufflink collection. Nor was she pocketing one of the many 8" × 10" framed photos of himself he had displayed around the room. Instead, she was carefully making his bed with perfect hospital corners.

Who's out of whose league now?

---

83 *To nick*: to steal

Twenty-one

"To arrive at Claridges is to have arrived."

—Unknown

"Those who are to meet, will meet."

—A Course in Miracles

Date: 23 Feb 2002 15:38:25 +0000 (GMT)

From: Jerramy Fine

To: Mom

Subject: "Survival Guide"

Dear Mom,

I've been trying to read the "Survival Guide" for 2012[84] that you sent me and I was doing okay with it until I got to the part where it says (and I quote), "It's not August, but the Magnetic Bat Moon of Purpose."

Sorry, but I couldn't take it very seriously after that.

Love,

Jerramy

Date: 24 Feb 2002 16:11:58 +0000 (GMT)

From: Mom

To: Jerramy

Subject: RE: "Survival Guide"

---

84 According to the Mayans, 2012 is a crucial juncture, signifying the culminating point of the 26,000-year cycle of human evolution.

Dear Jerramy,

As the human race enters this global and spiritual transition, the survival guide will become more and more important. *Please try to keep reading.*

I'm actually trying to wean myself off the Gregorian calendar and onto the thirteen-month Mayan moon calendar as the guide suggests. (Lots of our friends have done this already.) Try it!

I miss you.

Love,

Mom

⌐

Unlike Ezra, my charmingly pacifist brother, who cleverly agreed with everything our mom ever said (mainly so he could avoid arguments and go snowboarding), I simply wasn't blessed with that kind of patience. Whenever she mentioned something insane to me (be it about Mayan calendars, shape-shifting lizards, or whether or not water had feelings), I usually made the mistake of asking her what on earth she was talking about and why. Admittedly, this was guaranteed to trigger a high-volume session of mother-daughter combat, but I just couldn't help myself.

But now that there was a three-thousand-mile ocean between the mother and me, I was beginning to see the advantage of Ezra's appeasement techniques. I mean, was it really worth telling her that Microsoft would have to add "The Mayan Moon Calendar" to their drop-down menu options in order for her new time-keeping system to be compatible with Outlook? Probably not.

In any case, I had yet to "wean" myself off the Gregorian calendar and I have to admit I was still using passé, non-Mayan words such as "March" and "April" to organize my busy London life. That said, I couldn't tell you if it was the "Cosmic Turtle Moon of Presence" or the "Planetary Dog Moon of Manifestation" when I found myself attending a swanky book launch at the famously grand Claridges Hotel.

⟶

When Claridges first opened back in 1812, it quickly gained a worldwide reputation among aristocracy as *the only* place to stay when one was visiting the British capital. During the aftermath of World War I, many aristocrats were forced to sell their splendid London houses and move into Claridges on a permanent basis. (Believe it or not, without the expense of maintaining a large household staff, to many, this arrangement was actually *cheaper*.) And during World War II, when many of Europe's royal families were dramatically exiled from their countries and palaces—once again, dozens of noble families sought permanent refuge at this luxurious five-star hotel.[85]

So basically, if you're of royal blood and have nowhere to go—Claridges is the place for you. Quite frankly, considering the hotel's history of adopting royal orphans, Claridges also sounded like just the place for me. And in retrospect, instead of enduring the trauma of that bomb-shelter dorm for a single minute, I should have headed straight to Claridges and announced that I was a victim of royal exile. Granted, I hadn't been thrown out of any particular kingdom, but I *had* been separated from my aristocratic parents when I was only an infant, and made to suffer a life very different than that of my birthright. So, if you ask me, exile was not that far from the truth.

But as I entered Claridges' opulent art-deco lobby on that chilly spring evening, I displayed superb self-control and neglected to share any of this with the hotel's concierge.

The book everyone was launching that day was a celebration of

---

85 Crown Prince Alexander of Yugoslavia (son of King Peter of Yugoslavia, who was exiled in 1941) was actually *born* in Claridges—Suite 212, July 1945.

the founders of Savile Row, and boy, was I looking forward to meeting a roomful of well-dressed, traditional English gentlemen! If anything could make royal abandonment bearable, it was them.

My heels clicked across the black-and-white-checkered marble of the hotel floor until I arrived at the designated room. Upon producing my cream-colored invite, I was handed a glass of champagne, introduced to the host, and before I knew it I was surrounded by a bevy of distinguished old men—all of whom had dedicated their professional lives to maintaining the standards of State Liveries[86] and Shrieval Court Dress.[87] Luckily, I held a lifelong interest in all things made of velvet or satin, a genuine fascination with dress swords and gold-buckled shoes, and an endless rapture for anything involving royals, their ceremonies, their staff, and their uniforms. And whereas many girls might have felt out of their depth, I was quite able to hold my own throughout most of the conversation.

As usual, I was the youngest person in the room and as usual, this was because I was the only one in the office that consistently volunteered for such priggish-sounding publicity events. But I *loved* the prim and proper stuffiness that filled these conventional English functions! So to me, attending them was hardly a chore. And besides, it gave me a chance to meet new people. I could scarcely keep my social life buzzing if I relied solely upon impromptu tea parties with the occasional late-night stripper.

As I glanced around to see when the next champagne tray might be coming my way, I noticed a flurry of activity near the entrance. Whispers rippled through the crowd and then suddenly the party fell silent.

---

86 Liveries are the official garments worn by coachmen, footmen, chauffeurs, and so on.

87 Dress code prescribed to High Sheriffs when in the presence of a Royal court or a court of law.

Call it happenstance, call it serendipity, call it years of pure and relentless royal stalking—but yet again, I found myself face to face with my future mother-in-law.

In addition to the hundreds of charities The Princess Royal officially supports, she is also the president of U.K. Fashion Exports.

I knew this. And therefore I shouldn't have been so shocked to see her at a party dedicated to some of the most traditional apparel in the country. Nevertheless, she was there. Meaning that Peter's mother and I had found ourselves in the same country, in the same city, and in the same room—not once, but *twice*.

This was no fluke.

Not in the slightest.

What you think about, you bring about—and there was no doubt that I had brought this exquisite moment upon myself.

My heart pounded violently against my chest as my brain went into overdrive. Maybe this time I would actually get to talk to Princess Anne. Maybe this time I would be able to capture her attention for more than just a few moments. Maybe *this time* would be the chance encounter that would cement my place in her son's future once and for all.

I watched in a daze as Her Royal Highness walked to the podium at the front of the lavish reception room. She looked exactly the same as she had three years ago. Same conservative English suit. Same white gloves. Same retro chignon.

The princess began her speech and I listened as she praised the history of English tailoring, praised the legendary shops of Savile Row, and of course, praised the book's esteemed (and furiously blushing) author. But the more I listened to the princess speak in her wonderful cut-glass accent, the more my insides seemed to tremble. Toward the end, I could barely keep from spilling my champagne.

What was wrong with me? Why couldn't I just relax and act normal whenever I was confronted with my destiny?

Okay. Breathe. Just breathe and try to stay calm.

When presented to her, I will simply sweep into a graceful curtsy like last time. Then I will remind her of our last meeting at the House of Commons and tell her all that I've been up to since. I will be poised. Engaging. Demure. And when she goes home she will not be able to forget what a charming, intelligent young girl she just met and next time she sees her son (who is obviously miserable with his current girlfriend), she will mention me. Simple as that.

Once The Princess Royal finished speaking, everything began to move in slow motion. I watched as she gracefully stepped down from the small platform and joined her awestruck audience. I watched as she shook (gloved) hands with the author. And then with the host. And then, with a mixture of panic and delight, I watched as she started walking right toward me.

And then right past me.

And then right out the door.

〜

I'm not going to lie to you. I was disappointed. Very disappointed.

But, if I'm being honest, at the same time, I was oddly unfazed. I mean, let's face it: Souls are not thrown together in this world at random. (And they're certainly not thrown together randomly at Claridges.)

But deep down, I knew that every encounter, no matter how small, had a purpose. And that day, for those few seconds, Princess Anne reminded me of my own. Her very presence reminded me not of what I thought I must be, but of what I already was.

And the minute she came into my view, she had dared me to become it.

The word *manifest* means "obvious"[88]—and all I can say is that it was pretty obvious to me that I was *meant* to be at that party at Claridges at that very moment on that very night.

So while I would never admit it to my mother, perhaps the Planetary Dog Moon of Manifestation did have something to do with it.

---

88 *Manifest* (adjective): "clearly apparent or obvious to the mind or senses," from the Latin *manifestus*, "clear or evident," c. 1374

Twenty-two

"Courage is going from failure to failure without losing enthusiasm."

—Winston Churchill

I didn't know when socializing had stopped feeling like fun, and more like obligation. Even though it was a Saturday night and I should have been out on the town searching for royal connections, I was actually very much looking forward to ordering Indian takeout, watching the complete boxed set of *Sex and the City* series three, and having the flat to myself. I knew staying in over the weekend was hardly going to help me meet my English soulmate but there comes a time when a party girl just needs to rest.

But no such luck.

"Jerramy," Sophie asked sweetly, "would you like to go to this James Bond party with me tonight? It's at some banker's house in Knightsbridge and I know it sounds a bit cheesy, but a friend from work invited me and I'm not going to know anyone else there. Please say you'll come!"

Seconds later I was in my room searching for a suitable Bond girl outfit. (What can I say? I'm a sucker for dry martinis.) I didn't exactly own a leather catsuit and I'd already decided against the traditional go-go boots and bikini combo—but eventually I settled on a simple yet glamorous black cocktail dress and hurried my hair into the tidy blond bouffant of my all-time favorite Bond girl, Honor Blackman.[89] I had no idea how to go about fastening a dagger to my hip, but I figured I could always pretend that I had a gun tucked into my garter belt.

⟿

The neighborhood of Knightsbridge, with its mews houses and majestic redbrick buildings, boasts some of the highest property prices—not just in London, but in the entire world. When we arrived at the party and I saw how beautiful and spacious the flat was, I had no idea how someone my age (and the owner was my age) could afford such a place. What on earth did these bankers do all day to make so much money?

Anyway, don't get too excited. The flat's owner wasn't English. He was French. And as far as Sophie and I could tell, so was everyone else at the party. Either French or Italian or Eastern European. And all in 007 tuxedos.

Call me crazy, but uber-rich European guys just didn't do it for me. They loved to dance, they loved to flirt, and judging from the amount of expensive champagne that always flowed so abundantly around them, they clearly loved the finer things in life. But for me, something lacked. Let's put it this way: Would James Bond be so devilishly irresistible if he wasn't English? Exactly.

Sophie went off to find her friend while I stood on the sidelines swigging ice-cold vodka martinis. (Shaken, of course. Not stirred.) Martinis are ingenious inventions when you think about it. There is no other way to down large quantities of neat liquor without looking like a tramp. But pour the fiery concoction into a martini glass, and suddenly drinking straight gin becomes stylish. It might taste like lighter fluid, but it looks

---

89 Honor played Pussy Galore in *Goldfinger* (1964).

beautiful in the glass and you feel elegant holding it. Besides, after drinking the first one, you rarely notice what the second one tastes like.

Still, for once I just didn't seem to be in the party mood and after about an hour of watching drunk people dance around in their spywear, I was kind of wishing I'd stayed home and watched *Sex and the City*. I mean, even with my martini enhancement, there are only so many Euro-playboys you can chat to before it becomes tedious.

Right around the time I was thinking of cutting my losses and heading home, another guy came up to me. He was less tan and more portly than the others. German perhaps? Austrian maybe?

"Hello," he said, eyes twinkling.

He was English! At last I might be able to talk with someone who doesn't want to discuss sports cars or St. Tropez!

"Are you a liar like everyone else at this party?" he asked skeptically.

"I'm not a liar!" I replied with mild indignation. Seriously, the opening lines some guys came up with left a lot to be desired.

"Not *a liar*!" he chuckled. "A lawyer! I asked if you were a lawyer."

"Oh." I smiled bashfully. "Sorry. It's just been a long night, that's all. And um, to answer your question, I'm not a lawyer. There's no way I could spend my whole life arguing with people."

"Because you're too nice?"

I blushed. "Something like that."

"I'm Dougal," he said. These British names killed me.

"I'm Jerramy,"

"Really? Jeremy? Why, that's a boy's name in this country!"

"It's a boy's name in all countries," I replied.

"Well, you certainly don't look like a boy!" winked Dougal.

I laughed like it was the first time anyone had ever said that to me. "That's a relief."

"So, *Jerramy*—would you like to join me on the roof terrace for another martini?"

What did I have to lose? Sophie was nowhere to be found, and so far this was the first guy that had held my interest for more than a nanosecond. He was a little on the husky side, but his accent was right up my street and there was something about him that was quite charming. At the very least he could keep me amused through the next drink.

We wandered up to the roof terrace, but it was packed with chain-smokers. Actually, the whole party was heaving at this point and the two of us struggled to find any place to sit down despite the banker's giant apartment. Finally, we came across a spare bedroom. Just like everywhere else in the house it was filled with people and blaring with music, but we were able to perch ourselves on the edge of the bed. (I know what you're thinking: Sitting on a bed with a guy can be dangerous. But I wasn't worried. We were just talking.)

"So, *Jerramy*," Dougal began, once we were firmly ensconced with our new martinis, "I couldn't help noticing your accent. Are you Canadian or American?"

"American," I answered, "but please don't hold it against me."

"I wouldn't dream of it! My great-grandmother was American, and by all accounts she was witty and charming and everyone couldn't help but adore her. Much like you, I'd imagine."

I blushed again. What was it with this guy? He wasn't even that cute. Why did I feel so tongue-tied around him?

"Have dinner with me," Dougal blurted out.

"Excuse me?"

"Jerramy, I'd love to have dinner with you this week. When are you free?"

"I barely know you," I countered.

"Well, then. Let's get to know me then, shall we? What would you like to know?"

"How about you start by telling me what you do," I said.

"Well, that one's easy. I work in local politics. Dreadfully boring, I know. But no way around it really. It's in the blood."

"But I love politics!" I exclaimed.

"Really? Jerramy, for an American girl you are *full* of surprises. Tell me you'll have dinner with me."

I ignored him.

"I've spent time working in both Congress and Parliament," I said, trying to change the subject.

"How extraordinary!" declared Dougal. "I *also* used to work in the American Congress! I do adore D.C. Such a remarkable city."

I nodded vigorously. "I agree. I love D.C. If I had to live in America, that's where I would be. Whom did you work for when you were there?"

He proudly named a very prominent, very conservative member of the Senate.

My heart sank. "Oh. I see. A Republican."

"Don't tell me I've just lost my chance of taking you to dinner."

"You very well may have," I teased. "I'm sorry. I'm just not a fan of Republicans. Here or in the U.S."

"But Republicans in England aren't even a political party!" exclaimed Dougal, slightly confused. "They're just a bunch of batty people who want to abolish the monarchy."

"Precisely," I said. "That's exactly why I'm not a fan of them."

"Ah. Well, I can live with that. We may not support the same politicians, but at least we can both support Her Gracious Majesty the Queen."

"God Save Her," I smiled.

"Jerramy, you must let me have dinner with you!"

"And you must stop mentioning dinner with me!"

If truth be told, I was tired of pinning my hopes on every English guy that happened to flirt with me in a heart-stopping accent. Who's to say they wouldn't drop me within minutes—just like Fergus and Alex? Who's to say they weren't secretly bringing home strippers every night after work—like George and Oliver? Quite abruptly, I had reached a phase in my life where men were guilty until proven innocent. And unless I was face to face with Peter Phillips himself, at that moment I just wasn't in the mood to have my heart trampled upon by yet another sweet-talking Englishman. One measly dinner was hardly worth the heartache. Or so I drunkenly told myself.

"Jerramy, you are impossible! Tell me. Who would you consider to be your ideal dinner date?"

"Hmmm," I pondered. "That's a good one."

I wasn't about to reveal my royal crush to a perfect stranger, so I went with the next best thing.

"Okay," I said. "My ideal dinner date would be a cross between Hugh Grant and Tony Blair."

"Jerramy! I expected slightly more from you!"

I looked at him innocently. "But why? I'm just being honest!"

"Jerramy, Hugh Grant I can vaguely—and I mean *vaguely*—understand. But Mr. Blair? Please don't tell me that grinning nitwit is the only British politician that you admire."

"Well . . . I do love Churchill," I said truthfully. "I used to cry whenever I read his speeches in college."

Dougal looked at me approvingly. "I can't tell you how happy it makes me to hear you say that."

"But Churchill is dead!" I reminded him. "I was trying to think of the perfect *living* dinner date!"

Dougal moved closer to me. "You know, Jerramy, Churchill once said that there are only two difficult things in life: climbing a wall that is leaning toward you, and kissing a girl who is leaning away from you."

"Kind of like now?" I laughed.

"Why, yes. Exactly like now." He moved in closer. "You know, Jerramy, for an American, you really do behave like a proper English girl."

I smiled modesty and lowered my lashes. Dougal didn't know it yet, but that last sentence had just clinched the deal.

"Now Jerramy, I won't have any excuses. I *insist* that you have dinner with me. I'll even *cook* you dinner, if that's what you prefer. How does Friday evening sound?"

"I suppose Friday evening works for me." I know I said I wasn't in the mood, but at the end of the day, a girl's gotta eat.

"Superb," said Dougal. "I knew you'd see sense in the end."

Then Dougal inched even closer to me and (martinis are evil!) we kissed.

But it wasn't just a kiss. It was amazing. An utterly amazing, out-of-this-world, forget-who-you-are-and-where-you-are kind of kiss. It was brief, no more than a few seconds, but its impact was so unexpected that I was completely and utterly floored by it.

"I will make you my famous shepherd's pie," Dougal whispered into my ear, "and as soon as I get home tonight . . . I will begin chilling a few bottles of Pol Roger . . . Churchill's favorite champagne."

"How do you know so much about Churchill?" I asked.

Dougal stopped his nuzzling and looked me in the eye. "He's my great-grandfather," he said softly.

⌒

Okay. I did some major Googling, and to the best of my knowledge, Winston Churchill's great-grandson was making me dinner on Friday night.

My heart may have been set on the Queen's oldest grandson—but until then, I figured one of Churchill's great-grandsons would certainly suffice.

Twenty-three

"Failure comes only when we forget our ideals and objectives and principles."

—Jawaharlal Nehru

One cloudy Sunday afternoon I was having lunch with Adam and his mother—perhaps the only woman in his life besides me that knew his true sexual orientation. To her credit, she hadn't disowned Adam when he told her the "gay news," but nor had she altogether accepted that his homosexuality was a permanent state of affairs.

"Why, Jerramy's perfect for you, Adam," she said. "Can't you two at least *try* to be boyfriend and girlfriend?"

"I've already asked her to be my wife and she refused," Adam grumbled. "I daren't ask her to be anything else."

His mother turned to me. "You know what Adam's problem is, Jerramy?"

"What?" I asked eagerly. Adam rolled his eyes and kicked me under the table.

"Adam doesn't have any *normal* friends. He's always insisted on hanging around with these high-flyers. Politicians, academics, millionaires—that sort of thing. Nobody *normal*. Why can't he be friends with a simple shop assistant or a dustman?[90] Nice

---

90 This is a nice English way of describing a person whose job it is to empty people's dustbins and take the rubbish away. The U.S. equivalent would be "garbageman."

normal people that will keep his head out of the clouds and help bring him down to earth?"

She looked pointedly at Adam, who was looking right back at her with irritated bewilderment, as if she were absolutely insane. I knew that look well; it was exactly the way I looked at my own mother.

"My mom says the same thing about me!" I laughed. "In fact, she hopes that one day I will fall in love with a homeless man!"

Adam's mother didn't look at all appalled by the idea.

"You kids need grounding," she continued. "All these expensive restaurants and fancy nightclubs that you go to. It's not the real world. London is *not* the real world. I don't know about you, Jerramy, but Adam tends to forget that."

"I've got it!" shouted Adam, sitting upright in his chair. "Mum, I have the solution!"

She looked at him skeptically.

"I'll become friends with a dustman, just like you want me to. And then Jerramy can marry him! See? That way both of us will be grounded and both mums will be happy!"

Just then the waiter brought the bill to our table.

"Know any eligible dustmen?" Adam asked him.

"Sorry, mate," the waiter mumbled.

"That's a shame," sighed Adam. "Well, Mum, when I'm prime minister and Jerramy's living a miserable existence at Buckingham Palace, at least we can say that we've tried."

⌐

Meanwhile, I was about to spend an evening with a politician, an academic, and a millionaire all rolled into one. According to Adam's mother, Dougal was the stuff of her worst nightmares. But to me, he was a dream. A dream that stepped into my life just when I was beginning to think that all Englishmen were nothing but superficial cads and heartless bounders.

But Dougal was different than the others—he seemed more like the English guys I'd read about in Jane Austen novels, rather than exact replicas of the devious (yet gorgeous) Daniel Cleaver in *Bridget Jones's Diary*. I mean, Dougal didn't just *say* he would call me later that week—he actually called me! It's quite sad that a guy can earn brownie points these days simply by doing what he says he will. But nevertheless, I was impressed.

"I sure hope he has a great personality," Adam said after I e-mailed him a picture of Dougal I'd found on the Internet. "Because you sure as hell aren't with him for his looks."

"It's a bad picture," I insisted. "He's cuter in real life. And the best kisser I've ever encountered in my entire life."

"With a face like that, he had better be a good kisser!" Adam joked.

"Will you look out for him at the party conference[91] next week?" I asked. "I'd love for you to meet him."

"Jerramy, I refuse to make friends, professionally or otherwise, with your posh love interest of the week. Your taste in men is just so bloody predictable. I can tell just by looking at him that he's a typical Tory[92] wanker."

"And you speak as a friend?" I teased.

"Absolutely. I'm telling you, Jerramy—I *know* you. And despite what you say, I know you'll never be able to sustain a relationship with someone who's at the opposite end of the political spectrum. I don't care whose great-grandson he is."

"You underestimate me!" I insisted.

"No, Jerramy, I don't think that I do. I know all things English and royal mean more to you than life itself—but I also

---

91 Party conference: A national symposium given annually for each political party in the U.K. and attended by everyone who's anyone in British politics—regardless of political leanings.

92 *Tory*: U.K. slang for a member of the British Conservative Party, which is traditionally right-wing.

know that deep, deep down, social issues mean much more to you than you care to admit. But if you want to snog your brains out with another Tory who cares nothing for the plight of the poor, then go right ahead."

⤳

I decided on a pleated beige skirt, baby blue cashmere, and pearls for my Friday night dinner date and when I arrived at Dougal's small but expensively located Victorian flat, I was giddy with lust (and the small feeling that I was making some kind of political history).

I eagerly tucked into the proffered Pol Roger and made myself at home as Dougal moved expertly about the kitchen and amused me with his enchanting repartee.

"Jerramy," he said seductively over our candlelit dinner, "I *must* take you to Chartwell[93]—and show you the rooms that mere members of the public are not allowed to see."

"What kind of rooms are those?" I asked.

He winked. "Bedrooms mainly."

Once the shepherd's pie was demolished, we moved to the sofa where Churchill's great-grandson proceeded to spoon homemade chocolate mousse into my mouth.

It may have had something to do with all the champagne, but I have to say that by this point I had become borderline delirious. I mean, passionate attention from the progeny of my favorite English hero—combined with chocolate? What more could a girl want?

Dougal and I kissed that night until our faces were raw. Literally raw! And when my bruised lips could take it no longer, I insisted that it was time for me to leave.

---

93 Chartwell, a Victorian manor situated on eighty acres of English countryside, was Sir Winston Churchill's family home from 1922 until his death in 1965.

"Forget the bedrooms of Chartwell!" Dougal protested. "We haven't even made it into *my* bedroom!"

"Exactly why I need to leave at this very moment!" I laughed.

Dougal reluctantly went off to call me a cab, and while he was gone, I noticed two old Christmas cards sitting on the bookshelf. I reached over and sneaked a look at them.

All at once, I felt stone cold sober.

They were from Ronald Reagan and George Bush—*personally signed.*

I carefully set the cards back on the shelf and smiled weakly as Dougal kissed me good-bye.

Damn it, Adam was right. I had more principles than I realized.

⌒

Sadly, I never made it to Chartwell as anything other than a tourist.

As with most fledging relationships, it didn't take long to realize that other than a mutual fondness for trivial banter and kissing marathons, Dougal and I had very little in common.

Believe me, I would have happily carried on snogging the boy for years to come. But we couldn't kiss forever. Unfortunately, there were times when we had to come up for air and actually talk—and the more we talked about politics (which, quite frankly, was a subject impossible to avoid considering his family, his job, and my own political background)—the less we enjoyed our time together. And alas, in the end, we went our separate ways.

My lips still miss him, though.

⌒

Based on her own harrowing experiences (including an adulterous father and a string of two-timing boyfriends), my friend

Charlotte was a firm believer that men were inherently unscru-
pulous and intrinsically useless—except as stepping-stones for
women determined to elevate their own lifestyles. And strangely,
while many accused me of antifeminist leanings, she was one
of my greatest advocates when it came to following my English
dream.

"I live vicariously through you!" she always told me. "Never
give in! Never give up!" (Now that I think about it, her inspira-
tional tirades sounded a lot like Winston Churchill's.[94])

Needless to say, Charlotte was horrified when I told her my
brief affair with Dougal had come to an end.

"You did *what*?" shouted Charlotte over the phone. "You finished things with possibly one the world's most eligible bachelors
because you disagreed with him about *politics*?"

"Well, kind of," I answered. "But it wasn't all down to me. It
was very much a joint decision."

"You mean you annoyed him so much with your save-the-
world views that he had to send you packing," Charlotte said
dryly.

"I guess you could say that," I giggled.

"*Jerramy!!* I have no sympathy for you! You obviously don't
know a good thing when you see it! You'll never marry a rich
English guy if you carry on like this!"

"But I've told you a million times! I'm not *trying* to marry a
rich English guy," I argued. "I've *never* been attracted to a guy
purely for his money."

"Well, I can see that now. You *clearly* have far too many *principles* to marry for money." I love that this annoyed her.

"So I've been told," I mumbled.

---

94 "Never give in, never give in, never, never, never!"—Winston Churchill, October 29, 1941

"But if you're not marrying for money," Charlotte continued, "then why do you insist on pursuing this royalty guy?"

I smiled. "That has nothing to do with money," I told her calmly. "*That* has to with destiny. And true love."

"Jerramy," said Charlotte.

"What?"

"You're even crazier than I thought."

Twenty-four

"The heart wants what the heart wants."

—WOODY ALLEN

As I left for work the next morning (running extremely late as usual), I realized in horror that somehow I had become locked *inside* my own flat. How was this even possible? I had my key to the front door, but I didn't have a key for *inside* the front door!

I called Duncan in a panic.

Typically, all he did was burst out laughing.

"Classic!" he chuckled. "I *told* Oliver never to use both of his keys—or at least to make sure everyone had left the flat if he did!"

I rolled my eyes at him over the phone. "Well, do you have a spare key so I can leave the flat and go to work?"

Duncan carried on laughing. "No, I'm afraid I don't."

"Duncan! You're *the landlord*! Don't you have keys to your own properties?"

"Unfortunately, no. Classic, isn't it!"

"Well, what do you suggest I do? What if there's a fire? How am I supposed to get out?"

"You Yanks!" He laughed. "Such alarmists! I love it!"

I tried to stay patient. "Duncan, really—what am I supposed to do?"

"Call a locksmith."

"But that's like sixty-five pounds!" (For me that was almost three weeks' spending money.)

"Probably," Duncan snickered.

"Will you reimburse me?"

"Don't be daft! Now, I've got to go—I'm a terribly important man around the office, you know—can't waste all my time listening to the trivial complaints of my tenants. Cheerio!"

And he hung up on me.

I quickly called work and told them I probably wouldn't be in until lunchtime, because I, was, um, locked *inside* my own flat.

"You mean locked out?" asked the receptionist.

"No, locked *in*." If anything I guess they gave me credit for providing such an original excuse.

Then I called Sophie who worked in an office building near Oliver, and being the stellar friend that she was, she fetched Oliver's "special" key, put it in an envelope, and gave the envelope to a black cab. An hour later, the cab driver pushed the key through the letterbox and I let myself out.

Still, not an ideal way to start the day. Especially since the cab fare cost me £20.

I just couldn't believe that U.K. fire codes allowed doors that locked from the outside, but required keys from the inside. Nothing like a good measure of Old World incompetence first thing in the morning.

⌒

When I finally arrived at the office, I volunteered to attend yet another grand-sounding invitation-only event: a celebrity auction to benefit teenagers with cancer—taking place at the swankiest cocktail bar in South Kensington later that week.

Seriously, what was there not to like? I had no idea why my dreary colleagues always turned down such fantastic free tickets. Sophie couldn't get her hands on my extra invite fast enough.

Located in a converted warehouse, the auction venue was considered one of the hippest nightspots in the city—especially if you're anyone who's anyone in the world of fashion. So of course this prompted the eternal question: What on earth was I going to wear?

After much agonizing, I went with a black pleated wool miniskirt and fitted argyle jumper from Pringle. (I figured it was understated, yet still chic and traditionally British.) Meanwhile, since Sophie possessed the lissome stature of a couture model, she managed to look stunning in simple designer jeans and a plain white top.

Keeping with the fashion theme, entering the bar involved walking down an elaborate eighty-foot catwalk and then emerging into a soaring loft-style space packed to standing room only with trendy young fashionistas. (We couldn't wait to tell George and Oliver about it all—they would be seething with jealousy!)

Sophie and I gleefully dove into the fashionable throng and downed glass after elegant glass of Campari cocktails as we admired the designer auction items (including garb donated by Dolce & Gabbana, Pucci, and John Galliano), all the while pretending that we had enough money to place even a single starting bid.

We scanned the room for celebrities and to our delight spotted several B-listers, including the hunky star from the U.K. version of the *The Bachelor*. Sophie was discreetly pointing out the two super-stylish women from *What Not to Wear*, when I stopped dead in my tracks: Standing no more than three feet away from me was Sarah, The Duchess of York!

I didn't say a word to Sophie (who was momentarily distracted by the South African barman and lecturing him on apartheid).

Instead, I just watched.

With her flaming hair, large sparkling eyes, and fabulous legs, the Duchess was infinitely more beautiful in real life than she was in any of her photographs. Dressed in a classic tailored suit that showed off her new streamlined figure, I thought of her exceptional roller-coaster life and marveled at her amazing tenacity. Once again, I knew that serendipity had put me in the same room with her. After all, this woman was Peter Phillips's aunt!

Peter's mother (Princess Anne) has three brothers: Prince Charles, Prince Andrew, and Prince Edward. Miss Sarah Ferguson (aka Fergie) met the dashingly handsome Prince Andrew (the Duke of York) when her dear friend, the newly married Princess Diana, invited her to a party at Windsor Castle.

Sparks flew between Sarah and the Duke—and within a year, Fergie and Diana became sisters-in-law. In a huge televised wedding (at which nine-year-old Peter served as a page boy), Fergie married Prince Andrew in Westminster Abbey and became the Duchess of York.

Happily ever after, right?

Well . . . not quite.

Like Diana, Fergie was a vivacious free spirit and she struggled with the strict protocol of life at Buckingham Palace. Also like Diana, Fergie had a terrible time coming to terms with the ruthless criticism of the British tabloids. (One cruel headline went so far as to dub her the "Duchess of Pork.")

Nor did it help that Prince Andrew, her beloved husband, was away at sea with the Royal Navy almost ten months a year—leaving Fergie to look after their two small daughters, Princess Beatrice and Princess Eugenie, all by herself. Normally an extremely exuberant young woman, the duchess eventually found the combined pressure too much to bear—and with much sadness and heartache, the royal couple divorced in 1996.

Devastated by her broken marriage, Fergie tried to cheer herself up by plunging headfirst into a jet-set lifestyle and went on to spend millions (that she didn't have) on designer clothes and exotic vacations. Publicly banned from the royal family and constantly subjected to widespread public ridicule, it's no wonder Fergie finally hit rock bottom: Despite her best-selling children's books[95] she was nearly $8 million in debt and tremendously overweight.

But this is what I love about the dazzling Duchess of York: She may have stumbled, but when she finally faced up to her mistakes and pulled herself up, she arose with new power.

The penniless Fergie moved to America to escape the venom of the British press, and eventually, through her own efforts[96] she became a millionairess in her own right. How many royal family members can say *that*?

But even more amazing was this: Through all the ups and downs, Fergie managed to maintain an honest and loving relationship with her ex-husband, Prince Andrew—sparing their young daughters the traditional trauma that so often comes with bitterly divorced parents.[97] In this modern age of broken families (of which royals are clearly not exempt), I found it incredibly inspiring to see how Fergie and Andrew rose above the fray and kept their family unit intact.

Despite her royal title, Fergie refused to conform to everyone else's ideas about what her royal life "should have" been. Instead, she became the Michelangelo of her own destiny. She now happily lives out a storybook existence that *she's* designed and created—and does so with dignity and grace. Staying true to yourself like that takes guts—and I loved that about her.

---

95 The duchess authored a series of animated children's books called *Budgie the Little Helicopter*.

96 Which included losing 50 pounds and becoming an official spokeswoman for Weight Watchers.

97 The couple's friendship is so strong that they continue to share their original family home in the U.K.

I knew immediately why the duchess was at this event. Her own father[98] had suffered a painful battle against prostate cancer, and in 1998 she had endured a frightening breast cancer scare herself. Although the lump she found turned out to be benign, Fergie used her own startling experience to become a public advocate for self-exams and cancer awareness. And as a mother of teenage daughters (Beatrice was fifteen and Eugenie thirteen) this fund-raiser for teens with cancer was precisely her kind of party.

I was deep in royal thought when Fergie caught me staring at her (admittedly, I *was* staring). But instead of ignoring me and quickly looking away like most people would have done to an annoyingly awestruck stranger like me, she paused momentarily in her conversation, looked me directly in the eye, and *smiled.*

Thrilled by the royal acknowledgment, I turned to tell Sophie. And as the two of us exchanged awed whispers, Fergie calmly took to the podium and began to speak about her passion for the Teenage Cancer Trust. In those moments, I felt the audience respond not only to her words or to her royal position, but to Sarah herself. Life had given her a royal title—but Fergie used her title to give to others. And as I stood in that noisy cocktail bar, I knew deep down that that's truly what royalty was all about.

I'd been getting a lot of these royal reminders lately: Earl Spencer, The Princess Royal (again), The Duchess of York . . . all clear signs from the universe that I was moving in the right circles and headed in the right direction. As I've always suspected, like attracts like. Not only do you eventually *become* what you think about most, but I was certain that you also *attract* what

---

98 Major Ronald Ferguson had served as polo manager for both the Duke of Edinburgh and the Prince of Wales.

you think about most—how else would you explain all these royal personalities walking through my life?

⟶

I sat at my desk in a daze, unable to concentrate on anything. I desperately needed something to take my mind off all these royal appearances and my various theories on their potentially life-altering meaning.

From what I could tell, most people were lured into the world of online dating due to pure unadulterated boredom, but for me it was the urgent need for some kind of distraction. (My mind could spin itself into royal knots for weeks upon weeks if I wasn't careful.)

The way I saw it, there was no downside. The taboo of meeting someone over the Internet had completely disappeared for my age group and suddenly almost every girl I knew, on both sides of the Atlantic, was forever raving about this new e-pool of eligible men.

Besides, Peter Phillips was just as much a part of the digital generation as I was—so why not give it a try? Perhaps *this* was the way we were destined to meet. At the very least I figured it would get me through the working day. And with London social barriers being what they were, if I managed to meet new people through this untapped technology, even better.

Like most bored employees, within minutes of logging on to the various dating sites, I was hooked. It wasn't uncommon for me to spend hours surfing Match.com and Friendster, eternally devising the perfect profile and constantly analyzing everyone else's.

I saw no point in trawling through hundreds of undesirables, so when it came to composing my own profile, I was extra specific about what type of guy I was looking for. And after a handful of drafts, I settled on this:

Blond American bookworm/partygirl seeks privately educated Englishman (aged 25–30) with James Bond accent and Oscar Wilde wit. Must enjoy black-tie galas, debaucherous dinner parties, intellectual debates, and long walks in the country. An appreciation for fine wine, classic literature, and nonstop adventure goes without saying. Aristocratic lineage and Hugh Grant looks highly encouraged. No others need apply.

Pretty straightforward, right? Once it was posted, I sat back and waited for the flirty fun to begin. But despite my rather explicit dating requirements, I didn't get a single e-mail from anyone even closely resembling my carefully described ideal!

Instead, I received dozens of e-mails from every nationality you can think of—Italian men, Australian men, Jordanian men, Fijian men, Swedish men, even Icelandic men—each one naïvely thinking that they could persuade me to drop the "English" part of my criteria!

But I was strict. Any guy who wasn't English was deleted immediately.

Except once.

If his profile was to be believed, his name was Sebastian. Although he was born in northern California, he was now living in London. He listed fencing and rowing as his hobbies, had attended the Sorbonne and Oxford, and claimed to be both the CEO of his own consultancy and to be writing a novel in his spare time.

You had to hand it to this California boy—my interest was piqued. So I broke my own rules and opened his brief message.

"Can't help noticing your overt Anglophilia," it read. "Am curious to know what makes such a well-educated American girl possess such insular desires."

Ouch!

Partly in my own defense, something made me pour out my soul to this Internet boy. (That's the beauty of the computer-dating world—it can serve as excellent anonymous therapy.)

In a flurry of typing, I told Sebastian about my deep love for England and mysterious passion for all things royal; I told him about my crush on Peter Phillips; I even told him all about my crazy hippie parents and how sometimes, just sometimes, I wondered how much of my personality was actually a severe case of reverse rebellion. Then I pressed send.

Sebastian's reply arrived ten minutes later. And let me tell you, what it contained was the *last* thing I expected.

"Quite astonishingly," he began, "I believe that you—a girl I assumed would be snobby and inflexible, are in fact my mirror image."

In an e-mail filled with as many confessions as my own, Sebastian told me how his dad (with a beard and blond hair down to his waist) used to sit on their kitchen floor playing acoustic guitar. He told me about his *own* childhood of tie-dyed pillows, organic gardens, and raising chickens and how he was pretty much left to raise himself—spending most of his youth running stark naked through the forest plotting revenge against his parents for making him eat alfalfa sprouts.

He told me that once he hit adolescence, he took to wearing knickerbockers and smoking a pipe. (Take *that*, hippie parents!) He even had a monocle with a chain attached to his waistcoat, and when someone met with his disapproval, he would let it drop dramatically from his eye. He told me how he dreamed of moving to Paris, and being adopted by a family that would teach him to use cutlery instead of chopsticks. And best of all, he admitted to a life-long admiration of Zara Phillips (Peter's striking younger sister).

I sat at my desk in shock.

After all this time, was the person who understood me better than anyone *an American*? It was a dizzying thought.

In our very next e-mail, Sebastian and I exchanged pictures (he was preppy and cute with classic aquiline features) and we agreed to meet for a drink the following week. When he suggested my favorite London bar, I got goosebumps and it wasn't long before I became a nervous wreck. I mean, this guy seemed *amazing*. What if I wasn't good enough for him? What if I wasn't pretty enough? What if I wasn't smart enough?

I went to the bookstore and bought the cheater's guides to French literature and art history. I also read everything I could get my hands on about fencing. During the next few days, I ignored my work entirely and spent hours composing note-perfect paragraphs in response to Sebastian's seductively cerebral e-mails. (For godsake, the boy actually asked me if I had a *trousseau*!⁹⁹)

My heart raced wildly with every e-mail exchange and my stomach filled with endless butterflies at the thought of our pending date. But as I walked into the dimly lit bar situated ten stories above the sparkling lights of the River Thames, I knew—within seconds—that I shouldn't have bothered.

There was zero chemistry between us.

Not a spark of physical attraction.

Not even enough basic compatibility to sustain thirty minutes of small talk.

Although our e-mail discussions had flown off the keyboard at lightning speed, we now struggled to make a simple face-to-face conversation last as long as a single glass of wine. Like 99

---

99 *Trousseau*: nineteenth-century French word referring to the expensive collection of clothing and linens that an upper-class Victorian woman brings to her marital home. (Not many boys have even *heard* of this word, much less are able to use it in casual conversation.)

percent of relationships born on the Internet, ours should have stayed there. The magic of our fleeting cyber connection was gone. And never to return.

On the lonely taxi ride home, I marveled at my heart's gullibility. I couldn't believe I had let myself get so worked up about this random American guy! To become so emotionally involved! So unsure of myself! To think I was devouring French literature in order to impress him! *He* should have been devouring things to impress *me*! He wasn't even English! What in God's name was I thinking?

I vowed never to succumb to that sly online love trap ever again and removed my profile from those silly Web sites the very next morning. I seriously doubt Peter Phillips surfed the Web that much anyway.

⌐

The next day, I arrived home after work to find George and Sophie watching the latest episode of *Big Brother*—the mundane, eviction-based reality show that had taken the U.K. (and our flat) by storm.

"Jerramy, do you smell gas?" asked Sophie as I walked into the sitting room. "The boys keep telling me that I'm crazy."

I sniffed the air and definitely detected something that smelled like sulfur. "Yes!" I answered.

"That's it," exclaimed Sophie, jumping off the sofa and grabbing the phone. "I'm ringing Duncan."

"Good luck," I said sarcastically. I flopped down on the sofa next to George and settled in to listen to yet another of Sophie and Duncan's infamous screaming matches.

"Duncan!" she shouted. "Can't you at least come over here and smell it for yourself?"

Pause. "But you live five minutes away!"

Pause. "Duncan! If it *is* a gas leak, the flat could burst into flames at any second!"

Pause. "I can't believe you have so little regard for the safety of your tenants or your property!"

Pause. Slamming of phone onto receiver.

"What did he say?" I asked tentatively. I could tell Sophie was seething.

"He said don't light any matches and he would call in the morning to see if we're still alive."

"Can't say I'm surprised," I said.

"I'm going to bed," said George.

"Well, *I'm* calling the fire department," said Sophie, and she started dialing.

Less than ten minutes later, a fire engine pulled up outside our flat, sirens blaring and lights flashing. And before I knew what was happening, no fewer than *eight* firemen burst through our front door. Sophie explained the situation while the fleet of uniformed men circled through the various rooms.

Finally, one of the burly men spoke.

"Smells to me like you pretty little girls spilled some nail varnish," he said with a grin.

If Sophie's eyes could kill, that fireman would have dropped dead on the spot.

We emphatically denied such condescending allegations (could they be any more patronizing?). But eventually, after the whole fire brigade insisted we make them cups of tea, they finally gave us an official all-clear. No gas leak. We could sleep safely and without fear of spontaneous combustions.

The next morning I got a text message from Duncan: "STILL ALIVE?"

It took me less than two seconds to respond: "NO THANX 2 U."

Duncan replied even faster: "UR HOT WHEN UR ANGRY."

I shook my head in exasperation. The things I put up with for possible polo invitations.

Twenty-five

*"It's the soul's duty to be loyal to its own desires.
It must abandon itself to its master passion."*

—REBECCA WEST

Rupert and his friends had finally graduated from Oxford, accepted high-flying jobs, and at long last, everyone had arrived in London.

England is weird like that. In America, you graduate from college and depending on job prospects or grad school, close circles of friends suddenly disperse to just about every city in the country you can think of. But in England, you graduate from college and everyone moves to London. Simple as that.

When I was at the University of Rochester, my five closest girlfriends had moved to five different cities practically the day after we graduated, and as result, I was still coming to terms with the pain of being separated from my college friends quite possibly for life. I wholeheartedly envied English people who were lucky enough to strengthen their college friendships for decades to come—merely because they all lived in London.

In retrospect, I realized this weird migrating phenomenon might be part of the reason that meeting English people in London was so maddeningly difficult for me. In large American cities, everyone comes and goes so quickly that there is a general openness to new blood and new friendships. But in London, everyone is already firmly and happily ensconced in their college social circle, so there is very little incentive for them to make new friends. Newcomers (like me) are rarely accepted unless (like me) they have virtually punched their way in.

Still, because of these social boxing skills of mine, I was invited to Rupert's housewarming party. It was in SW, of course. And I could hardly wait. It'd been a long time since I'd been to a party swarming with boarding-school accents, antediluvian attitudes, gold signet rings, and those adorable pink button-down shirts with sleeves rolled to just below the elbow.

Far too long.

The moment I entered the large three-story townhouse (Rupert was sharing with three flatmates), I was in my element. Oh, how I'd missed this extraordinary level of charm and insouciance, this contagious neglect of all common sense and responsibility! And I no longer had to travel by that blasted Oxford bus for the privilege! It was now on my London doorstep!

I joyfully circled the party like a drunken butterfly. But amid the intoxicated sea of young college graduates I noticed a dainty old lady, possibly in her seventies, gulping down white wine with as much vigor as the rest of us. I pulled Hugo aside and asked him what this elegant, beautifully coiffed woman wearing a Chanel suit was doing at such a depraved social event.

"That's Lucinda," he answered, "Tom's mum. Cracking good fun! Former It Girl, apparently. Still can't get enough of the night life!"

Indeed. In fact, it wasn't long before Lucinda pulled out her digital camera and started snapping pictures of all the guests—and then promptly informing them if they did or didn't possess photogenic qualities suitable for the society pages. She was hilarious and I loved her. (Especially when she deemed me to be appropriately photogenic.)

It was good to see Rupert again although he was immensely distracted by what appeared to be a relatively serious girlfriend. Still, I was genuinely happy for him. I know it's not saying much, but I still thought Rupert was one of the most deserving English guys I'd ever met.

"Jezza!" Rupert bellowed drunkenly. "There is someone here you must meet!" Rupert grabbed my shoulder and began to steer me through the crowd.

"His name is Nick," he whispered loudly into my ear, "and, you're going to *love* this—he works for Buckingham Palace!"

"Rupert!" I laughed. "Stop it!"

"No! Jezza! Really he does!"

I rolled my eyes. "*No*, he *doesn't*. You really have to stop making fun of me in front of your friends!"

By this time, we were standing in front of Nick. He was cute—dark hair, roguish grin, big broad rugby shoulders.

"Nick," Rupert stated dramatically, "*this* is Jezza. The girl I was telling you about. She doesn't believe me that you work for Buckingham Palace."

"Oh, but I do," Nick replied, winking at Rupert. "Lovely to meet you, Jezza." I smiled in exasperation. I knew the two of them were just kidding around at my expense.

"I'll leave you two monarchists alone," teased Rupert.

Nick just laughed.

"So, Nick," I began, with mock seriousness, "what is it that you *do* at Buckingham Palace?"

"I work as an assistant secretary to Her Majesty the Queen," he replied.

He answered without skipping a beat. Maybe he was serious. No—*couldn't be*. He was far too young to hold such a position.

"And what does that involve?" I asked with amusement, happy to play his game for a while.

He shrugged and said smoothly, "Assisting with planning the official engagements carried out by my Sovereign."

Oh, be still my pounding heart!

"For instance?" I squeaked.

"For instance, this week I assisted Her Majesty in receiving His Excellency the Ambassador from the Republic of Turkey into the Court of St. James's."[100]

"Very impressive," I said flirtatiously. "But how do I know you're telling the truth? For all I know, you merely memorized today's Court Circular."[101]

"Very well then," he said, lowering his voice. "How about I tell you something I'm working on that has yet to be formally announced?"

"I wouldn't want to get you in trouble," I said coquettishly.

"I think obtaining your favorable opinion might be worth the trouble," Nick replied.

I blushed.

"Alright then," I whispered, "tell me."

"Well," he leaned closer, "at present, I am busy preparing logistics for the upcoming arrival of your very own illustrious commander-in-chief."

My eyes widened in shock. "You mean George W. and his entourage are descending upon Buckingham Palace?" I found the whole image rather disturbing. Royals and rodeos simply didn't belong together.

---

100 The royal Court of St. James's is considered to sit wherever HM The Queen happens to be.

101 The Court Circular is the authoritative, historical record of duties undertaken by members of the Royal Family. An account of the previous day's royal engagements is printed daily in three British newspapers.

Nick shook his head gravely. "I'm afraid so. Who would have guessed that one of my first assignments would be orchestrating royal protocol to fit the needs of a Texas cowboy?"

Just then, a rather drunken Hugo appeared. "Jerramy! Piers and I need your expert opinion on something *this instant*!" He grabbed my arm and attempted to drag me away.

I quickly pulled a business card out of my purse and slipped it into Nick's hand. "Call me if you ever want to divulge more royal information," I said softly, and then disappeared with Hugo into the crowd.

Hugo pulled me upstairs to find Piers. And as soon as our trio was assembled, the issue on which my expertise was so urgently required was revealed.

"Okay," slurred Piers in his wonderfully upper crust accent, "this summer, Hugo and I are planning a road trip across your grand United States of America. And we would like to ask you several critical questions regarding the itinerary."

"Jerramy," said Hugo sternly, "please don't take this lightly. As our honorary American friend, and perhaps the only American we are not embarrassed to be seen with—your expertise is invaluable. I implore you to listen carefully to our proposal, and to give us an honest answer regarding its viability."

"I'll do my best!" I laughed.

Hugo began by taking a deep breath, "Jerramy, you may not know this, but from the moment we learned of its glorious existence, Piers and I have dreamt of going to prom. In fact, going to an American prom is perhaps our deepest and most heartfelt desire."

Piers nodded earnestly. I did my best not to dissolve into drunken giggles.

"So," Hugo continued, "this is our plan: We will pinpoint

several strategic small towns in the Midwest and time our arrival exactly one week before prom night. Then, Piers and I, dressed in our most dapper English daywear, will linger about in search of a date."

"We already know that the foxy girls will be taken," Piers said matter-of-factly.

"*But*," Hugo grinned, "the geeky girls will be desperate!"

Piers nodded with enthusiasm.

Hugo carried on with his tactical explanation. "*So*, we will strike up a conversation with these desperately dateless girls—in the library, or perhaps in the car park[102] after school—and we shall introduce ourselves as earls or perhaps young viscounts."

"But we'll also be sure to casually mention how we'd *love* to be invited to a real American prom!" said Piers dreamily, stumbling into a simulated waltz with an imaginary American partner.

I laughed again. "And when these geeky American girls are face to face with your matchless English charm and hear your delicious English accents, you hope they'll be falling over themselves to take you to their prom?"

"Precisely!" Hugo exclaimed, a look of triumph on his face.

"They won't believe their luck!" added Piers.

"In all seriousness, Jerramy," asked Hugo gravely, "you know us—what girl could find it in her heart to turn down such a pair of distinguished English gentlemen?"

I could not stop laughing at their idea. It was genius. I wish I had thought of it a few years ago to get into dances at Eton!

"But do you think it will work?" asked Piers, gulping directly

---

102 *Car park* means "parking lot."

from his wine bottle. "We want to be sure before we put the plan into action."

"I *know* it will work," I told them. "If I were a young geeky girl looking for a prom date—and *you two* came along?" I shook my head wistfully at the thought. It was the kind of the thing I dreamed about happening to me in high school!

"Excellent!" shouted Hugo, raising his wine glass. "To senior prom!"

"To senior prom!" I toasted.

I considered telling them that some kids from my hillbilly high school actually arrived at our prom on a tractor—and that not all proms were as glamorous as the one portrayed in their beloved *American Pie*—but I decided it was best to let them discover these cultural anomalies for themselves. So I left Piers and Hugo alone with their wine and their road map of the United States and went into the bathroom to reapply my lipstick.

As I opened my purse, I saw a new text message (from an unknown number) blinking on my cell phone. I read it immediately:

"UR LOVELY. IF STILL HERE, MEET ME ON BALCONY @ MIDNITE. NX"

Nx? It was from Nick! (And the *x* was a kiss!)[103]

I looked at my watch. It was 11:50! My God, how long had I been listening to prom-crashing strategies? I quickly powdered my nose, smoothed my hair, and stopped in the kitchen to refill my wine glass. Here goes.

Not wanting to appear as if I had rushed to our rendezvous point, I slowly made my way through the inebriated crowd and stepped onto the large balcony at the front of the house.

---

103 This was actually a very common U.K. sign-off. Even I had taken to ending most of my personal e-mails and text messages with an affectionate "Jx."

There were a few smokers enjoying the unusually warm night air, and sure enough, there was Mr. Buckingham Palace—standing patiently at the corner of the railing and watching the nightlife traipse by through the streets below.

I walked up to him and lightly tapped his shoulder. "Hi."

His eyes lit up when he saw me, and he smiled. "Hi."

He put his arm around me and together we gazed into the starry spring night and then (hey, the wine was flowing, we were young, and it was midnight) we kissed. It's amazing how close a bit of royal chitchat can make you feel to someone, and to make a long story short, I accidentally spent the night with Her Majesty the Queen's assistant secretary.

Back at his flat, Nick showed me his royal security pass and palace photo ID. Apparently his mother was a former debutante[104] and through her tweedy family connections, he had landed the coveted palace position. Nick admitted that his job was mainly one of glorified admin, and didn't pay particularly well, but like most members of the Royal Household, he didn't really need the money—and primarily carried out his daily work due to pure allegiance to the Crown.

Such loyalty! Such duty! So incredibly romantic!

These were my drowsy thoughts as I rode the tube home the next morning. (Albeit I did have to alight several times throughout the rattling train journey as my stomach appeared to be suffering from acute alcohol poisoning. And in those terrible nauseous moments spent doubled over on the train platform, I vowed for the

---

104 Prior to 1958, young upper-class English girls were formally presented to the Queen to symbolically mark their debut into aristocratic society. This was followed by a string of formal balls and social events (including Royal Ascot and Henley Royal Regatta) known as "The Season."

billionth time to boycott white wine for the rest of my life. And, unlike those other times, this time I really meant it.)

My phone buzzed with a text message from Rupert: "JEZZA— WAS IT ME OR WAS UR LIPSTICK SMUDGED WHEN U LEFT? RX"

I sighed and held my aching head. Whenever I started to think that I might be in danger of turning into a real grown-up adult, I always proved myself spectacularly wrong.[105]

---

105 By the way, several months later, George W. made his first ever trip to England—which included an official State Visit to Buckingham Palace. Needless to say, I never saw nor heard from Nick ever again.

Twenty-six

"When you hate what is happening, something marvelous is happening. Something is changing."

—BARBARA DE ANGELIS

The splendid fluted ballroom with its Italian Renaissance stylings bustles with a flurry of pastel satin and gloved elbows. Glittering girls in swirling floor-length dresses dance fox-trots with debonair gentlemen wearing silk tailcoats and white bow ties. Beneath the soaring gilded ceiling and crystal chandeliers, the air is filled with the glamorous fission of soft laughter, warm candlelight, and sparkling tiaras.

Our eyes meet and the orchestra swells.

Standing on the landing of the Grand Staircase, he breaks into a wide smile. I smile back.

"There you are!" I mouth playfully through the buzz of the party. In his black evening clothes, he takes my breath away.

Looking at me with tender eyes, he slowly descends the curving marble steps until he is by my side. Confident in his intimacy, he kisses me gently on the lips and my hand slips effortlessly into his.

Together we walk into the palace garden, the golden brown stone glowing in the fiery light of the flaring torches. The powdered, liveried footmen bob graciously as we pass. We linger a moment, laughing quietly in the dawn air before he leads me swiftly through the portico, out of the gates, and into the hushed blue light of the winding London streets.

"We can't stay out all night!" I laugh.

But he just pulls me into his arms and says mischievously, "Why not?"

And then my alarm went off.

⟶

Normally I hate the mornings—but this one was different. I was practically whistling with joy as I floated cheerily through my working day.

Considering the extent of my passion I know it's hard to believe, but other than childhood nightmares about how my parents might behave at a royal wedding—I had yet to have a single dream about Peter Phillips. But last night's dream had been the most vivid I'd ever experienced in my entire sleeping life.

I could still recall every detail as if it had happened minutes ago. I could still hear the orchestra violins, I could still see the sun rising slowly above the palace, and I could still feel Peter's warm hand wrapped firmly around my own. Every sensation had been incredibly, astonishingly, arm-tinglingly real. And I wanted to hold onto their memory with all of my soul.

By the time my lunch break arrived, everything was clear.

There had been a crucial new development on the royal scene and once again, I had the eternally wondrous *Hello* magazine to thank. Once again, it had become my benevolent personal messenger, a glossy envoy from the heavens—this time alerting me to the glorious words I'd waited years to see.

The small article was tucked away in the back pages, but still, there it was in black and white:

Peter Phillips Splits with Girlfriend
Peter Phillips, Princess Anne's twenty-four-year-old son, has

split up with his American girlfriend of three years. The couple,
who lived at Peter's three-bedroom flat in North London, met
at a three-day equestrian event. No reason has been given for
the breakup.

I could have cried with happiness. (See? I *knew* he'd see sense
in the end! I *knew* everything was going to be okay!) With life-
shattering news like this taking place, it's no wonder I dreamed
about him. In those slumbering moments, Peter and I had something magical. And that magic was seeping into real life.

～

Max called from New York to wish me a happy birthday.

"So how are things going with the London love life?" he asked.
"No, wait, don't answer that. Let me guess. You're dating some pale
skinny Brit named Nigel. That, or some inbred prince with terrible
teeth and no chin named something ridiculous like Pip."

I laughed. "Actually, I had a really amazing dream last
week."

I told him all about the palace ball I had attended with Peter
Phillips and how wonderful it had been.

Max paused before saying anything. "Well, Jerramy . . . I'm
glad to hear things are going so well for the two of you . . . but
you *are* losing your mind, you know that, don't you?"

～

The guy who quietly occupied the desk next to mine was named
Conrad. With his sturdy thighs, his stocky build, and his weekly,
positively gruesome rugby injuries[106]—Conrad was somewhat
out of place in the fluffy publishing world and pretty much kept
to himself.

---

106 Seriously, his constant black eyes and broken bones reminded me of the movie *Fight Club*.

But it was later that week, as I was gleefully discussing the miraculous *Hello* article with one of my gossip-loving female coworkers, when I heard Conrad grunt something under his breath.

"Do you have something you'd like to add?" I asked playfully.

"I saw Peter Phillips this weekend," he mumbled.

I swiveled around in my chair and stared at him in shock, *"What?"*

Conrad shrugged. "I was drinking at a pub in Wandsworth this weekend and I saw him there with his mates." He said it as if it were the most boring thing in the whole world.

Wandsworth was less than ten minutes away from where I lived! My heart was pounding so hard I could scarcely hear myself think. (See what I mean about magic seeping into real life?)

"Which pub?" I breathed.

"The Ship."

"And you saw him this past weekend?"

"Yup."

"But Conrad! Today is Thursday! How long were you going to wait before telling me this?" I tried to feign anger but for the life of me, I couldn't stop smiling. "You *know* how much I like Peter! He's my screensaver, for godsake!"

Conrad looked at my computer monitor and chuckled. "Sorry. I guess I just forgot to mention it."

Of course, I forgave Conrad instantly and left him to nurse the latest egg-sized bump on his forehead. But still, no one could argue that the trajectory of my royal destiny seemed to be speeding up at quite a dizzying pace. First in my dreams, and now in my neighborhood? Soon he would be in my arms.

⁓

Remember all that uncertainty about my work permit? Well, for my own sanity I had shoved the entire topic to the back of my mind and carried on with my London life as if everything was absolutely fine—as if my very existence in the country that I loved wasn't wholly dependent on some silly paperwork that may or may not be approved. But that Friday morning, my boss sat me down and the look on his face told me everything I needed to know.

He said that word from the Home Office was expected some time next week, and based on what the company's immigration lawyers were telling him, I should expect the worst. Unless I could financially support myself without working, I must be prepared to leave England within the next ten days. Still, I was not to forget that I was a fantastic employee and it would be a terrible loss to them all.

How tremendously comforting.

Practically choking with emotion, I could barely breathe as I left the office that night. How could this be happening to me? How could this be happening to me *again*? Right when things were going so well? Peter Phillips was finally, officially single (not to mention hanging out in my neighborhood)—yet I had to leave England in the next ten days because of *another* stupid immigration rule? Just as I was getting so close to them, I had to walk away and leave my dreams behind? Just because of the place I had been *born*? It took all my strength not to sob hysterically the whole train ride home. What on earth was I going to do?

Ninety minutes later, I walked into the flat, visibly distraught and close to tears. George, Oliver, and Sophie were gathered in the sitting room and Sophie didn't look very happy.

"Christ," said Sophie when she saw the gloom on my face, "don't tell me Duncan called to tell you personally."

"What do you mean?" I asked.

She looked confused. "You mean you don't know about the letter?"

"What letter?" What was she talking about? And why were the boys behaving so strangely?

Sophie handed me a thick cream envelope. Inside was a type-written letter on Duncan's personal stationery, as well as a second letter from his solicitor. I scanned them quickly, then fell onto the sofa in disbelief.

According to the two very courteous letters, my rental contract expired next week and categorically was not going to be renewed. (Duncan's cited reasons for my eviction included, among others, an inappropriate obsession with fire safety.)

I had to move out by the end of the week.

"Am I the only one being kicked out?" I asked, trying not to cry.

"No," Sophie said curtly. "I'm also being forced to leave. But not surprisingly, the boys' contracts have been extended for the rest of year."

"It's a real shame," said George, solemnly shaking his head. "You know how much Oliver and I detest interviewing prospective flatmates. We'll probably have to speak to hundreds of new girls in order to fill your rooms."

"How horrible for you," spat Sophie.

It was clear to both of us that the boys couldn't care less about Duncan's petty property games and as they left the flat to embark on their usual Friday night of clubbing and strip joints, we were left to commiserate in private.

"What are you going to do?" I asked Sophie. "Do you think we can find a place to move into together with such short notice?"

"Well," she answered quietly, "I'd never admit this to Duncan, but for me this surprise eviction is really a blessing in disguise. For a while I've been thinking about moving back in with my parents so I can save money for a down payment. . . ."

"You mean you're moving out of London?" I asked incredulously.

Sophie nodded. "The commute to the office will be hell, but I think it's something that I have to do before it's too late. If I wait any longer before buying a flat, I will be priced out completely. . . . *Poor you, though!* I don't envy your search for a new set of lunatics to live with."

⌒

I cried myself into a fitful sleep that night. I tossed and turned as my dreams were filled with a blizzard of rejected work permits, eviction papers, and student loan bills. They piled up higher and higher around me until I was trapped beneath their weight. And as I lay there, helpless and suffocating and unable to escape, evil voices chanted incessantly around me: *"We told you so. We told you so."*

At dawn, I woke with a start. It was no use—I was a basket case and far too upset to sleep. I got dressed quietly, crept out of the house, and bought a newspaper. Then I groggily sat in a coffee shop with my mobile and made my first appointment to view a studio flat that very morning. I couldn't face living with more insane strangers; I had to find a place I could afford on my own. And this was the first studio I'd found in my price range that was available next week.

A fat, unshaven man wearing a tatty undershirt opened the door, gruffly introduced himself as the landlord, and then half-heartedly showed me around the microscopic one-room apartment. But it was hardly necessary; the place was so tiny I could see it all without turning my head: There were no windows; the stained and yellowing carpet was covered in thick layers of dust and looked like it had never been vacuumed in its life; the miniature "kitchenette" (which consisted of a fridge and stove the size of a shoebox) was encased in decades of black grease; and I don't even want to know the state of the flimsy single mattress that was lofted directly above the dirty kitchen sink. I never thought I'd say it, but the bomb shelter looked like a palace compared to this place.

"Where's the loo?" I asked.

The creepy old man dramatically opened a narrow door to reveal a space the size of a broom cupboard. I couldn't believe my eyes. It was like some kind of bizarre nautical wet room you'd find in a third-world youth hostel. The toilet was actually *in* the shower and the cupboard itself *was* the shower. And needless to say, it was covered, floor to ceiling, with dried urine and rusty water stains.

"Are you looking for a two-year contract or just a year?" the landlord asked, eyeing me lecherously.

Right then, the reality of my situation hit me like a ten-ton truck. A year? I didn't even know if I was going to be around for more than a few days! I felt dizzy and sick. And for a terrible moment I thought I was going to pass out.

"I'm sorry," I said quickly. "This isn't for me."

I bolted out of that filthy flat and in a blur of tears, I headed toward the riverbank. It was high tide and the shimmering, tree-lined Thames looked tragically beautiful. I crossed the footbridge, found an empty bench, and sat down.

And then—I completely fell apart.

I may have been in the country of my heart's desire, but I could no longer function normally. And in the moments that followed, I proceeded to have what many would call a nervous breakdown.

Hot tears tumbled down my cheeks as I silently screamed at the sky. For the love of God, how many times did I have to go through the same heartaches? How many work permits did I have to beg for? How many weird places did I have to live in? How many deranged flatmates did I have to live with? How many pointless kisses, empty promises, and bastardly boys did I have to endure? And how many trillions of dollars in debt did I have to rack up for the pleasure?

I tried to wipe away my runny mascara but it was no use.

Was this how the universe rewarded those who followed their dreams? God, how I envied people without dreams! How I envied their unlimited choices! Their freedom to do whatever they liked without betraying their hearts.

I thought of my childhood friend Chloe. I had seen her briefly last Christmas and she lived in a gorgeous, sparkling clean, three-bedroom American house with a gigantic backyard and a dog. She had a job that she loved and paid her well, she had a handsome husband who adored her, and the cutest baby son you've ever seen. Chloe wasn't stupid like me. She wasn't crazy. *She* didn't sacrifice her whole life to move across the world and chase after some boy she cut out of a magazine!

Chloe knew better. She had stayed in the real world. And because of that, she was a million times happier than I'd ever be. My God, who was *I* to lecture about dreams? Out of the two of us, *Chloe* was the one fulfilling her dreams.

My tears were unstoppable now.

Why was my heart so cruel? Why did it demand so much of me? Why wasn't I allowed to have normal dreams and normal ambitions like everyone else? Why wasn't I allowed to be happy in my own country? Why wasn't I allowed to fall in love with nice, normal American guys?

Just look at what following this stupid heart of mine has brought me. Just look at how my blind obedience has been repaid! Right then and there, I methodically forced myself to go over the facts: I was nearly two hundred thousand dollars in debt and yet I couldn't even afford third-world living conditions. In ten days, I would be jobless and unable to legally work without becoming lawfully bound to a homosexual. I had a résumé that most American companies would laugh at. I was an ocean away from my closest friends and an ocean away from my family. I was boyfriend-less, most definitely prince-less, and now I was homeless.

Maybe I should call up my mom and admit that a homeless man was actually an ideal match for me! Maybe I should call her up and congratulate her on knowing me so well!

I was nearly hysterical now. The afternoon sunshine swirled madly around me. The river sparkled, the rowers rowed by, and the herons watched me intently—but the tears kept on coming.

I thought back to the night I had wept endlessly in front of Buckingham Palace and I laughed bitterly. Yet again it had come to this: sitting in a public park and bawling my eyes out. Exactly like last year. Who was I kidding? Nothing had changed since that night. How many more years could I go on like this? Fooling myself that everything was just fine? How much longer could I go on convincing myself that all of this heartache was simply part of my so-called destiny? Deluding myself that I lived in some kind of Disney fairytale and that I would live happily ever after if only I persevered for that little bit longer?

My whole life people have told me that I was crazy—and I always ignored them. But you know what? Maybe they were right. Maybe I *was* crazy. Maybe the real world truly was as good as it gets. Maybe it was time to give up on my stupid English obsession and move back to America. Maybe it was time to give up my ridiculous royal dream and become a nice, drama-free housewife in some nice, drama-free place like Omaha.

Passersby glanced at my swollen red eyes and tear-stained cheeks—and then looked away. I didn't blame them. There was nothing new to see. I was just another maniacal crazy person sitting on another park bench. I wasn't special. London was full of people like me.

Twenty-seven

"How long 'til my soul gets it right?"

—INDIGO GIRLS

*B*ecause Adam was one of England's youngest and fastest rising political stars, he had been invited to attend the Queen's annual Garden Party. I nearly kissed him when he told me.

Held every summer on the grounds of Buckingham Palace, these elite social events were infamous. Just imagine a glorious afternoon filled with military bands, massive tea tents, and hundreds of specially chosen guests (wearing morning suits and cravats, military uniforms, or pretty hats and day dresses) milling around the enormous Palace lawn hoping to be spoken to by Her Majesty.

I'd waited years for someone I knew to invite me along as their guest! And with Adam's bottomless luck and infallible charm, he was bound to be selected by the Queen for a personal chat! At long last, I was going to be introduced to Peter's grandmother! Finally!

Then Adam confessed that he was taking his mum to the party instead of me.

I was still quite angry at this treacherous snub, but that night (approximately six hours post-nervous-breakdown) I called him up anyway. I desperately needed someone's shoulder to cry on. (Even if this someone refused to introduce me to Elizabeth II.)

Curled up in the bedroom that I was soon to be evicted from, I sobbed to Adam over the phone, filling him in on the tragic turn my life had taken at the hands of Duncan and the Home Office.

Adam listened patiently until I was finished.

"It's so weird," he said sympathetically. "I feel like you experience the same problems over and over again."

"I know," I whimpered, still sniffling.

"Jerramy, maybe you should look at all these events as some kind of sign."

"Sign pointing to what?"

Adam proceeded with caution. "Jerramy, don't kill me for saying this, but maybe all of this means you're supposed to go back to the U.S. for a while. Perhaps something else, a new job for example, will bring you back to England."

My tears turned to anger. "Adam! How can you say such a thing! You of all people know the power of dreams! How can you possibly suggest that I surrender?"

"Jerramy," Adam said gently, "don't be cross with me. I just don't know what else to say. I feel awful for you, really. But I don't have the answers. Relying on me to produce a magical solution to all of this is about as useful as relying on your horoscope."

"That's not a bad idea," I said quietly.

"What?"

"My horoscope." For the first time, I saw a glimmer of hope. "Adam, you're a genius! That's just what I need! Some kind of spiritual guidance!"

"*Jerramy*," Adam said sternly, "we've talked about this before. You know how I feel about those crazy clairvoyants. How can you pretend for a single second that you're not in charge of your own destiny?"

"Well, Adam, as my bank manager told me only last week—it's quite clear that I'm no longer in the driver's seat."

Adam laughed. "Did he really say that to you?"

"Yes! He also took away my checkbook and threatened to cut my debit card into eight pieces if I didn't start conforming to some sort of completely impractical budget."

"Christ! I thought mine was bad when she asked if I wanted to move in with her to save money on rent. Talk about sexual harassment."

"Adam, we are getting off the subject."

He sighed. "Jerramy, the answer is no. I don't know any tarot card readers that I can recommend to sort out your life."

"What about that guy Dimitri you were dating? He loved that paranormal stuff! Can you ask him if he knows anyone reputable I can go see? *Please?* You don't want me to end up calling some random psychic in the back of a magazine, do you?"

Adam was quiet. "Okay," he said finally. "I'll give Dimitri a ring."

⌒

A few hours later, Adam called me back and grudgingly recited the contact details of an elderly woman in east London named Estella.

I called her immediately.

"Most clients book three months in advance," she said sweetly, "but as luck would have it, I've just had a cancellation. Can you come to see me tomorrow at 3 P.M.?"

"Yes," I exclaimed, "that would be perfect."

"And I assume you know that I charge forty pounds per sixty-minute session?"

I hesitated. I barely had that amount to get me through to (quite possibly my last ever) payday.

Estella sensed my reservations. "If you are having financial difficulties," she said kindly, "I'm happy to take whatever you can afford to pay me tomorrow—and you can give me the rest when you have it."

I gratefully agreed to her offer.

"And one last thing," she continued. "I'm not a fortune teller. I'm a channeler. The master that speaks through me can offer you spiritual counseling, but please keep in mind that he can't predict your future."

"That's not a problem," I told her. I have to say that I found Estella's specific psychic skill set to be somewhat irrelevant. Let's face it: With my world crashing down around me on almost every level, I could hardly afford to be choosy when it came to divine guidance.

And so the very next day I boarded an eastbound train to her house. At least my emergency spiritual outing gave me something to do. It was either that or spend another day sobbing on a park bench.

—

Estella's modest house was located in one of the grittier London suburbs. She answered the door wearing a bright raspberry pink sweater and I saw that her nails were neatly painted in exactly the same shade. She had white hair, rosy cheeks, and a kind twinkle in her eye that instantly put me at ease. Still, I was careful not to reveal anything about myself.

She led me through her back garden and into a little shed that her husband had built for her. ("He doesn't like to be disturbed by my work," she explained.) The shed was warm and bright and filled with comfy pink chairs and dozens of pink candles. Needlepoint pictures of Jesus and the Star of David covered the walls. It was just like a room you might find in your religious grandmother's house. A bit cutesy—but not spooky in the slightest.

While Estella tottered around the shed preparing her things, she babbled cheerfully to me about her husband. "They were out of grapefruit juice at the local shop this morning. It's Simon's favorite, you see, so I walked all the way to the large supermarket to buy it for him."

I sat down in a pink overstuffed chair and she sat down in one across from me. Until then, I'd only ever had my fortune told at fancy London nightclubs by women dressed as gypsies who sat in elaborate Moorish tents, looked intently at my palm for a few seconds, and then told me something barely discernible through the blaring house music. That said, I wasn't entirely clear as to what a channeling session actually involved so I politely asked Estella to explain to me what I might expect.

"I have been channeling the spirit of Joseph of Arimathea for the last thirty years," Estella replied. (I had no idea who Joseph of Arimathea was—but I made a mental note to look it up when I got back home.[107])

"When I am channeling," she continued, "I am aware of the fact that I am speaking, but I can't actually make out what is being said—it kind of sounds like background radio noise to me—so everything discussed during the session is strictly between you and the master."

I nodded as if I had the faintest clue what she was talking about.

"Some people become frightened because the sound of my

---

107 My Google research later revealed that Joseph of Arimathea was a disciple of Jesus. According to apocryphal legend, he was also the Virgin Mary's paternal uncle and (most interestingly!) a supposed ancestor of many British monarchs.

voice changes and so do some of my movements. But I guess that's understandable," she smiled. "After all, it is a man taking over my body."

It was around this time that I started to freak out. I mean, seriously, what kind of creepy thing had I gotten myself into? A man taking over her body? Was this going to be like *The Exorcist* or something? My stomach began to knot. I was suddenly really nervous. And really quite genuinely frightened.

"Make sure you interrupt him a few minutes before the hour is up," Estella told me, "otherwise he will go on talking all day."

I nodded again, too petrified to speak.

She pressed play on her small tape recorder (the whole session was being recorded and yes, I still have the tape), and then, cradling a large white crystal in her hands, Estella closed her eyes and took a few deep breaths. For the next hour, her eyes stayed closed. She did not blink *once*. And to be honest, I found this enormously comforting, because I don't think I could have handled another soul peering out at me through her body.

Her breathing slowed tremendously and almost a full minute of silence passed before Estella's elderly body softly jolted in her chair, and then spoke: "Shalom, my child."

And in that unearthly moment, all my fears subsided.

⌒

Those first three words were deep and resonant and steeped with an overpowering love. All at once, the small wooden shed was bursting with a new energy—strong, calming, and unbelievably wise. And as it surrounded me, and as it humbled me, I knew—in my heart, in my head, and in my gut—that whatever was happening was real. And that it was going to be *nothing* like *The Exorcist*.

Estella's voice *did* change, but it wasn't scary or demonic or fake. And I know this sounds crazy, but the sound of it was so echoey and so ethereal, that it was almost like it was coming from some other plane. Or some other astral dimension. I don't know how else to describe it.

But even more noticeable than her slowed breathing and ghostlike voice was the drastic change in Estella's lexicon—she now spoke in a curiously succinct, almost poetic manner. And her subtle movements had become so unmistakably masculine that for the entire duration of our session, I *completely* forgot that there was a petite woman sitting in front of me rather than an extremely wise and kind-hearted old man.

"I do not see your fleshly self," Joseph began, "only your aura. And it is a deep indigo blue. The color of intellect and intuition."

That's because I'm an Indigo Child, I thought to myself. Wouldn't my mom be happy to know that someone else besides her realized this about me!

I felt so comfortable in Joseph's presence that I wanted to jump right in and tell him my whole harrowing story—my inexplicable love for England, my quest to find Peter, my work permit, my eviction, and how I had to leave the U.K. in less than ten days and what on earth I was meant to do about it all. But a small part of me was still wary of this psychic phenomenon and didn't want to give too much away. So I decided to keep my questions as vague as possible at first.

"Can you tell me about soulmates?" I ventured shyly. "I mean, do they actually exist? And will I ever get to meet mine?"

Joseph answered patiently, his words deliberate and unrehearsed. "Yes, my child. They do exist. But you do not meet these souls in every lifetime. You must remember that there are other kinds of love that can be just as fulfilling. You are so young, so desperate to rush into love, so desperate to find, as you put it, your soulmate. Do not forget that it can take several lifetimes to find this soulmate. Learn from all relationships, my child. There are very specific lessons to be learned from every individual you encounter. And you will continue to encounter the same lesson in different forms until it is learned."

Hmm. I sensed some hidden truths in there but it wasn't exactly what I was hoping to hear.

"Then what about my career?" I asked, already cringing at the banality of my question. "Can you tell me where I'm headed on that front? Is there a specific job I should be pursuing?"

"I cannot make a judgment on that, my child," Joseph replied. "You have free will. You control what you will do next."

I have to say that I was getting ever so slightly impatient with this wise spiritual master. What was with these ambiguous answers? They were practically as vague as my questions! I sat silent for a moment, trying to think of something to say that might bring a more detailed response.

"All souls are like genetic codes," Joseph started telling me, his powerful voice filling the room. "Your character and your nature stays constant and carries over into all of your lives."

I was still confused. Was this information supposed to help me?

Joseph continued talking: "You are an advanced soul, my child. You have had many, many lives in the physical state. But there is one in particular that is bothering you in this life. I have access to your Akashic Record[108] so I can tell you about it if you would like."

I perked up instantly.

"I would like that very much," I said.

Joseph nodded and continued. "Despite the fact that your soul chose to be born elsewhere, you have had a longing since birth to return to Britain. Yet you are confused as to why you

---

108 The Akashic Record is a theosophical term referring to a type of universal filing system that records the entire history of every soul since the dawn of creation. Mentions of these Akashic Records can be found throughout the Old and New Testaments and it is said to be traceable at least as far back as the Assyrians, the Phoenicians, and the Babylonians.

are here. And feel deeply unfulfilled for reasons you do not understand."

I felt like the air had been knocked out of me. And confronted with such startling accuracy, my eyes filled with tears.

I reached for a pink tissue from the box beside me and proceeded to listen in excited awe as the story of my past life was recounted to me in one continuous stream of thought. There were no pauses, no ums, and no ers; nor was there the slightest trace of storytelling bravado. Events were simply recited to me, as if they were truly nothing more than a matter of complete fact.

"The past life that is affecting you now did take place in Britain. You lived as a female, five hundred years ago. You were born under the reign of Henry VIII and died soon after Elizabeth I came into power. Queen Mary reigned in the interim after the young king[109] died and you were unusual in that you lived through four reigning monarchs. Your family were considered nobility and were highly respected members of the royal court. . . ."

My entire body was covered with goosebumps. Strange, disjointed visions flashed before my eyes and tears trickled quietly down my face.

"You were the eldest daughter, just as you are now. Your parents were nonconformists, just as they are now . . ."

I couldn't believe what I was hearing. How could this man, this *being*, know so much about me? My hands were trembling so hard I had to clasp them tightly in my lap to keep them still.

"Your parents were Protestant, but under the strict Catholic reign this was forbidden and therefore they were forced to practice their faith in the privacy of your family home. As a young girl, you watched your parents' constant struggle with hypocrisy

---

109 King Edward VI died when he was only sixteen years old. He had reigned since the age of nine.

for the sake of keeping their elite position in court. Although you were unreligious yourself, you were unusually academic for a woman of those times, and very much aware that being a woman held you back. Still, you read all you could on religion, politics, and history and by the time you reached your twentieth year you had become fascinated with Eastern religions. During this time, Britain was just beginning to navigate the spice routes of India. Your father was a merchant trader and knowing you were unhappy in the stifling environment of court life, he arranged for you to travel to India where you could stay with a wealthy family and continue your studies at your leisure."

My heart was pounding and my mind was spinning. So many uncanny parallels! My political science degrees, my recent trip to India . . . I really wished that my parents could have been in the room to hear all of this with me. They always suspected a past life was the reason for my odd behavior—they would be so pleased to see their long-held theory being validated, and so proud of me for seeking it out on my own accord.

Joseph's ancient, raspy voice continued to stream from Estella's mouth and I remained completely transfixed.

"You met a young Indian man who you liked and eventually convinced him to return to England with you. Upon your return, you were horrified at the racism he encountered despite his wealth and position. Furthermore you were unmarried, and both were the cause of much gossip. Your family convinced you to marry, to lessen the scandal. Finally, Queen Mary, who had been one of the most judgmental about your choice of husband, asked to be introduced to him. She was instantly charmed by his intelligence and his worldliness and took a liking to him herself. At that time, the monarch could take anyone they liked as a lover. To refuse meant banishment to the Tower and quite often death . . ."

I have to admit that I was sort of tempted to laugh at this

point. Was I supposed to believe that five hundred years ago my husband had an affair with chubby Queen Mary? Well, men weren't exactly universally known for their fidelity so I guess it was possible. Still, it was a pretty surreal turn of events.

But Joseph's steady narrative didn't stop for my musings and the story continued. "You were terribly upset by this and the whole affair was again causing new court gossip and jeopardizing your family name. But the Queen quickly grew tired of your husband. They had a falling out and he fled to India to escape her wrath, leaving you with no forwarding address. You gave up on the idea of love entirely and your parents begrudgingly took you into their home once again."

My heart twinged painfully with recognition. How many times (and in how many different centuries?) was I going to be abandoned by guys and left without a forwarding address? Was I simply not destined for love in any lifetime? It was all too familiar and all too emotional and new tears started sliding down my cheeks.

"Then," said Joseph evenly, "another man came into your life. The love and connection you felt was like a blinding flash of light. He was your soulmate."

The hairs on my arms stood on end. Still quietly sniffling, I leaned forward in my seat.

"He was an Englishman and had spent the last few years in China working as a Catholic missionary. The first conversation you had with him was comparing how upper-class women were treated in China compared to upper-class women in India and Britain. You continued to be fascinated by the oppression of women everywhere despite their position. You fell deeply in love with him. However, you were still a married woman. Annulments were unheard of and divorce meant certain death. The only way you could remarry was if your husband died and you had no way of knowing if this had happened. So your love for each other had to remain hidden. As a man of faith, he would allow nothing more than friendship despite his unbearable love for you. It was torture for you both. Finally, he went back to China and left you longing for him until your death. It is that same soul that has drawn you to Britain in this lifetime. And it is that soul you have desperately been looking for. It is an agreement that is unfulfilled and when you finally come together, even if only for a few minutes, the circle will be complete. When this meeting takes place you will no longer feel such longing and such unrest. You will be at peace."

I sat there in my pink chair, wiping away the tears and trying to catch my breath. Finally, my bizarre longings had meaning. Finally, all of my weird royal memories had context. Finally, my aching desire to be in England made some kind of sense! But more than anything, I could finally begin to understand what my heart had been trying so long to tell me. And all at once, the tears of sorrow that flowed from my exhausted eyes turned to tears of joy.

"It is very important, my child, that you do not spend all of this life focused on unfinished business from the life I have just described. You have many lessons to learn in this life as well, and you often get the two confused."

I didn't realize it at the time, but that last statement was possibly the most powerful piece of advice anyone has ever given me.

⤳

I looked at the small pink clock on the table.

"I only have five minutes left," I told Joseph.

"Do you have any last questions, my child?" he asked kindly.

"Can you tell me when I will meet this other soul? Or about

any other past lives?" Now that the floodgates to my metaphysical psyche had been opened, I wanted to know more.

"I cannot," Joseph replied. "Only what is important is revealed to you. Only what concerns you in this life."

I nodded in acquiescence. I wanted to ask something else, but my mind was still reeling from all that I'd heard and I was so exhausted and emotionally drained that I couldn't really think straight—much less think of another question that made sense. Then suddenly one just popped into my head out of nowhere.

"If you could tell our current world leaders one thing, what would it be?" I asked.

Joseph smiled. "I have not been asked that question in years. It is refreshing for me. I would tell them not to be frightened of mixing religions. They are all the same religion. Do not be frightened of mixing the races. Everyone is born in the same way. I would tell them that freedom and tolerance are important beyond all else."

I nodded in agreement. Our current world leaders could certainly do with a crash course in Joseph's wisdom.

"I have enjoyed our talk, my child. You have a long life ahead of you and it will be one of achievement. Please return again. I will remember you. Even fifty years from now, I will remember you. Shalom."

Another minute passed in tense silence. Estella took a few deep breaths and then slowly opened her eyes as if awaking from a deep sleep. My lap was filled with crumpled pink tissues.

"He has that effect on people," she smiled. "That's why I always put a box right next to the chair. Now, would you like to see my flower garden before you leave? The crocuses are coming up quite nicely."

As she showed me her collection of spring bulbs, I marveled at the gulf between Estella's conscious mind and the profound, timeless wisdom I had just witnessed in the shed. I have to say that if channeling Joseph was just an act, it was quite the skilled performance. For one, it was unbelievably consistent. For two, the historical knowledge alone was impressive. And even if that entire hour spent with her eyes closed was merely a clever piece of theater, Estella was still an amazing reader of people—the specifics of that story would not have made sense for anyone in the world but me.

～

What other people may think happened that day is of little consequence. What counts is how *I* felt. And all I know is that for the first time in a long while, I no longer felt crazy. I now knew why seeing ancient royal objects affected me so deeply; I now knew that my insistence on finding Peter Phillips was so much more than a madcap obsession; and I now knew that when I was two years old and told my hippie mother that she wasn't "the woman who dresses me"—I meant it.

Twenty-eight

"The meeting of two personalities is like the contact of two chemical substances; if there is any reaction, both are transformed."

—CARL JUNG

Learning that my royal obsession wasn't entirely Disney's fault certainly had a calming effect. I mean, for a girl who'd had a nervous breakdown on a park bench less than two days ago, when I walked into the office on Monday morning, I have to say that I was remarkably composed.

But that lasted approximately twenty-five seconds because my boss pulled me aside the minute I walked in the door.

"Sorry to bring this up so early in the morning, Jerramy," he said, "but a courier just arrived with an envelope for you. I think it's from the Home Office."

Oh God. Not now. Not today.

Not when I'd only just discovered that my soul was in England for a reason. And needed to *stay* in England for reasons those lackeys at the Home Office couldn't begin to comprehend!

My throat began to tighten and I hoped I'd be able to hold it together for just a few minutes longer so my boss wouldn't see me cry. My emotions were all over the place these days—and based on my track record, I knew that tears could spill at any second.

He held out the envelope and with superhuman strength, I willed my hands to take it from him.

"Aren't you going to open it?" he asked.

I was too upset to answer. Too upset even to look at him.

"Jerramy, I know it's probably not the news we want to hear— but I'm away for the rest of the week, and I'd like to know what the final verdict on all this is."

I stared at the flat package in my trembling hands.

I knew he was just doing his job and trying to manage my expectations, but did he have to be so cavalier about everything? Didn't he realize the root of my very happiness was on the line? I didn't want to open it in front of him, but I had to. If he wanted to risk a gush of tears, so be it.

I said a silent prayer to whatever entity was crazy enough to still be listening to me, took a deep breath, and ripped it open. With sweaty palms and a woozy stomach, I pulled out the letter and forced myself to look at it.

> *Dear Miss Fine . . . The Home Office is pleased*
> *to inform you . . . that your application has been ap-*
> *proved . . . and your Leave to Remain has been granted . . .*

The rest of the text blurred before my eyes.

Oh my God! I've been approved!

Then I said it out loud. "Oh my God! I've been approved!"

I looked up at my boss with shocked delight. I wasn't going to be deported! I could *stay* in England! My soul could *stay* in England! I wanted to hug everyone in sight and shout my new legal status from the office rooftop. But instead I just stood there with a dazed grin on my face. Once again, the gods had intervened on my behalf. And

I was so happy and so grateful and so relieved, that in the end, my poor boss still had to witness quite a large gush of tears.

⟿

Later that afternoon, I was still reeling from the jubilant news when the phone rang. It was Tigger (aka Arabella, aka the one whose father was on *The Times* Rich List).

"Hi, sweetie," she cooed in her hyper blueblood voice. "I know this is a bit unexpected, but you see, my silly sister decided only yesterday that she is going to spend the rest of her life in Sydney— leaving me with the *arduous* task of looking after her empty room. Since Daddy is making me rent out *all four* London bedrooms and I simply can't face the *vile* idea of living with strangers, you instantly came to mind. You're not by chance looking for anywhere to live at the moment, are you?"

"Well, actually I am," I replied in amazement.

"Oh, Jez, darling—you're an absolute *star*! I promise to make the rent whatever you can afford. Do pop round this evening and I'll show you your new room!"

I hung up the phone, and for the second time that day, sat in a state of blissful shock. I just couldn't believe it. In a space of five hours, I had learned that I no longer had to live in fear of exile *and* that I no longer had to live in Duncan's stupid flat!

I called Adam immediately and quickly related how suddenly, and quite miraculously, my life had turned on a dime.

"Don't you mean a shiny sixpence?" he asked.

It's funny. When you spend all your time desperately hoping that something will happen, you lose sight of the fact that something *is* happening. And has been happening all along.

⟿

That evening, when my parents called (probably to make sure I hadn't checked into a mental institution), I told them the wonderful news.

"Well, I have some good news myself," my dad said when I was finished. "I've just been ordained as a minister."

Allow me to point out that my dad is agnostic at best, and with his peace-loving ways he has always refused to acknowledge organized (and therefore war-mongering) religion of any kind.

"What kind of minister?" I asked suspiciously.

"A cannabis minister!" he exclaimed happily.[110]

"*Dad!* That's the kind of good news that's going to get me deported! Didn't I just tell you how I've finally been allowed to stay here?"

He chuckled. "Freedom of religion, honey. Freedom of religion."

And quite frankly, at that moment I couldn't have been happier to live in a country where religion was in the hands of Her Majesty the Queen.[111]

〜

Even though I was positively beaming with contentment, the following day was pretty much just like any other day in the office. Like always, I poured myself a cup of mediocre British coffee, sat down at my desk, and commenced my usual routine of scanning the morning papers. I was supposed to be looking for press coverage relevant to the company, but I (ever the multitasker) also utilized this daily assignment to look out for any news about the Royal family that might be relevant to me.

Just as I was finishing up and making my way through the last of the tedious sports sections, my eyes were drawn to a small blurb at the bottom of the events calendar:

---

110 http://www.thc-ministry.org. I wish I were joking.

111 Queen Elizabeth II, like all British sovereigns, is "Defender of the Faith and Supreme Governor of the Church of England." (But she also formally promotes tolerance and understanding of all other faiths and religions.)

May 28: Professional Rugby Players' Awards 2002
Peter Phillips, Jason Robinson, Johnny Wilkinson, Kieran
Bracken, Matt Dawson (Royal and England Rugby squad,
respectively) attend annual ceremony. Lord's Cricket Ground,
St. John's Wood, 7:30 P.M. Media Reception, 5:45–7:30 P.M.
Invite only.

I figured I was hallucinating so I read it again.

And again and again.

It couldn't be.

No one, *no one*, could have this much good luck in one week.

I read those few sentences over and over. I checked, and double-checked, and triple-checked my Outlook calendar. But there was no mistake: Conrad and I were scheduled to attend that very same media reception. And the 28th of May was *tomorrow.*

But before I allowed myself to completely hyperventilate, I picked up the phone and called the awards organizers.

"Hi," I said casually, "I'm just checking to see if Peter Phillips will be appearing at the awards dinner only, or if he will be at the media reception as well."

"Oh, Peter will be around all evening tomorrow," the man replied cheerily, "at the dinner *and* at the reception."

I nearly fell out of my chair.

⁓

It is not an exaggeration to say that I didn't sleep all night.

Not one wink. I just lay there, frantic with nerves, staring into the darkness.

After twenty years (and possibly twenty lifetimes) of searching, I was finally going to meet the boy I found in that library book. I was finally going to meet the boy I had once Scotch-taped to my wall. I was finally going to meet the boy (quite literally) of my dreams. How was I going to approach him? What was I going to say? How on earth was I going to cope? Despite my seemingly endless preparation, it began to dawn on me that at the end of the day, I was absolutely clueless. My destiny was less than twenty-four hours away, my fantasy was on the very brink of fulfillment, and I had no idea (*no idea!*) how I was going to get through it.

My one and only consolation was that Conrad would be there with me. At least he could catch me if (or more likely *when*) I fainted.

I was still awake and staring manically at the ceiling when my alarm went off. But compared to everything else racing through my frazzled and panicky brain, getting dressed that morning seemed almost easy. I decided on my black crepe suit; it had a slightly flared pencil skirt and an elegantly cropped jacket, which I wore over a fuchsia camisole (which revealed the tiniest glimpse of cleavage).

Still, my hair was simply refusing to cooperate with me and combined with my sleep deprivation and the billions of butterflies in my stomach, by the time I made it to work that day, I was a basket case. A queasy, quivering basket case with crazy hair and swollen red eyes.

When Conrad told me that he couldn't make it to the media reception after all and I'd have to go on my own, I really started to lose it. I was counting on him and his vast rugby knowledge to help me break the ice! The only thing I knew about rugby players is that they had big muscley shoulders, were always getting injured, and liked to iron urine into my carpet! That afternoon Conrad sat down with me and tried to explain the basics, but it was no use. Everything he said about mauling and rucking and scrums went right over my head. And when he started talking about something called a "blood bin" I completely gave up. There was no way I was going to become a rugby expert by 5:45 that evening.

"You can always just take a few swigs of gin and fake it," Conrad suggested.

I nodded hysterically, visibly shaking with nerves. "You're right."

I couldn't believe I was going to be in the same room with Peter in less than two hours yet I was on the verge of a bonafide panic attack.

"Looks like you could do with a few swigs of gin anyway," Conrad said, discreetly pulling a flask out of his desk drawer.

I gratefully took a few gulps.

"Jezza," Conrad continued, "you've been to millions of these crazy media events. Just because Peter Phillips will be there doesn't make it any different. He's just a normal bloke. You'll be fine."

I begged to differ about the normal bloke part but I nodded again, trying desperately to calm down.

"Just don't tell him that he's your screensaver, okay?"

I smiled weakly and took a deep breath. "Okay."

⌒

Around 4 P.M., I quietly left my desk, went into the ladies bathroom, and locked myself in one of the cubicles. Leaning my forehead against the cold metal wall, I held my throbbing temples, closed my eyes, and tried to regulate my breathing.

This is too important, I told myself.

You can't be nervous. You can't panic. You must take control.

Keeping my eyes closed, I began to visualize exactly how I hoped meeting Peter would take place—the eye contact, the smiles, the easy conversation, absolutely everything. I made myself feel every sensation and every detail as if it were already happening to me. And then I played the scene over and over again in my mind's eye until both my brain and my body believed it was real.

Then I retouched my makeup, put on my coat, hopped in a black cab, and headed to Lord's Cricket Ground.

⟶

I'd been to Lord's several times before. You might have noticed that I'm hardly the sportiest girl in the world, but I actually enjoyed going to cricket matches. And the beautiful, Victorian setting of Lord's was home to some of the most famous matches in the sport's history. Admittedly, the rules of cricket are a minefield if you haven't grown up with them (from what I can tell, one player's sole task is to hold onto his teammate's sweater for safekeeping), but what I loved most about cricket is that people dress up for it. On summer days, the stands of Lord's are filled with spectators in floral dresses and linen suits—leisurely reading *The Sunday Times*, munching on delicate finger sandwiches, sipping pitchers of Pimm's and lemonade, and stopping only occasionally to glance at the scoreboard to see how England is progressing. And of course the game pauses at 3 P.M. sharp to allow for afternoon tea. You can see why it's my kind of sport. Believe me, if baseball involved a semiformal dress code and a civilized tea break, I might be more of a fan.

I had no idea why a rugby event was being held at a cricket ground, but at least I vaguely knew my way around the venue. One less thing to worry about.

As I walked shakily into the hospitality suite, I was overjoyed to see that the bar was already open. I wasn't going to risk having more than one or two, but my God did I need something to calm my trembling limbs. That gulp of Conrad's gin didn't quite cut it.

I held onto my glass of wine with both hands (begging it to

grant me strength) and attempted to mingle with the other media types. Everyone was pretending to take notes or write serious things on their clipboards but it was obvious everyone was there to meet the England rugby squad[112] and get a few free drinks. The rugby players themselves were just as expected: sturdy, stocky heartthrobs with big smiles and even bigger thigh muscles. But I didn't pay them the slightest bit of flirtatious attention; my eyes constantly scanned the room for one guy, and one guy only.

Still, in spite of the friendly banter surrounding me, my stomach continued to churn with a lifetime's worth of nerves and my heart was pounding so hard I thought I was going to choke.

And then—I saw him.

He was standing casually at the bar, bottle of beer in his hand. And wearing a black dinner jacket. Exactly like the one in my dream.

Friends told me I might meet him this way or that, but when the moment arrived, he just appeared. And I was extraordinarily calm.

Everything around me moved into this lucid, luminous, almost dreamlike focus. Colors were brighter. Sounds were clearer. My whole being was attuned to the task ahead and it amazed me that there was a time when I was at all frightened or nervous about any of this. I knew *exactly* what to do. The instructions for that moment had been etched, eons ago, into my heart. All I had to do was follow them.

I made eye contact effortlessly.

Peter held my gaze.

And as his blue eyes locked onto mine across the crowded

---

112 England went on to win the Rugby World Cup the very next year. Unfortunately, I was so distracted I don't remember meeting many of the now quite famous players.

room, I could feel the chains around my heart unwinding. And slowly, joyously releasing.

There were no magical lightning bolts, no cosmic fireworks. It was simply as if I had always known him. Just like in my dream, the only thing that went through my mind, the only thing I wanted to say was, "Oh! There you are!"

Still inexplicably calm, I turned and walked confidently onto the long empty balcony overlooking the cricket pitch. Gradually, others began to join me in the open air and soon I was happily chatting away with four or five rugby players.

He will come to you, my heart whispered.

And he did.

Peter stepped onto the balcony and suddenly the boy I had cut out of a magazine and Scotch-taped to my wall was standing right beside me. Inches away.

I reached out and touched his arm lightly with my fingertips, having no idea what I was going to say until I heard myself say it. "Did I see you at The Ship in Wandsworth a few weekends ago?"

"Why, yes," he replied. "I was there."

"I knew you looked familiar," I smiled.

He smiled back. "Hi, I'm Peter," he said, extending his hand. I took it. "I'm Jerramy."

He didn't let go. "Delighted to meet you."

If anyone was watching me, I appeared utterly composed. But underneath the serene façade was my heart. And it was roaring with happiness.

⟶

We chatted, easily and naturally, about everything: loving late nights, despising early mornings, how we secretly missed college, how we couldn't stand the silly stereotypes of north and south London. We talked about cricket, the Rocky Mountains, and the Scottish

Highlands. I drank in every second; acutely aware, even as it was happening, that soon it would be no more than a memory.

Not once did I mention my screensaver or password. Not once did I mention that I found him in a library book when I was six years old. In fact, through it all, I pretended like I had no idea who he was.

Part of me worried that he might be different than the boy I had fallen in love with as a child. But there were no surprises. Peter was exactly as I knew he would be. What I had always known he would be. Same voice. Same rosy cheeks. Same height. Same impeccable manners. Same quiet sense of humor. And as we stood above Lord's Cricket Ground, shoulders touching, eyes locked, I could feel all these little mysterious pieces inside of me falling back into place. I know it sounds weird, but it's like I could feel my soul repairing itself. The chains that always held my heart so tightly and inexplicably to this one person and this one country were releasing. My heart was free.

And I was becoming whole again.

Nearly an hour had passed before Peter and I realized we were the only ones on the balcony. Our entrancement was such that we hadn't even noticed the others leave and we laughed at our mutual oblivion.

But the newspaper photographers weren't oblivious. They soon took notice of the starry look in our eyes and started snapping away. In their professional opinion, this was a royal moment worth capturing on film. And with Peter at my side, I smiled for the cameras like I never smiled before.

"Get closer," they kept telling us. But they were fighting a winning battle.

In my mind, the world was standing still, but outside it was flashing by—the reception was ending, the hospitality suite was closing down, people were leaving, and suddenly we both knew that it was time to go our separate ways.

"May I have your number?" Peter asked shyly.

My heart leapt.

"Sure," I answered breezily.

I handed him my card and he smiled sheepishly. I looked at him and right then and there I made a conscious effort to always remember that smile, to imprint it within my psyche forever.

"Good-bye," he said.

And then he kissed me on the cheek, and I watched my prince stride across the green grass of the cricket ground and disappear into the hazy London sunset.

Epilogue

"There is nothing noble in being superior to others. True nobility lies in being superior to your former self."

—U<small>NKNOWN</small>

*Y*ou know what the silliest part of this whole story is?

Peter Phillips is not a prince. He doesn't even have a title.[113] In fact, he was the first royal baby to be born a commoner in nearly five hundred years. Of course when I was six years old and found him in that family tree, I didn't realize this. And once I made up my mind about what I wanted, there was no stopping me.

But for all intents and purposes, Peter was just an ordinary guy—whose grandmother just happened to be the Queen. And the thing is, I could have made my mind up about anyone, about anything or any place and if I had gone after it with the same ferocious hunger, I would have had the same result.

Five years later I look back at that surreal and enchanting rendezvous and I am filled with wistful dreaminess—not because I finally met my childhood crush or collided with a cosmic soulmate—but because, well, it is the moment I grew up.

---

113 Royal titles pass only through the male line, and since Peter is a descendant of Princess Anne, he is not entitled to become an HRH. It is widely believed that the Queen offered to make Peter a prince, but Princess Anne declined the proposal, not wanting her children to be unnecessarily burdened. (Moreover, Peter did not inherit a courtesy title from his father, because Captain Phillips also declined a title from the Queen upon his marriage to Princess Anne.)

I still live in my beloved London and I still think it's the most breathtaking and beguiling city on the planet. I still believe, quite fiercely, in the power of dreams, and I still wouldn't touch the real world with a barge pole—but slowly, ever so slowly, I've begun to realize that when it comes to guys, royalty isn't everything.

Despite my "wise" middle name, I guess it's taken me longer than most to recognize this simple truth. But, bit by bit, I've come to accept that my personal fairytale (at least in this life) is not only about finding romance in a faraway kingdom, it's also about the majestic adventures, the splendid characters, and the valorous lessons that I encounter along the way.

I know you're dying to ask, so I'll tell you: No, Peter never called. He may have been well versed in royal protocol, but when it came to dating etiquette, Peter was just as hopeless as any other guy. I'd spent my whole life tracking down what I thought was the perfect male specimen, only to realize that he was still *just a guy!* I was so bowled over by this incredible realization, so liberated by it—that I practically threw a party.

Still, as I watched Peter walk away that evening, something inside of me said, "You know, if he doesn't call, I'll be okay."

And that's when it hit me: I will *always* be okay.

Royal or otherwise, I didn't need a guy to complete me. So I stopped looking for one. And as every girl knows, the minute you stop looking is the minute you find exactly what you're looking for.

Yes, this new boyfriend is English (I haven't totally changed in that respect!) and while he's not a prince, I have to say that he certainly acts like one. He treats everyone he meets—regardless of their class, their background, their accent, or their nationality—with exactly the same courtesy and respect. (Even if they happen to be hippies.) He always makes sure everyone else's needs are attended to before ever thinking of himself. He is handsome and romantic and generous beyond measure. And when I suddenly and without warning found myself battling a fierce, dragonlike foe bent on my destruction—he rescued me, and looked after me, until it was over.

It's been a rocky ride (and in some ways it still is), but my unique transatlantic journey has taught me that kindness and compassion are far more regal than pedigree and charm, and that happily ever after doesn't magically occur the minute you find yourself a prince or palace. I've learned that happily ever after is a state of mind that you have to create—every day, every moment— for yourself. And it is that noble knowledge, that enchanted power, that can turn any girl into a princess.

A lot of things have changed since that day at Lord's Cricket Ground. For starters, I can't drink white wine like I used to. (Not even close!) And I have to say that in the last few years, Tony Blair has lost almost all of his dreaminess. Still, as I look back on my childhood, I'm beginning to wonder if I've spent my whole life running away from something that was never really chasing me.

I wasn't allowed to watch TV, but because of my parents I could read almost by the time I could walk. Because of my parents, I was at the local library almost daily, and it was there that I checked out that fateful book containing the royal family tree. My parents may have embarrassed me to no end; they may have walked around the house naked and made me eat tempeh; they may have disapproved of the materialistic and capitalistic life that I went on to create for myself—but even when they didn't believe in what I was doing, my parents taught me to always believe in myself. They gave me the freedom of possibilities, the gift of an open mind, and the chance to take my life in any direction that I desired. And despite all the tipi and tofu trauma, I always knew that I was loved.

In the late 1960s, my grandfather worked at the Pentagon, while my teenage, bell-bottom-wearing mother joined massive peace demonstrations right outside his building. And this makes me wonder if perhaps my own reactionary tendencies are in the blood. And if so, how will *my* children turn out? Will I end up with a daughter who hates Barbie dolls and insists on wearing hemp fiber instead of cute little outfits emblazoned with Disney princesses?

It's certainly possible.

But on the other hand, she could turn out just like me. And if one day she begs to be sent away to English boarding school, I just might send her.

Special Thanks

To Angela Tsuei, Karan Raichand, Heather Bigley, Amy Gray, Lindsay Chamow, Jane Finette, Erin Lettman, and Olivia Vandyk, for crazily volunteering to read so many of my first drafts.

To Ezra, for always being so sane and supportive.

To my agent, Zoë Pagnamenta, and my editor, Lauren Marino (both of whom know what it's like to be in love with a prince!), for believing in me and my story.

To Buckingham Palace and the entire Windsor family, for accepting a book like this with such grace and good humor.

And to the incredible (nonroyal) parents who raised me, for teaching me that true royalty comes from within.